AFTER HAVING A BABY

AFTER HAVING A BABY

Diana Bert, Katherine Dusay,
Susan Keel, Mary Oei,
& Jan Yanehiro

A DELL TRADE PAPERBACK

Published by
Dell Publishing
a division of
The Bantam Doubleday Dell Publishing Group, Inc.
1 Dag Hammarskjold Plaza
New York, New York 10017

Dell ® TM 681510, Dell Publishing, a division of the Bantam
Doubleday Dell Publishing Group, Inc.

ISBN: 0-440-53492-5

Printed in the United States of America

May 1988

10 9 8 7 6 5 4 3 2 1

MV

To Our Husbands and Children with Love

Mel (Yogi) Bert, Benjamin, and Sosia
John (Jack) Dusay, Alexandra, and Deren
Richard (Dick) Katz, Natasha, and Ariana
Natalie Oei
John Zimmerman, Jaclyn, Jenna, and Laura

ACKNOWLEDGMENTS

Bettie Alvord

Diana Kay Annis

Cindy Averett

Kim Averett

Jutta Barion-Georgantis

Maralee Beck

Chris Beglinger

Joel Bert

Rose Bert

Carina Bjornfot

Cynthia Bowman

T. G. Brown, M.D.

Kathy Calcutt

Clients from Katherine's psychotherapy practice

Ana Gonzalez Crane

Suzanne Cummins

Melanie DeCarlo

Robert Dermott, M.D.

Linda Dancer DiLiberto

Debra Dusay

Floyd Dusay

Randy Dusay

Debbi Farbolin

Jack Futuran, M.D.

Yoel Haller, M.D.

Minnie Lee Harrow

Mike Herrick

Kristen and Hilarie Hinkle

Barbara Colvin Hoopes

Monica Hornell

Ellen Hornstein

Carina Jarl

George and Sylvia Katz

Alexander (Burt) and Betty Keel

Cheryl Kleder

Nona Wong Kline, C.A.P.

Jennifer and Jeanmarie Knight

Steve and Maribelle Leavitt

Mary Lyau

Cindy Martin

Connie McCole

Dorothy and Lois Moran

Linda Mugnani

Jamie and Janine Mulholland

Mike and Jan Mulholland

Richard and Sharon Mulholland

Richard F. Mulholland, M.D.

Winifred B. Mulholland

Mary Naylor

Andrea Novinski

Frank Oei

John and Irene Oei

Mona Olds

Renee Ortiz

Margaret Parks

Kathy Peralta

Dr. Richard Peters

Drs. Piel, Patton, Bolton, and Aicardi

Diane Proche

Melissa and Stephanie Quellette

Kita Ridgeway

Sandy Rowen

Dr. Steven Rubenstein

Nellie Sabin

Karen Scarpulla

Lynn and Alan Schuman

Lee Smith, M.D.

Dr. Patricia Soong
Barbara Standaert
Eva Elvemo Taylor
Henry Taylor
Gwen Telford
Jim Telford
John Telford
Kent Telford
Valerie Telford
Hans Thé
Hwie Tjong and Liem Loen Thé
Robin Thomason

Charlene Tims
Kees Tims
Elaine Tomkinson
Linda Uyehara
Dr. Harry Verby
Dr. Jimmie Westberg
Gwenda Williams
Jay Workman
Jeanette Workman
Ronald and Beatrice Yanehiro
Al and Ann Zimmerman
Laura Zimmerman

CONTENTS

CHERISHED MOMENTS

Funnily enough, there are two subjects I never read about. One is writing, because I somehow think that it is a God-given gift that flows through one's mind, and it cannot be taught to anyone, but only practiced through whatever lies in one's own soul. And the other is children. For years, I have collected volumes of wonderful-sounding books about everything from potty training to childhood nightmares, and for years they have gone unread and gathered dust on my desk. Not because they weren't worth reading—but because I never have the time. I have been too busy bringing up my own children to read what anyone else had to say about it. Yet when my friends began this book, I longed to join them—and this time, much to my chagrin, I was too busy to pitch in. With nine children of my own, and my books to write, there is never a spare minute in the day to catch my breath, let alone stop to think about how I do it. And with that small army of little people around me, I should claim to be some kind of expert—but the truth is that I am not. What I have learned, they have taught me, and what I have done is fly by the seat of my pants, and since everyone seems to be surviving, I guess so far we've done all right.

What the ladies who've written this book and I have discovered is that each child is different. Totally. All together, they have nine children, each lovely and special and unique and with nine of my own at hand to study closely, I can tell you that no two are alike. Each one is an absolute individual, each one is

1

totally different from the next, and I can only stand back and marvel at who they are and what they have taught me. The greatest blessing in my life are those nine people, the greatest gift the joy they have brought me, the greatest education the things they have taught me, rather than what I have taught them. I have tried to share with them my values, my beliefs, my own experiences in whatever way they can benefit them, but they are, have always been, and have remained, exactly who they are. You can influence them somewhat, you can attempt to bend their experience in the way that you feel it should go, but in the end they will find their own roads, and follow them in the ways they see fit. And the greatest gift I hope for in future is to be their friend when they have grown up. I am not always their friend now, in fact frequently I am not. I have been assured at times that I am the meanest person on earth and they hate me, I have been told that I am unreasonable and know absolutely *nothing*, I have been informed on many occasions that I *just don't understand anything* (and occasionally I wonder if they're right), and then at other times I have been told that I'm not as dumb as they thought and there's hope for me after all. More important, there is great hope for them. They are all wonderful people, and I admire them and love them. Luckier still I *like* them all—which is not to say that they don't have their eccentricities too—they have, lots of them, and undoubtedly your children do too. You will discover that with surprise, and even amazement—you will discover as they grow up that they are indeed people, and not always people just like you. And you will have the heartache at times of knowing that you cannot always spare them pain, cannot always help them, cannot even understand them all the time. But I feel certain that you will do your best, and one day they will remember that. It is also sad to realize that despite our best efforts, we cannot always hit the nail right on the head, and they will remember your failings, too, but with luck, when all is said and done, they will look back at their childhood with satisfaction and joy, and accept you for who you are, and accept the fact that you tried as hard as you could, even if you did lose your temper, or got exasperated, or even spanked them once or twice . . . but, by God, you tried. What I hope for myself, and for my children, is that one day, no matter how different they are from whatever design I have imagined for their lives, that I can accept them as

2

they *really* are, accept the paths and lives they've chosen, and be pleased for them. I wish them joy, and satisfaction, and happiness, and good lives ... and I hope that many, many, many years from now, we will still be friends.

But that is much later, and you are at the beginning ... but perhaps that is where it all begins. With their first steps, and yours, with nipples and night feedings and applesauce ... they will teach you the rest in time. You will teach each other a great deal. And each child will teach you something new. Just when you think you've got it down pat, they change, or a new baby comes along and you have to start all over again—learning from them. That is really the key. My children are a remarkable crew. Beatrix, my oldest (she's nineteen now), is a gentle, determined, persevering, scholarly child. She has always been serious, quiet, and very definitely has her own mind. At times I have despaired over the disorder in her room. At times I have made myself laugh when I threatened to put her on restriction if she didn't stop studying *right now* and go out and have some fun! Others have had to be begged, prodded, and cajoled to make them even open a book. (One of my children has never read a single one of my books.) Nicholas, who is nine, is an individual to the very roots of his soul. Somehow I had envisioned him in velvet suits and short pants, a mild-mannered child who would impress all my friends. And he has, but not for one minute in the way that I imagined it. By the time he was two he had his own ideas about clothes (at seventeen Beatrix was still relieved when I shopped for her), he detests anything that looks "cute"—all those adorable little suits with appliquéd giraffes made him gag the moment he saw them. He discovered disco music before he was one, hard rock when he was three, and by seven played the guitar and drums, and at eight had dreams of life as a rock star (as I gulped, but that's who he is). Now he wants to be a skateboard champion. He is a nonconformist in every possible way, and there is no changing who he is. But he is delightful too ... Trevor is handsome and charming and debonair, the pride of the family. Todd is full of mischief and fun and is allergic to socks ... Samantha wants to be a ballerina one day, and has a gentle soul. She is easily wounded and cares deeply about everyone she knows. I also can't discipline her as I would any other child because a firm no to her is a mortal wound, whereas the others are used to my marine sergeant voice. Victoria is good humored, and very shy, and quite a beauty. And Vanessa has a wonderful sense of humor all her own and can be as tough as she has to be to survive in a crowd. And Maxx is always laughing and seems to be always good humored. He falls into deep despair only when his dinner is late and he thinks he'll never see food again. But just as their personalities differ, so do their habits, their likes and dislikes, and their development has varied just as sharply too.

Nicholas walked at eight months, lurching forward into life at full speed as he has continued to do, getting into everything he possibly could. Beatrix didn't walk until fifteen months, advancing cautiously, and Samantha waited until sixteen months. Nicky sat up almost immediately. Samantha never did. I think she walked before she sat. If I sat her up, she just rolled over and collapsed as I secretly worried about it (needlessly!). Victoria and Vanessa and Maxx all walked at twelve months. Beatrix got teeth at five weeks, the others waited until five or six months. Victoria also developed an early and passionate interest in food (particularly anything red: strawberries, tomatoes, and raspberries were a big hit); Beatrix has always made us wonder how she survives. I think she still eats two grapes and a lettuce leaf approximately once a week. She has always absolutely *hated* to eat, but by the time she was six I decided to stop worrying about it. Beatrix took naps until she was six. Nicholas gave them up before he was a year old. To let Nicky take a nap meant that you had him on your hands until midnight, wide awake and raring to go. All of my children have woken up frequently in the night . . . until Vanessa, who began sleeping ten hours a night at six weeks, and that's fine too (actually, it's a relief, and I'm still amazed by it). And Zara is sleeping through the night now at four weeks. Nicky refused to sleep in a crib when he was exactly a year old, and Samantha did the same at fourteen months. Victoria was still a good sport about it at two, and Beatrix was distraught when I finally moved her out of her crib when she was three.

To Samantha the mildest shake of the head indicating no is a sharp rebuke that must be tempered by explanations and enormous apologies and assurances that I'm not too upset at her. To Nicholas the threat of murder and mayhem is unimpressive, and we frequently meet toe to toe—and I'm not always sure I've won.

Personally, I don't believe in spankings, but a handful of times, with each child, I've lost my temper and swatted their bottoms. And amazingly, in each case, it's been very therapeutic. But I generally bend over backward to avoid it. And as the old saying goes, it hurts me more than it hurts them. On a recent trip to Hawaii, Samantha sat in her seat on the flight without moving for the entire trip. She ate her lunch, watched the movie, played with her toys, smiled at the stewardesses, and literally never moved. Victoria walked up and down the plane, making friends, and taking apart everything she could for the entire trip. I felt as though I had walked her to Hawaii. To Nicholas to sit in one spot for more than eight seconds is torture beyond words. Beatrix has to be shouted into bed at 2:00 A.M. with threats that she'll get wrinkles and flat feet . . . but if you can't find Trevor by 9:30 P.M., you can be sure that he's sound asleep in bed.

Beatrix started school at five, and really didn't seem ready for it before that, Nicholas at two, and I would have started him sooner if I could have because he needed the stimulation and the company of other children. Samantha also started at two, Victoria won't start until she's three. In fact, the only thing they have in common is how different they are. And the benefit I have by now is in knowing that, in knowing that it's just as normal to walk at eight months as it is at sixteen (or earlier or later, as the case may be). Nicholas is absolutely fearless, yet the embodiment of terror for him as a tiny child was a swing. He was terrified of them . . . and then he hated bicycles. In fact, I think the only thing they all have in common is that they all hate milk. Passionately. And our pediatrician thinks that's okay too.

Our experiences with toilet training have been different too. At fifteen months Beatrix was totally trained, I will confess more in tribute to the nurse who was helping me than to any genius on my part. But Beatrix was ready for it. In sharp contrast, Nicky was not toilet trained until he was two, but continued to have accidents and wet his bed at night until he was five. I was in despair, convinced that it was a sign of some deep-seated problem. Eventually, we began discussing bed alarms and all kinds of elaborate systems to train him and help him avoid the night incidents that were beginning to distress us. But in the midst of our discussions, he simply stopped. We never made an issue of it with him, never made him feel guilty or naughty. He really couldn't help it. Even now he is a very heavy sleeper, and staggers to the bathroom on his own in the deepest sleep. But the "accidents" are long forgotten. Samantha, on the other hand, became totally trained at the age of two, put on a pair of training pants herself, and never had another accident. Victoria, at twenty-one months, desperately wanted to learn and would announce "Potty!" every five minutes, but she hadn't yet figured out what one did there, so she'd blow her nose in the toilet paper, and flush the toilet sixteen times before leaving, with a look of enormous satisfaction. But it was a beginning, and when she was ready, it went quickly.

Samantha also lies quietly in her bed in the mornings, waiting for someone to get her, while Victoria redecorates the house, wandering all over, making a party for herself at five-thirty in the morning. Vanessa wanders the halls late at night, looking for someone or something to play with. Nicky even went so far as to let himself out of the house one morning at daybreak, which led to gates, umpteen locks, and a lot of shocked speeches to him about going out alone. Beatrix also used to get up at the crack of dawn, and her favorite pasttime was "washing." She once washed my new coat and several pairs of shoes for me. Very helpful.

Even water has been a fascinating difference among them. Literally, at three months, Samantha adored going swimming. At one she was a little fish, at two she would sail off the diving board behind her older brothers and sister. At three we had to drag her out of the water under great protest, and at four she swims laps. Victoria, on the other hand, feels that water in anything but a glass is a dangerous and unpleasant experience. Her idea of a swim is to stand up to her ankles in water, looking worried and suspicious, clutching her life jacket to her. (When normally she is far more adventurous than Samantha.) Nicholas was terrified of the water until he was five, and is now an excellent swimmer. And at seven Beatrix was still struggling with her fear of the water. But Vanessa swims the width of the pool underwater at two. But no matter how they feel about it, if they're going to be around it, you should do your best to make them water safe. I am obsessed on the subject, and have life jackets in every size and color. The stories one hears on that subject are too terrifying and too final to bear any kind of laxity on our part, and even if you feel foolish being overly careful—it's a lot better to be overly careful about it!

Another area where we've had varied experiences was with nursing. I did not nurse Beatrix, because at twenty I found it unappealing and I didn't want to be that tied down, and it wasn't as fashionable then. With Nicky, I wanted to nurse, but he weighed ten pounds at birth and would have been happier with steak. I lasted three days, and with blood pouring from both nipples, I quit. I felt guilty, and as though I'd failed dismally, but I was also relieved. He grew to an enormous size on formula, and everywhere I went people said "Oh, you must be nursing him." Not at all. And I was just as close to him as to those I nursed. I have never believed the myth that you are closer to a baby because you're nursing. If you hold your baby and give him or her a bottle, the baby will still feel your warmth and love and closeness, and not everyone can nurse, for a variety of reasons. I don't think one should feel one *has* to. I've enjoyed it both ways. Samantha, Victoria, Vanessa, Maxx, and Zara were all nursed and it went very smoothly—but differently. Samantha took a supplement from the time she was four weeks old and was delighted with it. Victoria wanted no part of it, and we tried every bottle and nipple we could find, and it took four months until we could get her to take a supplement—we started by using an eyedropper, and finally settled on Playtex nursing nipples. Vanessa also wouldn't touch a bottle until she was four months old. Samantha and Victoria both abandoned nursing of their own accord at exactly five months. One day they looked at me with boredom and disgust, and that was it. I was sad, but they had the last word. At seven months Vanessa showed no sign of giving it up, and with great regret I had to wean her because I was once again pregnant.

Four of them were born by Cesarean, the others vaginally, and that didn't seem to make any difference. The babies were all lively and healthy, and my recoveries different. Sometimes I snapped back faster after a Cesarean than after a vaginal delivery, but not always.

The key to it all is that there are almost no rules. There are certain very obvious basic ones, like never leave a child alone, don't leave any plastic bags around (I tie all of ours in knots before throwing them out), don't leave chemicals or dangerous products within reach, *do* guard their health and their safety and

7

their lives zealously, because babies are quick, and you will never forgive yourself for an accident. But as for their preferences, who will eat lamb chops and who will hate eggs, and even who will eat, or what, or when they walk, or when they go to school— oddly enough, if you watch them, and let them teach you, you'll be way ahead of the game.

Another good rule is to try and make them fit into *your* life. I have not always been successful at that, and by sheer numbers, and as they get older and have greater needs, I have to make adjustments to them. But if you can, try to let them fit into your routine. You and your husband will probably be a lot happier that way. One thing I've refused to do over the years is adjust the noise for them. We live in a big family, and they have to adjust to that. You can't have ten people tiptoeing around because there's a baby in the house, it's not fair, so they learn to live with our chaos and clatter. My favorite memory was of walking into the nursery to see my cleaning lady vacuuming loudly under Nicky's crib as he slept on blissfully. That kind of thing has been a big help. And even there they will have their own style. Some of my children could sleep through an atom bomb, others wake at the drop of a pin. Samantha was passed around to family and friends, and I even walked in to find her in the arms of the TV repairman one day, but at the touch of anyone but my husband or myself, Victoria went pale—literally. Samantha adored men, Vanessa for the most part was afraid of them. Samantha loves the family's dogs, but had terrible fears about foxes and squirrels and even rabbits "coming to get her." Victoria is terrified of even our small dogs. Beatrix had an imaginary hippopotamus under her bed for several years. Amazing, isn't it?

On the subject of work . . . it seems to affect me more than them. When Beatrix was born I wasn't working yet, but got a job within the first year. I traveled a great deal, and was out a lot, and I was also very young so more outwardly directed than I am now. And I felt guilty about it even then, but I don't think it affected her as much as I feared. In Nicholas's case, I went back to work, writing at home, within eight weeks, and that seemed comfortable. But I never left him for a single day and that was a mistake. When I finally did leave him for a weekend when he was four or five, it was an enormous trauma. In fact, I haven't left any of them enough, and I do regret that. I think it's important for them to learn that parents go away and come back, that it's okay, and eventually it will give them permission to come and go too. You don't want them tied to you for the rest of their lives, it's not healthy for them. With my more recent children, I've gone back to writing after about four months and felt a terrible ache "leaving" them. In Vanessa's case, I took a year off and loved it a lot. But as I said, I think it makes a lot more difference to us than it does to them. They adjust to anything, as long as they're well cared for and well loved when you're not around. You can't be with them all the time—no matter how guilty you feel. I feel guilty for each moment I don't spend with them. And if I'm with one child, I worry about the others, but somehow they survive. They learn to fend for themselves if they can't always turn to you. They learn to depend on their fathers and their siblings and their baby-sitters and their teachers—and, better yet, themselves. My husband is a great believer in teaching the children to be independent. Eventually you're not going to be around to solve all their problems for them. Teach them early to stand on their own two feet, to dress themselves, make a sandwich, make a phone call if they have to. Aside from making your life easier, it will give them a tremendous sense of accomplishment.

In many ways I envy the journey you are about to embark on. With that tiny hand in yours, you are going to see the world with new eyes, you are going to discover your child, and yourself, and your husband, and new wonders you never dreamed of before. It will not be easy, at times it will be awfully hard, at times it will be frightening. I remember all too well every visit to the emergency room at 4 A.M., with my heart in my mouth and the worst possible images in my head. There are times when I've literally laid down my head and cried with exhaustion . . . times when I've been consumed with guilt . . . times when I've ached for whatever physical or emotional pain I could not take away from them. Times when I've been sure I've failed. But you can only do the very best you can. Trust your instincts, you know what's best—often better than anyone else—and don't be afraid to stand by your kids. That's what you're there for, to watch and love and guard over them, to help them grow, and keep them safe, and give them the kind of love no one else ever will. And when all is said and done, you will look back over these years and remember them as a special time. The sleepless nights will seem very few, the regrets will pale beside the rewards . . . and in the end, no matter what you do, or who you are, or how much money you make, or how successful you are, the very, very best gift you'll ever have are your children. Enjoy every minute with them. The years fly by like moonbeams on wings . . . much, much too quickly. And one day, when the last bottle is gone, and the last crib given away, and the last sock picked up, and the last toy is gone (and the last car from your garage!)—you will smile back at these cherished moments. Enjoy them to the fullest, and I wish you well. Remember that no one knows what's best for your child better than you do. You can't beat a mother and father's instincts! Good luck to you, and your husband, and the baby!

D.S.

Chapter 1

INTRODUCTION

We wrote our first book, *Having a Baby*, because we got so much support and information from each other during our pregnancies that we wanted to share it with you. After our babies were born, we found that this support continued and grew as we shared the joys and grappled with the difficulties of being parents. There's nothing like a heart-to-heart talk with another parent whose child is going through some of the changes yours is and who is experiencing some of the pride and fear you are—and that's what we'd like to offer you in this book.

For those of you who are joining us for the first time, welcome! *After Having a Baby* follows our children through the first three years of life. Many of us now have more than one child, which enables us to share more experiences with you—including such topics as second pregnancies and sibling rivalry. We're not writing as experts, telling you what is supposed to happen or how things are supposed to be done; we only want to tell you, as openly and honestly as we can, what we have learned from our experiences. We are learning as we go along, as are you. Even if we wanted to, we could not tell you how everything should be done with *your* child, for every child and every parent is different.

What did we do right? What did we do wrong? What tips worked for us? What were the rough times—and the humorous times? What were the surprises? What methods did we use? How do we feel about being parents? How have we fit parenting into our busy lives?

We hope that you will be able to benefit from our mistakes, and perhaps some of the things that worked for us will work for you too. More important, we think you will see from our varied experiences, attitudes, beliefs, efforts, and results that what you are doing is probably okay too.

Diana Bert 🦆

Hello, I'm Diana. I love being a parent. I learn more about myself and my relationships every day. Each day brings along a wonder of its own, something new and exciting to think about, or to be challenged by, or simply to giggle over. I am always learning more about parenting, myself, my husband, and all that parenting means to me. Of course some days are tough. I get tired, and I have pressures that a really perfect mother would probably be able to roll off her back. But the job of parenting is extremely exciting and the tremendous challenge it offers to create, mold, and fashion our own experiences and those of our children is wonderful.

My children are truly magic. They have given me an opportunity to remember and enjoy the true wonders of life. Together we discover for the first time the excitement and amazement of the moon showing itself during the day, a kitten lying in a sunny window, an ant carrying a crumb. My children have given me back a deep appreciation of everyday life.

In *Having A Baby* I shared much about my pregnancy and delivery of Benjamin, my second child. I also mentioned Sosia, my first child. During this book I will bring out the two different stories. Sosia was a first birth to a couple with established identities and lives. My husband, Yogi, is an ophthalmologist, and before Sosia was born I worked in public relations. The postpartum period was a phase of real adjustment that was tough on my husband and me. By comparison, adjusting to Benjamin was a breeze. I will be telling you about our various experiences with each of our children, who, to my surprise and delight, are very different.

I live in San Francisco, but I was raised in Salt Lake City. I learned to adjust to being a city person, but it was harder adjusting to becoming a city mom. There are no backyards for playing; no mothers next door to call in case of a baby-sitting emergency. I had to create a freestyle mothering technique, which I will share with you, and I will give you some reasons for my decisions. I hope that my experiences will give you some insight into the confusion I felt and the solutions I worked out. I can only tell you that as a mother you have complete control of your own little corporation. You can arrange and rearrange your household in any way that you like. It is a challenging role.

You will never refer to me as a historian. I kept records sporadically at best, and I still have boxes and boxes of photos and memorabilia that I will someday find time to sort. I enjoy the living part more than the historical records part. I just let it all flow. Someday I will put all the little locks of hair in a book and neatly write down all the little quips, but for now I am content to watch in amazement as my children transform before my eyes.

One afternoon Sue and I were having a cup of coffee in her living room when she announced that Natasha had just cut her third molar. She asked me if Benjamin had cut any molars, and I had to tell her that I really didn't know. I walked over to little Benjamin and did some exploring and sure enough he also had cut three molars—and all without an ounce of record-keeping on my part. With all due respect to those of you who keep immaculate records, there are those of us who are equally thrilled and amazed by changes or events in our children's lives, but we simply don't stop to write them down. I enjoy things like little ringlets of hair softly winding their way down the little baby's back while he sits in the bath, and the smell of baby breath, and the look of a little belly much more than keeping track of the date of the first doctor appointment or the day the baby changed from infant to medium-size Pampers.

I have a wonderful friend who kept a book called "firsts"—the first time the baby nursed, first time he smiled, the first time he gooed, the first trip to a restaurant. I want you to know that I look upon that book with amazement and awe. Guilt creeps up somewhere along my back. I just can't imagine myself during the first weeks of the baby's life doing anything other than surviving and taking sitz baths.

Hoping to assuage some of the terrible guilt I felt when I looked at my meager bunch of memorabilia, I asked another friend of mine if she felt all these stirrings to keep track of everything her baby did. I explained my philosophy to her with an almost impassioned plea: "Please agree with me." She blushed and said that she had fully charted the first six months of her baby's life. Oh well—further proof that there is more than one way to be a perfect parent.

I consider myself a stay-at-home mom. My first priority is to be there for my children, to supervise them and to see that they are well taken care of. As the children have become more independent, though, I have assumed additional roles outside the house. I manage Yogi's office on a part-time basis. It's a job with many rewards: It gives Yogi more time to share with us; it gives us a both a sense of well-being; it leaves me plenty of time to do my mothering. I also love to write, and in addition to *Having a Baby* and *After Having a Baby* I do as much free-lance writing as my schedule permits. I have therefore hired both live-in and intermittent baby-sitters, and I'll be talking more about my mixed roles and the help I've needed.

I am able to serve cookies in the afternoon, take the children to the park, and still be active in the adult world outside my home. I feel lucky to have found a niche that fits me so perfectly. Enough outside responsibility to keep my head pumping and enough free time to do my number one job—to be mom—to the utmost.

The joy of observing the growth of both my children has filled me with a new respect for the process of life. But did I say I knew anything about it? Did I tell you that I even knew what to look for? Let me clarify a point. I learned and continue to learn by watching, faltering, and listening to anything and everything put in front of me. I hope that my story will give you some new ideas and also comfort in knowing that we are all wonderful parents, that each one of our parenting styles is great, and that there is always the opportunity to learn something new.

Jan Yanehiro ≥

I can't believe that I have two children! But having Jaclyn and Jenna (aged three and one as I write this) are the two best "things" I've ever done. I've discovered there is no love like the kind of love one has for a child.

I remember my obstetrician telling me that every time he delivers a healthy baby he considers that child a miracle. They truly are miracles, as I have learned. Okay, not all the time, but let's save that discussion for another chapter. My two babies (I still think of them as that) are so much a part of our existence that I can't imagine life without them—and I can't imagine that at one time I thought life would be fulfilling enough without them.

I was thirty-four and a half (whew!) when I had Jaclyn, and thirty-six and a half when I had Jenna. My husband, John Zimmerman, and I had been married for nine years before Jaclyn was born, so we had lots of time to think about having children. We felt we had such a full life, lots of travel (somewhat restricted now), lots of eating out (only on special occasions now), lots of spur-of-the-moment outings (almost totally out), and challenging careers (still . . . hooray!). But there's nothing like children. I don't want to sound corny when I say this, but I almost feel sorry for people who choose not to have any children. There is nothing like the warmth of two chubby arms hugging your neck; those sleepless nights worrying over your sick baby; that first smile and first laugh; the first tantrum; the astonished look on their faces when they get a taste of grown-up food; the crying you hear when you tell them they can't have any more treats; the unexpected and provoked slaps that Jaclyn gives her baby sis; seeing big sis Jaclyn teaching Jenna to talk; the ache you feel for them (because you miss them!) when you're away; the agony of needing more time for yourself. There is nothing but nothing like the love you have for them.

15

Miracles? You bet. Each time. Each one.

John and I both work full-time. John is an investment adviser and president of his own company. I've often said that I consider my job to be the best in the world and that I am awfully lucky to have it. As a host of a television magazine show in San Francisco, I get to interview the everyday people who do extraordinary things as well as the rich and the famous. I get to travel and report from exotic and exciting places from Japan to China, to Europe and Hawaii. I absolutely love my job. I absolutely love my children.

I got a birthday card recently that congratulated me on being a working woman of the 1980s. It said something about being successful, forthright, hardworking—and exhausted! It's not easy doing it all, but I rather like all my titles—Wife, Mother, Working Person—and I wouldn't give up any one for anything.

But you do need help to accomplish all three jobs. And though it was a new expense and felt a bit odd at first, I have come to appreciate the verb "hire" very much. I now have a wonderful care-giver for my children (who lives with us), a housekeeper who comes once a week, and a manicurist who I see once a week (a lot cheaper than a psychiatrist, and she gives me beautiful nails!).

Sometimes I'm not sure that I fulfill any of my titles. Sometimes I feel guilty about not having enough time to accomplish creative feats at work or not spending enough time with my children or private time with my husband. But most times I'm so proud to be Jaclyn's and Jenna's mom, so happy to be John's wife, and very glad to be me.

I like to think (fantasize?) that I will have more children . . . given a younger body, twenty-eight hours in a day, Jaclyn sleeping through the night and Jenna waking up at a more reasonable time in the morning (8:00 instead of 5:30). But for now our two girls are perfect for our family. I'm already asking each of them what she would like to be when she grows up. An astronaut? Attorney? Adventurer? If a woman's place is in the house, how about the White House? (Much to my delight, Jaclyn is saying that when she grows up she'd like to be a doctor . . . and a mommy!)

Katherine Dusay ❧

I'd like to introduce myself and my family to give you an idea what we are like. My name is Katherine Dusay, and I'm an older mother (definitely over thirty-five) of two young children. I am also Jack's wife of many years, and I work as a psychologist with a part-time private practice which I limit to twenty hours a week. My husband is a psychiatrist and we maintain separate home offices for our therapy practices. We love the convenience of the one-minute commute!

Jack and I had been together more than nine years before we even considered having children, and our personal and professional lives included an enormous amount of travel. We loved to travel! Before marriage I was an international airline flight attendant, primarily because of my passion for travel and adventure. One of the biggest differences for both of us after having children was deciding to drastically curtail our worldwide trips. Now our outings stay within a fairly short driving radius from home for two reasons: (1) We don't want to go on trips *without* the children and (2) we don't want to go on trips *with* the children. After you read some of these chapters this paradox will become perfectly clear to you. One child was fairly difficult to travel with, and two kids seems nearly impossible! We have learned to enjoy the less obvious, subtle splendors of home life and will continue taking short-range field trips for another two or three years, or at least until the children are older.

At this writing our son, Deren, is a magnificent seven-year-old, and our daughter, Alexandra, is a glorious three-and-a-half-year-old. There's a wonderful age difference between them; they can relate and play together but they are not too competitive with one another in games. (They are competitive in wanting love and attention from Jack and me, and that is fine—usually!) See what I mean? Sometimes it's hard to make definitive state-

17

ments about children because the situations continue to switch—the rules change or the reverse becomes true.

Although both Deren and Alexandra were "wanted" children, both of the pregnancies were completely unexpected surprises for us. Within the first month after I stopped using the birth-control pill, Deren was conceived, and for two months I had no idea I was pregnant. Jack took a lucky guess about my rotten moods and exhaustion—and he was right!

With Alexandra, we had tried for over a year to become pregnant. When we finally gave up and were without any hope of having a second child, she was conceived. Again, I didn't know I was pregnant. When I became nauseated each morning, Jack thought I had the flu or a common cold. Danielle was the bright one who guessed I was pregnant. She had broken the news about her pregnancy the week before—maybe the condition was contagious!

With each confirmation of pregnancy, I had an extreme reaction of shock, fright, sadness, and a "Why-did-I-do-this-to-me?" attitude. Fortunately, these thoughts and emotions dissipated in the first three months and were happily replaced with an ever-growing wonder, joy, and anticipation for my new babe-to-be. My emotions of wanting/not wanting a child were at each end of the spectrum. I have since discovered that quite a few other women go through theses extremes as well.

I had great, noneventful pregnancies with each child; however, the births were like night and day! These birth experiences are recorded in great detail in *Having a Baby*. Deren was the rough birth, and Alexandra was the "piece of cake."

Well, enough about our present family for now. Let's take a trip a few years back in time to see how the children were as infants, babies, and toddlers, and how everyone managed.

Mary Oei ✒

Who is Mary Oei? She is the mother of Natalie, a three-and-a-half-year-old little girl, a career woman (though she never wanted a career), and the only single parent among the five of us. Well, that is me, but it sounds very different than what I always thought my life was going to be.

I'm from a conservative Chinese Catholic family. I was born in Indonesia thirty-two years ago and brought up in my teenage years in Germany and Holland. My marriage to Frank in 1974 brought me to this most wonderful country, the U.S.A.

I'm an aesthetician (a skin-care specialist), a profession I learned in Holland. Frank and I opened our own skin-care salon, Mary Oei Skin Care, in downtown San Francisco in 1979. I never dreamed I'd be a full-time career woman. I always wanted to be simply a good housewife and a mother. Even my father was reluctant at first when I had to go to work, since in our family the woman's place is at home. Now I am glad I have had the opportunity to develop my talent and contribute to our good life and I'm having fun doing it!

I am totally dedicated to my profession. Most of my trips abroad are for my work. Besides Natalie, it is now the most important part of my life. This dedication has helped us earn a reputation as one of the leading skin-care salons in the San Francisco Bay Area.

Natalie was born after Frank and I had been married for eight years. We did not know a child could give us this much happiness. We were mostly concerned that we wouldn't have as much freedom as we had.

Our friends were having babies and so were my clients—it almost felt as if everyone was expecting but me. Without too much discussion, we knew the time was coming. We wanted a baby as a symbol of our love for each other. Let's face it, we all

19

have problems from time to time—I never knew I was going to ask for a divorce four years later.

I had no problem getting pregnant. We planned it, and I got pregnant the next month. I had the easiest pregnancy of all my friends, and the delivery was, to my surprise, also not too bad. (In our first book, *Having a Baby,* we shared our experiences on this matter in much more detail.) Our life has changed now. Natalie had proved that I do have a motherly feeling; motherhood suits me very well. Even though Frank and I are no longer together, I have never regretted having Natalie.

Natalie lives with me, but spends at least one night a week with her father. Both Frank and I love her very much and she knows that well. She has a good time at home as well as at Daddy's place. At least there are no more arguments between the two most important people in her life.

Being a mother, a business owner, and a single parent can sometimes get to be overwhelming. I've been very fortunate to have wonderful parents, who give me lots of love and support. Thanks to them—they come from Holland to stay with me a good part of the year—and my live-in housekeeper, I am able to concentrate on my work and still have time to spend with Natalie when I get home.

Sometimes I do wish there were more time than twenty-four hours a day and more days in a week. Time goes by too fast.

Natalie and I have gone through many challenges in these past few years, but we seem to get even stronger when each challenge goes by.

Susan Keel 🐤

In our first book, *Having a Baby,* I introduced myself to you by saying that I was a lawyer beginning a practice in family law mediation, an inactive registered nurse and an active wife and mother. None of that has changed except that my mediation practice had begun and I'm much more active as a mother. The most important change is that now I have two wonderful children instead of just one. Although there are times when I still don't know who I am or what I want to do when I grow up, one thing is more certain than ever—I love having children! I still have trouble with the concept of motherhood and there are certainly things about being a mother that I don't like, but I do love having children and wouldn't trade the experience for anything in the world. Yes, they *are* worth it all.

Richard (Dick) Katz is my husband. He, too, is a lawyer. We have now been married for seven years and are still very happy with our decision to get married and have children. True, Natasha (now four) and Ariana (now one and a half) have added difficulties in our relationship and life would be smoother without them, but I believe that the problems are due more to the constant state of fatigue we both experience than to anything else. I expect that to pass, and the children have added a new dimension to our relationship that makes it better than ever.

I have tried lots of options when it comes to child care. Right now, if I need to meet with clients, attend meetings, or have lunch with a friend, I take Ariana to a family day-care home and leave Natasha at her school day care just long enough to accomplish my purpose. The rest of the time the girls are with me. As they've gotten older I have been able to do more work at home with them playing in another room, although this still creates some difficulties. And of course Dick helps out when I have nighttime or weekend appointments.

For me this book has been an attempt to give you an honest account of what it has been like dealing with the first few years of my children's lives. Sometimes I've tried to tell you not only what we did and whether it worked, but why we did it. Other times I've just related experiences—they often defy analysis. Writing this book has been difficult because parenting is difficult. I have tried to be honest—to tell you what it is really like—but I admit that this has been hard at times because I also want to come across as a good parent.

To write this book I have relied on a few notes I made when important milestones occurred. I noted precisely when Natasha and Ariana first turned over, sat up, stood, walked, and talked. Unfortunately, I don't have any of this information neatly recorded in a beautiful baby book that I can give to my daughters when they are older—all I have are scraps of paper waiting to be transcribed. So far, this project remains on the shelf next to the book on the history of the world that I haven't yet read.

Record-keeping is one of the things I wish I had done differently. Instead of *planning* on completing gorgeous baby books, I wish I had kept a little pocket calendar with me at all times and made short little notes about what the girls were doing and saying. Then I would have not only recorded when they walked, but also some of those even more precious moments—those crazy antics, hilarious statements, and brilliant thoughts. At the time they were occurring I couldn't believe that I would ever forget. But my memory is short and what isn't written down is lost, or at least blurred, forever.

I have not tried to write a treatise on child rearing. Please bear this in mind as you read. If my words are at times confusing, that is because I have often been confused. If my statements are inconsistent, it is because I have been inconsistent—or because circumstances have changed over time. The task of raising children is one of the most challenging ever. I don't have the answers; I only hope that my experience will help you to find your answers. And in the process I hope that you will enjoy sharing our experiences—our happiness, our sadness, our frustration, and, most of all, our joy.

Part One

PHYSICAL DEVELOPMENT

❧ ❧ ❧

Introduction 🐌

In our first book, *Having a Baby*, we described the first few
months of our children's lives in great detail. In Chapter 2 of
this book we look back and give you an overview of those first
three months. The one consistent theme is the fatigue we all
experienced and the fact that we expected too much of ourselves
during that time. But we differed a great deal, too, and herein
we tell you about the good and the bad, and about the different
techniques that helped us survive that difficult time. After this
overview we devote the rest of this section to the physical development of our children.

In Chapter 3 we tell how we experienced our children's progression from helpless infants to running, jumping bundles of
energy. It was different for all of us. Our children developed at
different rates and we all reacted differently. Some of our children had accidents during this period of time. We tell you about
those accidents; we hope you will learn from our experiences
and understand that it can happen to anyone.

Sleep, or more appropriately, the lack of sleep, is addressed in
Chapter 4. Some of our children slept better than others, but
many of us had difficulty getting our children to sleep through
the night. Among us we have tried many techniques with different degrees of success. Perhaps something we tried will work for
you. At the very least you will know that you are not alone if
your child seems to need less sleep than you do! We also talk
about naps and the pros and cons of baby sleeping with Mom
and Dad.

Breast feeding is a big part of Chapter 5. Although we all
breast-fed our infants, we varied on how long we breast-fed (from
two months to two years), how comfortable we were doing so in

public, whether or not we supplemented, and, if so, how much, with what, and how easily. We also talk about introducing the cup, solid food, bottles, pacifiers, thumb-sucking, and all the other issues and equipment associated with feeding our infants and children.

Our children all eventually sprouted teeth, and in Chapter 6 we talk about teething, brushing the teeth that are there, visits to the dentist, and our concerns about tooth decay. Since some of us have older children, we even mention the tooth fairy.

In Chapter 7 we cover growth spurts and slow spells and our reactions to the physical development of our children. We also speak of the types of clothing we used, liked, and disliked during the various stages of the first few years.

We have all now dealt with toilet training at least once—some of us twice. In Chapter 8 we tell you how each of our children accomplished this task and how we handled it. Some of our children were early by today's standards; some were late. You will read about our different approaches and different degrees of concern.

As you read this part of physical development please remember that we are not experts. We are not telling you what *should* be, only what was. We offer you our experiences as friends—to give you ideas and to let you know you are not alone in your frustrations and joys as you experience your child's marvelous development.

Chapter 2

SURVIVING THE FIRST THREE MONTHS

- How we felt as new mothers—our joys, fears, and ambivalences
- Techniques that helped us adjust to having a newborn in the house
- Who helped us
- How our husbands helped (or didn't help)
- What we expected to accomplish—and what we actually did
- What kind of physical and mental shape we were in
- How soon we went back to work
- Traveling with a newborn
- Whether or not it was easier the second time around

Diana 🙠

I became a mother instantly, fully, and completely in moments. My life was entirely changed, and it has never been the same since. As I lay in the birthing bed and heard the first cries of my brand-new daughter, I looked from face to face for help. The doctor? The nurse? Yogi? No, this little baby was crying for *me*, and not anyone else in the world. Every other time I had held an infant, I had loved and rocked and enjoyed the baby until the first sign of crying and then I would hand him or her quickly back to the mother and say, "Here, I think the baby wants you." This was uncharted, unfamiliar, and sometimes treacherous territory. This was being on the other side of holding a baby. This was new awe, new respect, and new understanding of the phrase "The baby didn't sleep all night." (And maybe not just last night—maybe the last four or five or fifteen nights.) This was a surprise. This was a *shock*. This was real. And this was my responsibility. This was supposed to come naturally. Aren't there things called instincts? Aren't the instincts supposed to kick in at times like these?

I waited patiently for my instincts to start pouring forth, to tell me what to do, how to feel, but I soon realized that if any instincts were there, mine were out of order. I seemed to have no instincts at all to fall back on. So I did what any new mother in my shoes would have done: faked it. I mean, aren't we supposed to know all of this? The one natural reaction that began to appear—and I mean it started parading around unabridged—was terror. "My God! This tiny helpless, totally defenseless creature is depending on me . . . *for everything!*"

I galloped back to the books. I bought every book I could get my hands on. I borrowed and checked out everything my friends suggested. I faced the fact that I could—I had to—work this thing out, somehow. I'm talking about walking through each and every step. There just had to be a list somewhere in those books, something entitled "The Perfect Mother's Perfect Guide to the Perfect Child." And you know, I found a lot of them. In fact, if you laid every book ever written on children and parenting end to end you could probably encircle the earth several times, and each book offers wonderful suggestions about the perfect way to be a perfect parent. The only problem is that they seldom agree. "Let the baby eat on demand." "The baby should follow a regular eating schedule of approximately every four hours." "Breast feeding is the best method." "Breast-fed babies seem to be more fussy and sleep less." "Talk to the baby constantly." "Talking to the baby during meals will eliminate the baby's ability to concentrate on eating."

I was looking for the perfect guidelines, and I couldn't even find a beginning format. It finally dawned on me: "Hey! The perfect way for me to be a perfect Mommy and raise a perfect baby is to do it in my own perfect way!" I just know that you will come to the same conclusion.

In addition to my total lack of instincts as well as practical knowledge, I also assumed that this little wonder was a guest. I live a great distance from my family, and whenever they visit I put all else in my life aside and devote undivided attention to them. Surprise! This little guest is going to stick around for about twenty years and the dishes and the laundry are just not going to keep.

Also (this is where the plot thickens), Sosia believed that life was meant to be cried through. During her first three months she seemed to be trying out for the crying-baby opera. All day, most of the night, and every spare moment in between she cried. At first we tried to find a solution: burping, feeding, bathing, burping, feeding, swings, music, and everything else we could think of. My life soon changed to living with Sosia strapped to my stomach in the front pack. Life as I had known it for the previous twenty-nine years ended. There was someone else who came before me. Although it was hard to accept, I soon learned that I could no longer lavish myself with solitude. I also realized that despite the crying and the abrupt changes, this little creature who was changing my life so drastically was a gem. The satisfaction of having her coo and gurgle was more wonderful than I ever could have dreamed.

I quickly learned that being a new mother meant not being able to count on anything. After spending a positively splendid morning doing all the things that a new mother and baby are supposed to do, we packed half the contents of the house and went to visit a friend. She made me a cup of tea. (Please be sure to make all new mothers a cup of tea, they will feel so good to be cared for.) My tea did not reach my lips before my little darling spit up her entire everything all over me and the couch I was sitting on, thank you. Life can be full of surprises. However, a few guidelines will help you weather the first few months. There are several ways to survive!

Remember that this is all temporary. Crying nights, sore nipples, flabby hips, and raging insecurity will disappear sooner than you would ever dream possible.

Don't take any of these early days or months too seriously. It is, after all, just the very beginning of your life together. There are going to be more moments to share, many more things that you will focus on beyond these first few weeks. If the baby cries a lot, he will stop soon. If the diapers leak, you will soon learn the perfect solution to that problem. If you make a mistake, you will learn from it. You are feeling your very worst right now, so give yourself an extra dose of self-love. Really.

Keep a sense of humor. Read joke books on new parents and the new life-styles afforded those who dare enter the ranks. Realize what a funny time it is despite it all. I promise that someday you will giggle about all the awful things that you don't even think you can live through right now. (We really do laugh now about how Sosia cried all the time and we just cried with her.)

Don't expect miracles of yourself. Lower your standards. Getting anything done with an infant around—whether it is folding the laundry or finishing a writing project—can be all but impossible, for the baby comes first. You just have to respond to the cries, and you can frustrate yourself to distraction if you set impossible goals. Slow down and enjoy.

Everything takes at least twice as long as before. Reduce your expectations. Don't set yourself up for frustration by thinking you'll take care of the baby and finish your needlepoint. Just take care of the baby, and appreciate yourself for doing such a wonderful and difficult thing. Believe me, it will keep you busy enough. Shrink your day. I can remember reducing my objectives to getting up and taking a shower and feeding the baby. That was enough! Once I really got the hang of that, I increased my day to include brushing my teeth. Work up from a basic schedule and you'll feel you are accomplishing something. You're doing a lot more than you're used to right now, and you'll soon be doing more than you have ever done in your life, so don't go hurrying into it.

Plan outings carefully. You will be taking a lot of stuff with you now. I've found that the best method is to pack your baby bag every night or every time you come home from an outing. This will eliminate any last-minute rush looking for things. It will also give you a sense of freedom. You will feel more mobile and "spur of the moment." (See Chapter 21 for more on traveling with baby.)

Remember to work the baby into your daily routines. He or she will enjoy your simple routines and being moved from room to room with you. Sitting on your lap while you talk on the telephone and walking around the house with you will be wonderful stimulation. This may be more difficult to do with a demanding baby, but the household does not stop running because a baby has entered it.

"Quality time" comes in different forms. You don't have to go to great lengths to stimulate or entertain your baby. You can provide sufficient stimulation simply by holding the baby a lot, by feeding and touching and talking to him or her. You can love and enjoy your baby without the stress of buying educational toys or taking the baby to classes and on different outings all the time. Schedule your week to include some quiet times at home.

Network with other new mothers. There are numerous ways to meet other women who are experiencing the same wonder, frustration, awe, and terror that you are. Sharing your feelings with someone else is the nicest thing you can do for yourself— and you'll pick up a tremendous amount of useful information as well. You can find connections through the YWCA, the adult education classes at your community college, or your local churches or synagogues. You may want to form your own play group. You will find that the women you befriend now with children the same ages as yours will be your best friends through the coming years. Be careful not to overschedule yourself, but do become involved with some networking.

Don't get overly excited if you are carrying some extra weight. Like all other conditions right now, being a bit heavy is a temporary situation that you will soon overcome. Be nice to yourself. The weight *will* come off again.

Keep a list of things to do. When you are exhausted and worried about so many things, writing a list helps eliminate the need to remember everything. Writing down when you last fed the baby will be a wonderful plus. The one thing you must remember is that *not* remembering (and even feeling a bit crazy) is normal—don't let it worry you.

Nursing mothers need clothes that allow nursing. Clothes that are absorbent and practical are an absolute necessity. The first time I took Sosia to the doctor I had to completely undress in order to feed her.

Make life comfortable for yourself. If it had not been for our futon, I probably would never have slept. With the futon I was able to nurse Sosia and the let her fall asleep next to me without worrying that she would roll out of bed. I took afternoon naps on it and sometimes used it at night if I was really exhausted. When Benjamin was born I moved him into our room in his bassinet. That way I was able to nurse him in our bed and quietly return him to his bassinet. If you don't have a rocking chair, this might be the time to get one. The main thing is to find what is the most comfortable and energy-preserving for you.

Be easy on those who try to help you in ways you dislike. Everyone has a different approach to childrearing and there will be many people with so much invested in your new baby.

The first few months of your new baby's life can be difficult. You are entering a new schedule and realizing a new rhythm that changes your daily life and every relationship in it. The exhausting demands and fragmented sleep patterns can leave you with a feeling that you have no controls and no routine. Just be assured that others have survived it all. I came out at the other end a much better person. Both of my children, Benjamin and Sosia, are wonderful, and my husband and I have reached new heights in understanding each other and our relationship. Be kind to yourself and those around you. Don't expect too much of yourself. I know that you will be able to come out of the first few months happier than you have ever been.

Jan ॐ

The hot, steamy showers saved me. I took more showers (twenty minutes at a time, three or four times a day) during the first few months after both girls were born than at any other time in my life.

It was pretty easy to sneak off to the shower after I had nursed my first daughter, Jaclyn, and knew she would be asleep for a while. But after Jenna, my second daughter, was born, it became very tricky timing their naps at the same time so Mom could have shower time!

My husband was assigned "baby watch" (both kiddies) during evenings and weekends, and our care-giver and sometimes even visiting friends were "volunteered" to sit while I took showers. It almost seems silly to talk about taking showers, but it took on new meaning for me right after my babies were born. Perhaps it has for you too?

Somehow, for me, taking a hot shower shut out all the new baby chaos that was going on. It washed away my tears. And it is so soothing to the body. It's also the quickest way to get clean since you're leaking from the top (milk from your breasts) and leaking from the bottom (I wore a sanitary napkin for six weeks to the day).

The hot water felt sooooo good on my episiotomy. Apparently heat speeds up the healing process, bringing more blood to the affected area. And I hurt. I couldn't imagine ever having sex again, let alone inserting a tiny tampon. Thank goodness nature does heal. Mother Nature understands, she being of the same gender.

After each baby was born I took three months off from work. Three months seemed like such a gift. I planned to accomplish so many things, so it was frustrating and disappointing when sometimes the only things I really did all day was nurse the baby, change diapers, eat, do the dishes, do some laundry if I was lucky, and take my beloved showers!

Exactly four weeks after Jaclyn was born I stepped out of the shower after a good crying bout and called Katherine. I told her how inadequate I felt, that I had accomplished nothing of magnitude, and that if my husband came home and asked me again what I'd done all day, I would divorce him!

In her warm and wonderful way, Katherine reassured me that *being a mother* was my job for the next several months, and that it was a very important one. She also told me something I've passed on to many new mothers: "Inch by inch, it's a cinch; yard by yard, it's hard." But the inches add up to yards!

I also called Danielle, who said with her remarkable humor (she with nine children!), "If you brush your teeth by noon and get out of your nightgown by five in the afternoon, you're ahead of the game!" Having friends makes having babies so much better!

And now a word—okay, several words—about husbands. I always knew John would be a loving and fun daddy. And he is. He gives the best horsey rides around; rows the best "Row, row, row your boat"; and plants the biggest kisses on "daddy's girls." He's not long on watching them—ten minutes seem to be his limit—but he does change poopy diapers (only when Mom is clearly busy).

But (ahh, here it comes) . . . during my first week home from the hospital, the little things John did and did *not* do bothered me. Actually, they really bugged me. Socks on the floor. Dirty coffee cup in the bedroom. One night he promised to cook dinner, and I remember getting a bowl of vegetable beef soup at ten, only after I had mentioned that I was starving.

My expectations were high; my disappointments great. John and I had two long talks during the first few months, and I discovered that it's just not in his genetic makeup (nature must have missed him) to do many of the domestic duties of the home. I still have hope, though, that someday an angel will fly overhead and bestow upon John a fraction of the desire to do the mundane things that make a house run.

After one of our talks John suggested that I make him a list of all the things I needed. What a great idea, I thought! Why hadn't I thought of this before? How could he have known exactly what I needed if we hadn't discussed it and gotten it down in writing? I gave him the list with a kiss, he gave it to his office partner's wife. *She* got everything I needed.

One more thing bothered me about John—what he said when he came home from work. "So, babe, what have you done all day?" I was already extremely disappointed in myself for being unable to accomplish heroic feats, definitely on the defensive, so when he said this, visions of divorce danced in my head. I felt his tone was sarcastic—that clearly he felt his world of high finance was far more important and exciting than what was happening at home. I thought he was insensitive, flippant, and definitely degrading and demeaning to me.

In truth, as I found out later, John really did want to know about my day, but not in the way I had imagined. He wanted to know how I was feeling, what things I had done with the baby, and how she had responded—not what feats I had accomplished.

And now just one more teensy thing about my hubby. It turns our that his socks on the floor, his coffee cup in the bedroom, and the dishes in the sink didn't bother him in the least. But since it did bother me, naturally we had arguments. Over the silliest things. And, of course, I would end up crying.

You can blame it on hormones, but there's also fatigue—and the newness of it all. A new baby, someone new in the home, new routines, new baby furniture, new baby clothes . . . and new parents. It takes about three months before the routine of a new baby becomes regular in our home. (Danielle says it takes about six weeks in her home, but then I've always accused her of getting things done much more quickly than most people.)

After Jaclyn was born two people helped me immensely during the first month: my mother and a dear friend with whom I had grown up in Hawaii, May Lyau (I call her my oldest living friend on earth). May came by every day for a week to help. She freshened up the house, picked up the socks, washed the baby's laundry, and cooked dinner. I'll never forget her generosity.

My mother flew in a week later and took her two-week "vacation" helping me with her new granddaughter. I've always felt close to my mom, but I felt even closer when she showed me how to bathe the baby, did the vacuuming before friends came to visit, and cooked wonderful meals. She came again for her two-week "vacation" after my second daughter was born. I hope someday I can take the same "vacations" for my daughters.

Katherine 🐦

Right before I gave birth to Deren, I was thinking, "I wish he could stay inside indefinitely. This way I can carry my baby and not have to care for another human being. I may be inadequate at it and everyone will suffer. I know nothing about caring for a newborn. How will I manage? How will I provide for every need of a helpless human being who is completely dependent upon me?" I had been agonizing over these types of thoughts daily, scaring myself and feeling ambivalent, yet my eagerness to see this infant that was growing inside of me was creeping more and more into my thoughts. My body knew how to care for this child physiologically; however, my personality might not! Deren, of course, was going to be born regardless of whether I had resolved anything or not. He did, to his credit, give me a small courtesy of coming five days late. This became the exact amount of time I needed because the actual day I went into labor was the day I bought the diapers, bassinet, baby basket, and stretch pajamas. I had no sooner lugged everything home and up the two flights of stairs to our bedroom when my contractions started. They were gently rumblings at first, and I was thrilled and scared instantly! "Oh, boy! My body works! " And "Oh no! There's no turning back!"

Shortly after Deren was born, I felt delight and a warm glow, in spite of an extremely difficult and painful birth due to a positioning problem in the birth canal. I was amazed how quickly I put all that pain behind me. I had a gorgeous, miraculous little baby boy, and all I could do was be in complete wonder and awe of this tiny baby. We were overjoyed! Jack and I stayed with Deren for hours after his birth. I had lots of hospital visitors, phone calls, and flowers. I loved showing him off. I wouldn't let him out of my sight. Because there had been several recent tragedies in the world, our local newspaper sent a reporter to interview a new mother and father as a front-page story entitled "Good News." Guess who was featured?

I slept no more than a couple of hours during the entire three days I was in the hospital. Even though my doctor told Jack he could take me home about six hours after Deren's birth, I decided to stay in the hospital with Deren to rest, be fed and pampered, and to take some of the neonatal classes the Red Cross offers for new mothers and infants. I loved the hospital food (yes—all that "yucky" turkey with mashed potatoes and Jell-O for dessert), all of the attention the hospital staff and visitors gave me, and I attended a breast-feeding and baby-bathing class. Life at the hospital vacillated between the leisure time of watching the baby sleep and the excitement of seeing him awake. I was thoroughly proud and pleased. I took pain pills so I wouldn't feel the episiotomy stitches too much. I had time to gain confidence in holding, feeding, and changing my new baby.

I remained on an enormous high and thought things were fine as long as I had no responsibilities except for cuddling and nursing the baby. My hospital meals came like clockwork. I pushed my nurse's button when I needed help.

When I brought Deren home, my husband, Jack, presented us with this fabulous surprise: an enormous, fully-decorated Christmas tree to greet us. I thought I was living in a dream.

Jack and I pretended to be on another honeymoon and moved into the baby's gorgeous room, which had been our guest bedroom. I had always loved this romantic room because it didn't get messed up with cups, dishes, newspapers, and clothes the way our own bedroom did. I enjoyed its charm—the flowery Victorian wallpaper, period furniture, and cozy fireplace. It also didn't have a phone. The three of us could cuddle all through the night.

We happily camped out in Deren's room and kept his bassinet right next to the bed. I hung sweet little mobiles that played lullabies over his bassinet and presented him with cute stuffed animals.

After the first three days at home I "hit the wall." My bubble of ecstasy burst. I realized that I had just completed a six-day marathon and was presently enduring exhaustion, sore breasts, continually interrupted sleep, and an aching, infected episiotomy (in that order).

In addition, Deren was colicky for his first three months. He began his shrieking and cramps after we brought him home from the hospital. I immediately felt helpless because I didn't have the trained professionals at the hospital to help us. Now it was just Jack and me on our own—and Jack worked all day. The only thing that seemed to help Deren was walking him around and bouncing him lightly on my shoulder, nursing him, and bouncing him on our bed vigorously while he lay on his back.

My brother Jamie, who is also my best friend, came to stay with us for the first few weeks to help us out. Jamie made an enormous difference to me because it seemed that Jack was working harder than ever, and I would see him only at brief times during the day as he popped in and out between his appointments. I had no energy to go out, and didn't know how I would ever manage to take a baby outside all by myself (even though I had been around the world, literally, several times by myself with no problem).

I would agonize over little things. How do I work the front pack? How do I set up the stroller? How do I do this while holding Deren? I was daunted by how complicated everything seemed. How do I carry him, the stroller, and the diapers down the stairs and then master opening the door? I would overwhelm myself with these questions, and since I would still be in my robe at three o'clock, I would figure the day was shot anyway. Perhaps Jack would help me or have a great idea about what to do. Instead, Jack would be full of questions like: "Are my shirts back from the laundry? What's for dinner? Did you remember to . . . ? What did you do all day?" I would feel defensive and want to cry. I thought miserably, "Who is going to take care of Jack and me? I can hardly take care of the baby, let alone anything else!"

Instead, guilt was everywhere. I would see the unmade bed, the pile of laundry, the messy kitchen, the empty refrigerator, the full trash cans of diapers. I started feeling helpless and like a failure. Everyone else was able to do things, and I was the "flake." I felt isolated and would nostalgically remember those few precious days I had spent in the hospital where I wasn't expected to do anything except show off my baby, enjoy my pretty flowers and gifts, and take celebratory phone calls.

I wanted to take my baby and go hibernate. I had thought that

I would have many hours to be peaceful, enjoy Deren, read books, and relax—but the closest I came to relaxation was nursing Deren in a bubble bath, where my episiotomy didn't hurt so much. Days would dissolve into nights, and then too soon the sun would send unwelcome rays of light into our room. I would shudder and wish I could become invisible. I hurt mentally and physically. The pains I had been trying to ignore suddenly took over: my episiotomy would ache and itch unmercifully, I had hemorrhoids for the first time in my life, my breasts were swollen and tender. They became hot and infected easily from Deren's irregular nursing patterns. "Oh, poor me," I would think. "Will I ever catch on?"

Thank goodness Jamie was there with me. He would bring me breakfast and light a fire in the fireplace. I would rock and nurse Deren in front of the fireplace while Jamie would talk to me and reassure me. He would spontaneously run out to get a pizza or fast food and prepare things that were easy. He would bring up trays of dinner for Jack and me and then the three of us would start laughing and lighten up. I began to realize how hard I was being on myself. I had just had a new baby; I had been through a major medical procedure called birth; I had an infected episiotomy; I hadn't really slept in weeks (if you add in the ninth month of pregnancy); I had never experienced being the complete caretaker of a brand-new infant, who was colicky to boot! What I learned from this experience is that I could have been much better prepared for these early months. I wish I had gotten someone to live in. Jack and I had wanted to do everything ourselves—every bath, every diaper, every burp—but what we didn't realize is how hard we were being on ourselves.

My parents came to visit and were sympathetic to my hurts, questions, and needs. Gradually, over these three months, I began to get a few days of restful sleep. Jack was wonderful and positive. His sympathy and cheerful attitude meant the world to me.

My very first trip out with the baby was to my pediatrician's office for a well-baby visit. Deren was five weeks old and I was so proud of myself. I dressed Deren and myself beautifully, took a big breath, and ventured out. Our appointment was at three, which gave me the needed time to get "the show on the road." Everything went smoothly and my confidence soared. I did it! I had gone out with my new baby and even understood the car seat.

I got lots of positive strokes from the doctor, the nurses, and other parents and passersby that day. I told myself it was worth it to consciously make a plan and get out of the house every day.

When Deren was born I didn't know anyone else who lived close to me who was in my situation, and that was a problem. I had met a great couple in Lamaze class, but they lived far away. With the birth of our second child, Alexandra, that all changed: I had six fabulous friends with whom to share experiences—and write a book.

Alexandra's birth was one of those twenty-minute wonders that many of us hope for. I was in little pain. She was a very easy baby, not fussy or colicky, which enabled me to spend more time with Deren, who needed the attention during his sister's early months of life. The second time around I was more experienced, I organized and planned better, and I hired a sweet college student to live in and help with the baby.

I had learned that when I went back to work, the right type of helper—one who will help shop, make dinner, and do the laundry so I could spend more time with the children—is invaluable. I delegated more things with the second child and found that I had more of me left—more sleep, more enthusiasm, and more confidence for the roles of motherhood and working mom. Having help at home and friends in the same stages of babyhood enabled me to do what is most important during those first three months—enjoy the baby to the fullest.

Mary 🦢

I had no idea that newborn babies were so small until I had Natalie in my arms at 6.1 pounds and 21 inches long, totally helpless and sweet. Now I know that the ideal-size baby in my imagination was at least four months old, cute, and cuddly.

When Frank and I came home from the hospital with Natalie, she was then only 5.9 pounds. We had no idea what to expect other than sleepless nights. Being pregnant and actually having the baby are totally different experiences. You stop discussing pregnancies the minute your baby is born. I had no idea how I would act as a mother and how this baby was going to change our lives. Basically we just let things happen naturally and tried not to worry about it. My mother lived with us for the first three months with Natalie, until we found our first au-pair (baby-sitter).

It turned out that I was the one who needed the most attention. It's amazing how much your body has to go through to give birth. I had problems with hemorrhoids. Sitting down became quite a chore for about five weeks. Katherine suggested taking warm baths. I love taking a warm bath but never seemed to allow myself to have enough time for it. One morning I finally did try one for about fifteen minutes. It felt wonderful, and I loved the hot water. Well, the rest of the day was wasted; I was dizzy and thought I was going to faint all day. Probably the water was too hot and fifteen minutes was too long.

We were very blessed with Natalie. She was a healthy and easy baby. There was no serious frustration in our household because of lack of sleep. Natalie had a pretty regular schedule for feeding and changing right from the beginning, and by the time she was six weeks old she slept four to five hours at night without interruption.

Frank was very helpful in chipping in with the night feeding and the first feeding in the morning. He continued this routine until Natalie was over one year old. Those moments with Natalie alone were very meaningful for him, and I am sure they were for his little girl too.

The first three months was a period of adjustment for us. We had a lot to learn about being parents. I couldn't believe how many diapers we went through in one day. We had bought disposable diapers two months before she was born, all with elastic legs. But when Natalie came home she was so small that the diapers were too bulgy and rough for her little legs. I really felt sorry for her. Then we got some plain Pampers for a while and went back to the elastic-leg diapers after a month or so. Basically we were more comfortable in handling our little girl by that time, understanding her strengths and weaknesses better.

I was born and brought up in Indonesia, where one is very conscious of keeping clean. In Indonesia we bathed twice a day. Water was the only source of cleaning, since toilet tissue was not widely available then. I've adapted to toilet tissue, of course, but I still think water is a safer and cleaner way to go. Therefore every time Natalie needed a diaper change, I used to wash her, using a squeeze bottle filled with lukewarm water. Then I would dry her with a cloth diaper. We were not confronted by diaper rash until she was a couple of months old, when she started some solid food. When that began Vaseline and A&D ointment were essential. The squeeze bottle was still our favorite, and eventually we did use some baby wipes as well.

When Natalie was three weeks old she developed acne all over her face. I was terrified. I was so sure that it wouldn't happen to my daughter—maybe to other babies, but certainly not mine. I knew it was normal for the skin to show a little outbreak when the little glands started to work, but this condition lasted six weeks with Natalie and all we could do was to clean her regularly with no soap and use cornstarch only if necessary.

When Natalie was two months old I went back to work. As much as my daughter needed me, my presence was very much needed at my business too. You can't help but feel somewhat torn. My work brings me lots of satisfaction personally, but so did my daughter, just differently. I need both. As a mother I am happier with myself and therefore effective at work. In turn, working helps me be a much better mother when I am at home.

The first month back at work was not easy. It was rather rough emotionally. I felt guilty leaving Natalie at home with my mother, even though I knew she was in good hands. My uniform did not fit me yet, since at that time I still carried an extra ten pounds, and I had to periodically express my milk at work to avoid the pain. . . . It was not easy.

Eventually we worked everything out. Natalie nursed only twice daily (in the morning and before bedtime at night); she had no problem taking supplement and was just as happy. I lost my extra pounds two months later and we all adjusted to our new routine beautifully.

Natalie was a happy baby, she smiled a lot, and it was wonderful coming home to her. No matter how hard a day we had had at work, Frank and I managed to get a complete new dose of energy when we got home.

Susan 🐦

As I think back over those first three months I recall two dominant and seemingly incompatible feelings: joy and misery.

It was a blissfully happy time when I had no responsibilities except to care for, love and nurture our beautiful new daughter, the most beautiful, alert, happy baby anyone could ever dream of having. I loved having visitors come by to see Natasha. I loved showing her off and hearing people exclaim about how alert she was and how much hair she had (she was born with a full head of black hair). And Natasha was an incredibly easy baby (I couldn't imagine an easier baby until Ariana was born). Natasha did require a lot of attention, but because she was our first child we were able (in fact, anxious) to give her the attention she demanded.

Natasha was not the kind of baby who would play quietly in her crib. She never stayed in her crib long enough to even notice the toys. The second she was awake she would cry to be picked up. Once she was brought into the center of things, she was very happy. She never cried unless she was hungry or wanted attention. She did not cry when her diaper was wet or messy, nor did she cry for no (or some unknown) reason (well, maybe once or twice, but that doesn't really count, does it).

That's the good news—having a happy, colic-free, cheerful, bright-eyed, beautiful baby, and no responsibilities other than caring for her. Those first three months held many good times.

The bad news is that I had never in my life (the future is another story) been so nonproductive, so absentminded, so . . . *tired*! It is the fatigue that I remember the most. It was torturous and, I believe, much of the cause of the nonproductivity and the absentmindedness.

Natasha nursed every two hours around the clock, and she would nurse for fifteen to twenty minutes. Unless you have a newborn at home, and thus are too tired to do simple arithmetic, you have already figured out that I had about one hour and ten minutes between feedings to sleep—or, during the day, to accomplish something. Needless to say, I didn't get much sleep and I didn't accomplish much. Many so-called experts recommend that you take a nap when the baby is napping. Sounds like a great idea, doesn't it? But I found that Natasha's nap times were barely long enough to take care of my personal hygiene—in fact, they were not usually long enough. Was it true or did it just seem as if *every* time I got into the bathtub Natasha would wake up and need attention? I would drag myself through the day, looking forward to the time when Natasha would sleep through the night. (I had a very long wait!)

Since I wasn't going to be working I had promised Dick I would try to take two years off—I was sure that after the first week or so of physical recovery I would have lots of free time. I planned to organize my desk—and thus my life. Then I was going to read a one-volume work on the history of the world (I have always felt that my knowledge of history is shamefully inadequate). Well, they were good intentions.

I soon found that there was no time during the day when I could give any task my undivided attention. My attention was *always* divided. And, I'm sorry to report, remained so until Natasha was off to school.

It was difficult to deal with the absentmindness. I don't like being unreliable, and I don't think that under normal (pre-child) circumstances I was absentminded, but for those first three months—and for some time thereafter—my mind was definitely absent! I couldn't remember anything. Dick said that during the birth process I lost some of my gray matter. My theory is that I was so busy taking care of the baby and being mesmerized with joy and fatigue that I just couldn't handle other complex tasks such as remembering to run simple errands or make telephone calls. One day I went to the grocery store with the girls, exited with my groceries in the cart, wheeled the cart to the car, put the kids in the car, and drove off without the groceries. I got all the way home before I realized that I didn't have them. Fortunately, when I drove back to the store I found the groceries right where I had left them!

I am very pleased to report that my absentmindedness didn't seem to compromise my ability to care for Natasha and Ariana. Nature seems to have a way of setting priorities. Although the babies caused my absentmindedness, they did not suffer as a result of it.

Before I got used to having Ariana around I *did* do something which I am truly embarrassed to admit. I mention it only to let you know that if you have done some stupid things, you are not alone. I came home from somewhere, took Natasha into the house, and started to make a telephone call when I realized that Ariana was still in the car! I had forgotten all about her! I rushed out to the car to find Ariana fast asleep. Fortunately, that was the only time that I forgot her and we were at home behind a closed gate, not in a public place where the consequences could have been disastrous.

We did do some traveling during the first three months with both children, and contrary to what many people think, it wasn't bad at all. In fact, it was easier than being at home, if for no other reason than Dick wasn't working and could help a lot more with the babies. Besides, what difference does it make whether you lose sleep at home or in a hotel room? And meals are actually easier when traveling because you eat in restaurants and are waited on.

As I look back on my calendar for those first three months of Natasha's life and see empty little squares and wonder what I did, I realize that I did accomplish something during that time—I survived.

With the second child the first three months were a little different. When Ariana arrived I had a very active, bright, demanding two-year-old at home to entertain me. Again, however, I was fortunate. Ariana was an exceptionally easy baby. Not only was she happy and colic-free, but she would entertain herself in her cradle. She did not call to be picked up the moment she woke up, and as she got a little older I understood the usefulness of crib toys. Some babies *do* stay in their cribs for a while with their eyes open. Ariana would be happy by herself while I showered, or combed my hair, or used the toilet, so I could use her nap times to be with Natasha and attend to other tasks associated with the presence of a two-year-old.

Having help during the first three months can be enormously useful *if* it is the kind of help you want. Right after both births my mother came to help for a couple of weeks. It was wonderful having her since she was willing to help with the mundane things and let me care for the baby. Dick was also a big help during the first three months. He's a great cook and did much of the cooking for the first few weeks and more than usual for several months. But since I breast-fed both babies there wasn't much that Dick, or anyone else, could have done during the night.

When Natasha was born I didn't want any help taking care of her. I wanted to do it myself and I would do it the same way again. When Ariana arrived I had gotten used to leaving Natasha with sitters and it was easier to leave Ariana at an earlier age. When Ariana was born I had a regular sitter. It was wonderful for Natasha to have someone who came and spent time with her while I was busy with the baby. And this also allowed me to leave the baby with the sitter while she was sleeping and spend time alone with Natasha. But no matter how much help one has, it is still Mom who bears the brunt of the responsibility and fatigue during the first three months.

I don't know if the first three months are the *most* difficult, but I do know that *they are difficult!* I lived through them, though, and so will you—and maybe even enjoy them!

Chapter 3

. . . AND THEY'RE OFF!

- How active our children were as infants
- How soon they became playful
- When they achieved their milestones—turning over, sitting up, crawling, standing, going up and down stairs, walking
- What we did (or didn't do) to encourage them
- What "firsts" we missed seeing
- How we felt—and how the babies felt—about their efforts along the way
- Accidents

Diana 🎐

From the time the baby is born, totally helpless, to the time he or she stands up and walks is *just one year*. It's a miracle to watch. Sometimes it's terrifying (such as when the baby is learning to crawl up and down stairs), other times hilarious. The changes are subtle. As infants my children enjoyed a good kicking session, their arms and legs flailing about as they strengthened each muscle. From there they began stretching, either arching their backs or pushing themselves up on their arms. I did little to encourage them, other than putting them on their stomachs for a while and then on their backs. I did give each of them things to look at and enjoy—big colorful balls, stuffed toys or mobiles that they could aim for and look at. But I did not involve them in any baby exercise classes or reward sessions; I have always felt that it is the baby's life and each one has the right to experience the adventure in his or her own way. I did not want to place importance on their accomplishments for my own edification.

Sosia was absolutely desperate to move around and was unhappy being unable to get around by herself. I walked her around the house a lot in either a backpack or a front pack, but my schedule just didn't coincide with her need to have private tours at all times. At the first opportunity we got her a walker so that she would be able to move herself about the house. I didn't try to restrain the children in any way. Intense childproofing (more about that in Chapter 10) allowed both children to scoot and crawl and climb throughout the house. Sosia was much more content and at peace once she was able to explore her environment. She loved the walker because she could scoot herself over to look at things. She was not a famous crawler because she disliked the feeling of different textures (sand or carpets) on her hands. She preferred to be seated with her toys within reach. Because of her aversion to crawling, Sosia seemed to go from sitting to walking without much formality in between.

Benjamin was not so desperate for stimulation, probably because he had his private tutor, Sosia, who would bring him wonderful things all the time, and then promptly take them away again. Benjamin was a classic crawler. He moved through the paces perfectly—push-up to all fours, and then he was off. He enjoyed his mobility in that position for a long time. With Sosia so very mobile, I think Benjamin also enjoyed the security of crawling. When he did decide to walk, he did that, too, in the classic manner—from standing alongside furniture to taking a few steps and then on to walking.

At the time the children are mastering each of these skills, it seems like the most important thing that has ever happened.

Some mothers put a tremendous amount of importance on the fact that their child walked at nine and a half months; another worries because hers isn't walking yet at fifteen months. Some children are encouraged constantly and almost pushed into walking too early. My pediatrician told me that his daughter didn't walk a step until she was sixteen months old ... and now she is number one in her medical school class. Each child learns to walk at his or her own pace—according to his or her private agenda as well as circumstances—but they do walk.

Katherine 🐦

Before Deren was born I read most of the pregnancy and child development books that were on the market. I had a rough idea when certain milestones would occur. Both children were able to hold their heads up from the beginning. From a few days old they would strain to lift their tiny heads up and peer around. Each of them could see and focus and even smile before the books said it was possible. I decided to put those books away for good and just enjoy my children.

Both my babies developed quite differently from day one, and each is still unique. At each stage—trying to sit up, crawl, pull up, and walk—I would see their frustration. It was clear that they continually wanted to master things that were beyond their abilities. Deren would crawl everywhere and pull himself up. Alexandra would stand upright and hold on to anything and anyone to remain upright. Both of them walked right about their first birthdays, but each had a completely different system for getting to that point.

I was pleased that both of my children actively related to the environment. Each time a child started to walk I felt that our family had reached a major milestone. They learned to be pool-safe by age three (which provides a tremendous relief for parents). Little did I know that soon each child would try to skip, hop on one foot, and jump down from high, precarious places. No sooner was this going on than they were experimenting with tricycles and eventually the big two-wheelers. Deren mastered his bicycle at age five after innumerable scrapes and bumps. Today I am amazed about all the physical ways they can transport themselves.

In high school I became a cheerleader because I love to cheer people on. With my two children I resumed this role, and I was delighted to see them take their first steps, swing on things, climb trees, ride bicycles, learn to ski, swim, ice-skate, skateboard, do tricks on the monkey bars, and so on. I am permissive with both children, and Jack and I made sure they got their share of bouncy horsey rides and roughhousing. Since Jack and I are pretty athletic and enjoy keeping in shape, it has felt natural to share our children's energy and enthusiasm.

We also believe in safety, and in having good equipment (ski bindings, crash helmets, and knee pads where appropriate). Each child has gotten a good dose of cuts, scrapes, and bruises. Deren even had a fractured wrist, and this is how he tells the story:

"I was skiing the steepest run in Squaw Valley and made lots of turns and did great! On the flat part where the beginners can ski, I took an easy spill and landed on my wrist. We found out later that day that I fractured it—and not even on the steep stuff!"

Alexandra, our self-proclaimed tomboy, takes fewer risks than Deren, but she still ends up with her share of skinned knees and bruised elbows.

We have found that their "owies" are temporary setbacks. They are ready to go again within minutes.

Jan 🐾

At six months Jenna was scooting all over the place on her tummy . . . backward. Any day now, I thought, she'll be crawling. I was given the glorious assignment of reporting on cruising the Mexican Riviera, and I left for ten days. When I came back Jenna was crawling (forward) everywhere! I thought, "I missed it!" She couldn't wait for me to come home. And rightly so. Her life won't and can't wait on ours.

Jenna had to "practice" sitting up. She's our "baby," so we tend to carry her, stroll her, and rock her. At her six-month checkup our pediatrician said she had the muscles to sit up, but wasn't using them enough. He suggested we "practice" sitting her up. In four days she learned how to sit on her own.

Both of my children started to sit up, crawl, and walk just about the same age. Jaclyn walked before her first birthday; Jenna, two weeks after her first.

You know in your mind and heart that each child is different, that you should not compare your children to each other, let alone to other children. You say it out loud, you repeat it to friends and family—but you still do it.

In our group Natasha Katz turned over, walked, and talked way ahead of all the other children, mine included. We were all sure she would be going to college by the time she turned five!

Of course you're proud when your children do things early. I'm pleased to know I have early crawlers and walkers. But Jaclyn, now three, still drinks from a bottle to fall asleep at night and is still struggling to be potty trained completely.

Jaclyn took to crawling up and down the stairs easily. Jenna loves to go up the stairs, but hasn't mastered the technique of coming back down, although we've shown her repeatedly. She can walk across the room and around tables but she still can't crawl down the stairs. Maybe before she goes to college she will have figured it out.

Jaclyn took a tumble down our stairs three months ago and broke her right forearm. She has gone up and down those stairs a thousand times! But one night, after her dad and I kissed her good night, I put her on the stairs and patted her bottom good night. She was in good spirits, singing as she walked up. I turned and was making a quick phone call when I heard her tumble down. I ran, only to reach her as she landed at the bottom of the stairs. She immediately went to her arm, crying, "It hurts!"

I took off her pajama top and saw instantly that her forearm did not look right. The bone had not penetrated the skin, but the entire arm looked slightly askew. We rushed to the emergency room and X rays indicated the arm was broken.

Of course I was a basket case at the hospital. The orthopedic surgeon explained the fracture; described exactly how he was going to set it, and sent us to the waiting room. He said it was advisable that parents wait outside. I could hear Jaclyn screaming for me, either from pain or fear. I started to cry too. Why did this happen? In our own home? Why didn't I simply walk her up the stairs myself this one night?

Our pediatrician advised me not to dwell on the "what ifs" and "why didn't I?" Falls and breaks occur when you least expect them, he said. Jaclyn was in a cast for five and a half weeks. She never complained. She easily adapted her left hand to eating, drawing, and picking things up. On several occasions she wanted me to take her cast off when we took her clothes off, but when I explained that she had to wear it for four to six weeks, she never argued.

Today she talks about falling down the stairs and breaking her arm. Doctors tell me they don't believe she will remember the trauma, this mother—at thirty-seven—will never forget.

Mary ❧

If we could all learn as much each year we live, as we do during our fascinating first year of life, we would all die geniuses.

In the first six weeks Natalie was mostly busy making her body grow stronger. She gained about one pound a week. She looked so peaceful and slept all the time. She did not care what happened around her and slept through any condition. I had to wake her up for feeding and changing time. I made sure I changed her head position to help her head shape. I did not want Natalie to have a typical Asian head, flat on the back, because when I was little Asian babies mostly lay on their backs and stared at the ceiling.

I wanted Natalie to recognize and play with me so badly. I did not mind her being a little fussy at all. When she was able to recognize us, showing her excitement by using both arms and legs and giving a big smile, it meant a lot to us.

We were anxious to see Natalie make progress, but we never felt there was a time limit or any rules on how or when she should do things. However, when she started to show interest in more serious development, such as reaching, pulling, and turning, we all became kids too. Many times we would find ourselves on the floor playing with her. This is when the fun began for me, and Natalie developed quite a laugh when she was only a couple of months old.

At five months Natalie was turning and crawling, but she couldn't sit until the following month. From then on Natalie followed us wherever we went. In our house we have many different levels, and you can't avoid the stairs. Fortunately they are all carpeted, just in case, and in no time Natalie could handle them like a pro. She crawled for six months, since using a walker would be dangerous in our house.

Natalie was a pretty careful child. She was not an active little girl who loved to climb and fix everything she saw. We did not childproof our house at all. I just made sure someone always knew where she was. She seemed to know what things she was permitted to touch and which she was not, so we were very relaxed about that.

There is one drawer in the kitchen she loved. It was full of towels and all kinds of pot holders in different colors. She took them out and put them in, and had so much fun while making excited noises. That was the only drawer she kept going after.

Music has been very important to Natalie since she was four months old. By six months she could move her body back and forth in rhythm. She loved to dance, and would sit on the floor uttering to music, moving her whole body and smiling. She danced as soon as she was able to walk. Now she sings and gives a free performance to anyone at any time.

Michael Jackson's "Beat It" was Natalie's first hit song. She recognized this song wherever we went, and we finally bought the record.

Stevie Wonder's "I Just Called to Say I Love You" was another hit. She will hold anything in her hands to pretend she has a microphone and will sing with full expression, just like the singers on TV.

The one big move Natalie made that we missed was when she started to walk at one year. It happened during the two weeks we left her (for the first time) with my parents in Holland. When we came back she was walking and she did not want me anymore. That really brought tears to my eyes. But the grandparents had so much fun watching her first steps.

Generally I don't believe in pushing Natalie to do something she isn't ready for. It never bothers me if I hear that my friends' children are able to do certain things earlier. Natalie is a healthy child and shows every sign of being a happy, normal little girl. It depends only on us, the parents, to be as perceptive as possible, to recognize what she needs and then to provide and encourage.

Susan 🐦

Looking at Natasha those first few months, it was hard to imagine that soon she would be running around and that I would hardly remember when she couldn't. But in an amazingly short time she progressed from being completely immobile, with no purposeful movements, to a little ball of fire who never sat still for a moment. I was truly fascinated with the process and watched each advance along the way with great joy.

I'm sure that everyone around me was bored with my effusive pride. I must admit that before I had children I had never been particularly interested in the fact that someone else's child could crawl, sit up, stand, walk, or run, and the fact that he or she did it early was equally unimportant to me. When my good friend Suzanne had her first child, she would report in every telephone conversation her child's latest accomplishment. I would listen politely and try to sound interested and duly impressed, but in fact I would have been just as interested in talking about the weather. Then Natasha was born!

Although I now understand the fascination parents experience as their children learn to move about, it is still unclear to me why we parents take such pride in our child's accomplishments. I was sure that I wouldn't do this, but I do. I am extremely proud that she was walking at eight months. It is an amazing accomplishment, but it wasn't *my* accomplishment. (My parents had to trick me into walking when I was fourteen months old. They pinned a clothespin to the back of my dress so that I thought they were supporting me.) And I didn't teach Natasha to walk—it just came naturally. All I did was watch and laugh and exclaim about how terrific she was. So what do *I* have to be proud of?

Ariana's progression was much slower than Natasha's and I found myself wondering if she would ever walk. But how and

55

when each child walks varies dramatically. Natasha was determined. As soon as she started to get the idea, she would work at it, practicing until she got it. Ariana, on the other hand, was more hesitant, more content to stay at the stage she was comfortable with. For a long time after she started taking steps, she was content to crawl most of the time. The differences make it almost as exciting to watch the second time as it was the first.

Children all do things at their own pace and in their own way. They each have different strengths, but it is hard not to compare children and be proud when yours do something early—or concerned when they do something late.

In retrospect it seems like just overnight from the time they are babies and you are anxiously watching their every move to the time when they don't need or want your constant attention. During the transition it can be difficult to judge just how much attention they do need and find a balance between carelessness and overprotectiveness. We experienced a very scary incident that demonstrates how hard it can be to find this balance. We had rented a condominium with two other couples for the July Fourth weekend. On the Fourth, Natasha, who was then three and a half, had been put to bed in one of the upstairs bedrooms and we were having dinner downstairs. One of the adults went upstairs to do something and discovered Natasha was out of bed and into a bottle of medicine.

The owner of the pills said that there were a lot missing and some of the pills had obviously been in Natasha's mouth. I couldn't believe that she had actually swallowed any. It just didn't seem like her, but then getting into other people's medicines didn't seem like her either. My heart skipped a few beats, then began to race as I realized the gravity of the situation. We questioned Natasha, who said that she had spit the pills into the sink. We checked the sink and could find no trace of any pills. Her story did not seem consistent, so we had to proceed as if she had swallowed some.

At home I keep syrup of ipecac on hand to induce vomiting, but unfortunately I had not put any in my travel kit, so off we went to the nearest hospital. After two doses of ipecac, Natasha vomited. There was no sign of any pills. The doctor assured us that we would have seen some trace of the pills if she had swallowed any.

Natasha was fine the next day, with no apparent residual effect other than the nightmares she had that night, probably due to all of our agitation over the event and having to force the ipecac down her throat over her violent objection. It was a very unpleasant experience for everyone concerned. From now on I will always carry ipecac with me when I travel and keep the poison-control telephone number with me at all times. Having these things only at home isn't good enough!

During the rest of our stay I kept a much closer watch on Natasha, but I believed it would be a mistake to hover over her too closely. There are risks that we must take in life. As our children begin to walk, they begin to walk away from our absolute control. Fortunately this is a gradual process, giving parents time to adjust, but it is difficult nonetheless.

I must gradually let them go. I will continue to try to control their environment to make it as safe for them as possible, but I know that I will not always be able to protect them from harm. I can only hope that the end result will never be much worse than that of the July Fourth episode.

Chapter 4

SLEEP

- Our children's sleep pattern
- How we dealt with lack of sleep
- How soon our babies slept through the night
- Advice we could have lived without
- When our children went from cradle to crib to bed
- Answering nighttime cries
- Sleeping with Mommy and Daddy
- Naps
- Effective bedtime techniques

Diana ❧

At this point my children sleep—whenever we go somewhere in the car. At home, they are awake. That is how Sosia has always liked to spend most of her time. She doesn't want to miss a thing. Sometimes she slept, she must have. She just didn't want me to know about it.

I am telling you about fatigue. When Sosia was born, I learned new depths of exhaustion. Something happens to people who wake up at two, four, and six A.M. I love to sleep. I treasure my sacred time for rest. Nothing is more wonderful to me than to wake up in a room filled with sunlight and feel I am rested and ready to face a new day. Once Sosia arrived, I no longer had any days when I woke up feeling fresh and ready for anything, and I almost never woke up when it was light outside. But I did wake up . . . a lot. I had a new alarm clock called "the baby" who had settings that I could not quite figure out. I kept waiting for the night when I could sleep in—or just sleep through. I would have been happy to sleep four hours straight! Days faded into nights that faded into days. I kept Sosia's feeding schedule on a little card because I had no idea when or where I was. Sosia had a long spell when she did sleep but it was between 6 P.M. and midnight. At first I just couldn't bring myself to go to sleep at six o'clock. Do you know how silly that feels? I had dinner and usually enjoyed a little time with Yogi. Sometimes I would revel in a bit of private time for myself.

I kept hearing stories about people whose babies slept through the nights when they reached four weeks or ten pounds. Sosia was eight weeks and twelve pounds. I was beginning to develop bags under my eyes. I experimented. I changed her patterns around. I bathed her at different times during the day. I took her out on long outings. Then I kept her home for long, quiet, nonstimulating days. She maintained the exact sleep patterns during all the variations. I realized that she simply had very different sleep patterns than I did, and that she didn't need so much sleep. Her sleep patterns were more like Yogi's—a little sleep went a long way.

Yogi and I talked about letting her cry through her wake-up spells, but we both changed our minds during the first three minutes of crying. We just felt that failing to answer her would go against all our feelings of the importance of developing trust. So we adapted survival techniques. We moved Sosia closer so that she didn't need to worry about us. We let her sleep with us, and we showed her the way people sleep. We were all a lot more rested. I also gave up my long evenings and started going to bed at the same time Sosia did. If we were out in the car and Sosia fell asleep, I would find a nice shady tree and pull over to the side of the road and read or rest. I keep a briefcase with a novel, my unanswered correspondence, a few stamps, and a pen. When Sosia fell asleep in the car seat I used her nap time to do the things I wanted to do. I did not continue driving and lose that time of solitude. Surviving through a time when your sleep patterns are interrupted can be a test in creative intelligence. The best thing I did was realize that my sleep was important and that I needed to take steps to secure it. Little luxuries had to be given up. I couldn't stay out until midnight and expect to be chipper the next day after waking up at 2, 4, and 6 A.M. Naps were not indulgences, they were mandatory. I would sleep on the futon on the floor with Sosia and then put up a child gate in the doorway. That way I didn't worry when she got up or began crawling around.

Before Benjamin was born I planned carefully for the possible sleep interruptions. I borrowed a wonderful little bassinet. I stocked the bottom with any necessary items (diapers, etc.) and moved it right next to our bed. When Benjamin began to fuss I just reached over and put his little pacifier into his mouth and I got another hour or so of undisturbed slumber. When he became hungry I just lifted him out of the bassinet and fed him in bed and returned him to the bassinet, *without ever getting out of bed.* It saved me, literally and completely. I was able to sleep and do my duty as a mother, and I didn't even have to get out of bed to do it. I also decided that if Benjamin didn't have diaper rash or a messy diaper, he would be okay until morning. And he was. He slept better and I think he got the message that night was for sleeping and day was for all the necessary items that make life function.

Sosia didn't sleep through the night until eighteen months, so when Benjamin was born I had no expectations. But he surprised me. At four weeks he was sleeping through the night. He took predictable naps twice a day. He has had periods when he sleeps less or when he prefers to stay up late at night, but his schedule can be predicted.

I never have regretted answering the children when they cry. Yogi and I believe that children cry because they need something. Maybe they just need to check to see if you are asleep. Maybe they are lonely. Maybe they need a drink or a hug. But we felt that their cries should be answered in some way. When one of us felt that we just couldn't keep answering the cries, the other seemed to get new energy. We never let either one of our children "cry it out." No matter how exhausted and frustrated we were, one of us found the strength to rock or talk or just be with them when they woke up. We both agree now that we did the right thing for us and our children. They knew then and they know now that whether they are cold, frightened, or simply lonely they can depend on us to be there. To this day we have an open-door policy on our bed and our bedroom. We sometimes get little visitors who are thirsty or frightened. Requests are rarely denied.

Now that both children are out of the crib and able to move about their rooms by themselves, I have taught them to respect each other's sleep and never to awaken someone needlessly. If they wake up early in the morning, they have instructions to sit in bed and look at books or play with puzzles until they hear someone up. This has really made a difference! They can sometimes play quietly for a little while.

We also have regular bedtime rituals every night. This helps set the tone for going to sleep and also sets a definite pattern for a quiet time out for everyone. We begin the bedtime ritual with baths and teeth brushing. Then we move on to storytelling. Both children get the same number of stories or chapters when we read separately. Big books are a family affair and we all read in the same room. After story time the children are allowed to read to themselves or to listen to a tape on their small bedside tape recorders. These small tape recorders are really the best investment I have made. We have tapes of stories that I have recorded for the children and we have tapes of music or books that they enjoy. They are able to maneuver the tapes themselves (as opposed to records, which require adult supervision) and they almost always fall asleep easily.

Jan ❧

I never knew exhaustion until I had my babies. We're not just talking lack of sleep, but physical and mental exhaustion.

It all begins with the lack of sleep. I often thought, "I can't get more tired than this!" But I did. Not often, just one time too many. After my second baby there were times I was so worn out that I felt feverish, aching, and sick. I thought for sure I was coming down with the flu. I would drop into bed, and by the next morning the symptoms would be gone.

"Sleep when the baby sleeps" is advice I often heard, and I really tried to do this. But after I nursed and put the baby down, there were dishes to do, laundry to wash, thank-you notes to write, a shower to take, and a bed to change. By the time I did all that, the baby would wake up. Sleep? Nap? During the day? Ha!

What really amazed me was how the lack of sleep colors your outlook—how you see things, how you feel. How you rationalize or not rationalize, how you're easily perturbed, how you lack patience. I'm sure there would have been fewer arguments with my husband had I been properly rested, fewer tears over the silliest things, fewer showers. I'm sure of all this. I'm just not sure how you can get enough sleep after you've had a baby.

Jaclyn slept in a baby basket next to our bed for the first two months. I was nursing and it was so much easier to reach over, pick up the tiny bundle, and nurse her when she woke up during the wee hours of the morn. I really was rather reluctant to let her sleep all by herself in her own room even after she was two months old.

Our second daughter slept in the same basket for two months beside our bed too. The only advantage in having babies sleep in their own rooms is that the parents aren't awakened by every stir and gurgle the baby makes while asleep. On the other hand, there is something secure about having them right next to you. I mean, what if there should be an earthquake?

I'm not sure how we came to the conclusion that two months was the magic number, and that after that it was "banishment" to their own rooms. No deep voice from above said "two months" and no white envelope with the winning number "two" was handed to me.

The gurgling and quiet whimpers never bothered my husband; he could (and did) sleep through an earthquake. It did begin to bother me. I felt I wasn't getting enough sleep (I woke up if they moved a finger!). But to "send" them to their own rooms seemed so cruel when they were so tiny.

Since I was going back to work after three months, two months seemed a logical time period. In truth, I don't think a baby really cares where it sleeps. It's we moms who seem to be the most apprehensive about our babies leaving our sides. Just think what it is going to be like when we have to send them away to college! At any rate, do what is best for you . . . three months . . . one month . . . one day. And try not to feel too guilty to bid them adios . . . and don't think about earthquakes!

Both babies slept just fine—for them, not for me. Jaclyn never slept through the night until she was past her second birthday. Now she is three, and on rare occasions she will sleep until morning. Thankfully, Jenna slept through the night her first day on earth. (It was a time of rejoicing!) But for the next three months I did get up for feedings, usually two or three times a night. Gradually I noticed she was sleeping longer and longer after her night feedings, and by six months she was sleeping almost from seven to seven. Today at age one she sleeps from about eight in the evening to six in the morning. I have tried many times to put her down at nine so she would sleep an hour later in the morning (a small favor for me on weekends), but it isn't working. Her body clock sets off her own personal alarm at 6 A.M. Since some mornings I barely function at this hour, I give her a bottle and she is usually content to play in her crib.

Jenna gets up quietly with a smile. Jaclyn gets up cranky with a wail. I never had any trouble hearing Jaclyn wake up from a nap or in the morning crying "Mommmeee." But many times Jenna wakes up so quietly, you don't know she's awake until you check on her. Sometimes I suspect she's been up for hours playing in her crib!

I had many long talks with my pediatrician about "encouraging" Jaclyn to sleep through the night. You do have options. He said to let her cry, but I couldn't do this. It bothered me too much to hear such sad crying at two or three or four in the morning or at all of these times.

Even if I thought it was a good idea in principle, I didn't have the strength to withstand the tears.

Other advice I got: Feed her cereal and milk for the last feeding, or feed her formula, since this tends to be "heavier" than mother's milk. Supposedly this would give her that extra bulk that would enable her to sleep through the night. Neither of those tricks worked. I was also advised to be businesslike when Jaclyn awakened at night. Don't hug or kiss her or give these kinds of "rewards" that may encourage her to wake up. I tried this, too (much against my mother's nurturing instincts), and it didn't work either. What I'm really trying to say is, listen to all the well-meaning advice, but *hear* your own instincts and do what you believe is right, and I hope it works for you!

Now that Jaclyn is older we're telling her that if she wakes up and looks out the window and sees it is still dark, she should go right back to sleep again. We even have a saying: "Sleep and sleep until it's light." This backfires during the summer months when it gets light very early in the morning and Jaclyn says at 5:30 A.M., "Look, Mom, it's *getting* light!" I've long wanted to talk to Mother Nature about keeping it darker on weekends.

We let Jaclyn sleep in our bed when she was a baby and for us it was a mistake. She seemed so cute, this tiny child in a great big bed. It was also a good time for John and me to look at our sleeping angel (finally) and marvel that she was ours. It seemed like such an innocent, nurturing, loving thing to do. After Jaclyn fell asleep I would move her to her own bed. If she woke up at night (Did I say if? I mean when), I would carry her back to our bed to fall back to sleep. Big mistake. Now she wants to sleep in "Mommy's bed" all the time. It's nice and cozy when Mommy has had lots of sleep, but when Mommy or Daddy get home late, Jaclyn in bed with us is not a picnic. She *wants* it to be a picnic . . . she wants to drink juice or milk, read a book, and sing or talk. Mommy and Daddy want to sleep! I really want to break her of this habit, but then she gets up crying at two or three or four, I don't have the strength to be tough. My only salvation is, I don't think she'll want to sleep in "Mommy's bed" when she's sixteen!

During the weekdays while I am at work, the girls take naps. Jenna takes a morning nap and an afternoon nap; Jaclyn takes only an afternoon nap. Both of their dispositions are infinitely better with naps. On weekends they must know their mom is a real pushover because Jenna will take only one nap—two hours if I'm lucky, one hour if I'm not. Jaclyn will nap for about an hour if I beg and plead and sometimes even bribe her.

Two months before her sister was born, Jaclyn moved from the crib to her "big-girl bed." We made a big deal about it. I took her to the store to pick out her bed and we said good-bye to her crib. We raved about her new bed and how wonderful it is to have such a big bed. It must have all worked because she never once asked about her crib again. When the crib magically appeared for the baby, it was as if she had never seen it before. She seemed to have no comprehension that she had slept in it for almost two years, and had given it up only two months before. But this new "big-girl" bed did not guarantee that Jaclyn would sleep through the night. It only makes it easier for her to slip out and into "Mommy's bed." Only thirteen more years till she's sixteen!

Katherine ❧

When Deren was born I thought, like many new mothers, that my new little sweetie pie would adopt a regular sleep schedule and at least sleep in his own crib. When Alexandra came along I knew better.

The only time I could count on my children sleeping was during their daily naps. Since I have never been a nap person, these naps did not do me—or my husband, for that matter—much good. With each child we went through nearly a year like zombies. On occasion Jack and I would get a sound sleep. I wonder sometimes whether we were both so exhausted that we'd slept through some crying and squawking. I sort of doubt it, but those few restful, deep-sleep nights provided us with a new enthusiasm and perspective for the day.

I read all my baby books on the subject of sleep and then went to bookstores and explored more, I found out little more than what I already knew. Basically there are two schools of thought: Respond to the baby or ignore the baby. I had a lot of trouble with the latter idea although it made perfect sense. I would do a mental trip called "My baby needs me" (he's hungry, wet, scared, hurt, etc.). I had to find out. The majority of the time the baby was hungry and lonely and wanted some cuddling. I would continue this quest for more knowledge because I thought there was something magical that I needed to know in order to assure everyone a peaceful, uninterrupted night's sleep. Other mothers had told me their babies were heavy sleepers from two weeks on.

When Deren was an infant we kept him in a bassinet by our bed. At his first whimper I would reach over and lift him into bed and nurse him. I would fall asleep with him nursing in the center of our bed so he wouldn't fall out, and the three of us (Jack, Deren, and me) slept just great.

Many books state that your children shouldn't sleep with you because they need to adjust to their own surroundings and get used to their own beds. I would say "hogwash" to this advice. Both Jack and I needed to sleep. We had regular jobs during the day and needed to be alert. I also loved having this special time with the children at night because I miss them. The practical solution was for us all to sleep together. By the time Deren was finally sleeping through the night in his "big-boy" bed and only visiting us a couple of nights a week, Alexandra was born. We went through the same system with the bassinet, and in those early days, the four of us would usually wake up together.

As you can tell, I am not a person who can let a baby cry unless it is an unusual circumstance where nothing I can do will make the baby feel better. In the middle of the night when each of my children wanted to nurse, they would invariably cry until they were cozily nuzzling at my breast. After I learned to accept that about them and myself, life went much more smoothly and I didn't read sleep chapters anymore.

Jack seemed to enjoy our system of being one happy family in the king-sized bed. He and I were the slices of bread and the children were the peanut butter and jelly respectively. Occasionally the jelly would get sticky when she would squirm and kick. The peanut butter slept like a rock, which was great. Sometimes Jack and I would carefully carry them back to their own beds so we could cuddle and have some personal time together.

On other nights when I was completely exhausted because of a fussy, unsleepy child, Jack would take either sleepless Deren or Alexandra down to the living room and listen to KJAZ, our local jazz station. I would nod off with a good feeling, knowing that Jack and Deren or Alexandra would be cuddling well into the wee hours of the morning. This became a magnificent solution for everyone because Jack loved the cuddling and the jazz; he also needed less sleep than I, probably because he wasn't nursing and I was the resident milk machine. "After all," I would ask myself, "why did we have children in the first place if it wasn't to hug and cuddle, tickle, enjoy, and play with them?" Jack experienced a huge boost in his relationship with each child when they would share their special late-night times together. Even today Deren and Alexandra will say, "Daddy, can we listen to KJAZ with you?"

During the day my babies would happily fall asleep in the automatic baby wind-up swing. The Gerry Bear type was my favorite because the others were too noisy. I notice many parents carrying sleeping children around in baby front packs or backpacks. Also, driving the child in his/her infant seat in the car usually worked like a charm as long as the child was sucking a bottle or pacifier.

When both babies were tiny I would rock them in their baby chairs, take them for walks in the stroller, and rock them to sleep in a cradle. The motion and the sucking became a tried and true combination. I would also put lots of pillows and stuffed animals around each child so they would feel well padded and "snuggled." I think this helped them to feel cozy and secure. I was given a record of actual sounds in the womb, and I would play this for Deren in his first weeks. I really don't know if the record worked or not. The noises from the recording "got to me" and didn't make me tired because it sounded like whooshing (blood through the arteries) and "boom-boom, boom-boom" from a heart pounding. I think I also heard some indigestion sounds from the stomach, but I wasn't sure.

When Alexandra was born Danielle lent me a darling stuffed teddy bear that also played "back in the womb" sounds. They seemed more palatable coming from a recording inside a cute teddy and the sounds were softer. Both children managed to sleep, but not specifically at the times I would have preferred.

It's important for you to come up with a strategy you feel comfortable with and can live with. Once we lightened up and went with the flow, sleep was not a problem for us anymore.

Now that the children are older, we continue a ritual we started when Deren became school age. I read the children stories at 7:30 P.M. and have lights out or soft lights at 8:00 P.M. We cuddle and hug each other during the stories and they sleep through the night, usually until 6:30 A.M.. At that time they both run down the hall to our room. Deren uses the bathroom first and usually wakes up Alexandra to come to our room with him. We go back to sleep for another forty-five minutes or an hour and then it's "up and at 'em" time at the Dusays.

Mary 🦢

Natalie's sleeping pattern was the easiest when she was a baby. She slept most of the time under any conditions, at least for the first two months. Often we had to keep her awake at feeding time. When Frank gave her the bottle he would keep Natalie awake by constantly moving it. Our house was peaceful and quiet then.

Natalie stayed with us in a basket bassinet in our room. This was easiest, especially when she needed night feeding. During the day I could move the basket all over the house with me.

Right around the time I went back to work, Natalie's sleeping pattern changed. The last feeding was at 11 P.M. and the first feeding was between four and five o'clock in the morning. By the time Natalie was one year old, she needed less sleep. She went to bed at 9 P.M., got up at 8 A.M., and took two naps of one hour each during the day. We did enjoy her going to bed a little late, since we came home rather late every day. This way, we had more time to play with her.

Bedtime was never a hassle for us until Natalie turned two and a half years old, when she did not want to go to bed unless we went to bed too. She wanted to stay up just like the grown-ups did. This time she was so determined that she made the effort to climb out of her crib. Our tricks and games began. Natalie would sometimes sneak out of her room very quietly and sit in the dark in the living room, where we were, sucking her thumb, afraid of being noticed and yet wanting us to notice her so badly. Several times we let her fall asleep in our bed and then moved her to her own bed, but she was really heavy by now, and half an hour later she would wake up and cry, feeling totally insulted. How could we play such a dirty trick on her? So she was usually back in our bed instead. Natalie refused to go to bed unless she was really sleepy, but when that happened she would sleep anywhere—she could not even keep her eyes open.

At three years old she now takes one nap in the afternoon for one hour and goes to bed at night at 10 P.M. She rarely wakes up during the night and gets up at 8 A.M. Our new sleep problem is that she is scared to be alone in her own room now. She never cared about this before, and used to sing in her own bed when she woke up in the morning. But when we came back from a trip—we went for a month to visit the grandparents in Holland— Natalie no longer wanted to go to bed in her own room at night. In Holland she was mostly sleeping with my parents and got a great deal of attention. Now she creates stories about lions, tigers, and dragons under her bed. She is scared of her own stories, and has been sleeping in our bed at night.

Shortly after our return from this trip, Frank and I decided to separate. First he moved to a different bedroom. Natalie slept with me at that time. I really did not want to shake her up even more, so I did not push her to sleep in her own bed.

When Frank moved out, four months later, I bought Natalie a

new twin-sized bed and linens with teddy bears all over the sheets, pillow, and quilt. She loves the teddy bears and was excited about her room, but at night I think she is confused, still scared of the dark, and needs the security of being with an adult on whom she depends most. I try to read her stories until she falls asleep in her bed, but one hour later she always gets up and comes to bed with me.

Everyone I talk to disapproves of my allowing my daughter to sleep with me, but I am sure that one of these days she will develop more security and will feel that it is also wonderful to sleep in her own bed surrounded by all her favorite stuff. I'll always try to find a way to tell her that whatever happened had nothing to do with her, and that I'm here for her always and she can feel totally secure that I will never leave her.

As much as I am waiting for the day when Natalie can sleep in her own bed peacefully, I am also enjoying having her sleep next to me. Her innocent face is so wonderful to look at, a real angel. And, after all, I don't see her as much during the day as I wish I could.

Susan ❧

Sleep? What's that? I don't think I've had a good night's sleep in the last three and a half years!

When Natasha and Ariana were newborns they slept in a cradle in our room, which made the nighttime feedings easier. I didn't have to turn on a light or stumble around in the dark. I merely reached over and lifted them into bed with me and let them nurse as I rested. There were many times when I would fall asleep while they nursed and wouldn't wake up until they were hungry again. As they became more vocal and started to move about more in the cradle, the noise disturbed Dick's sleep.

At that point we moved them into a crib in their own room, just next to ours.

Although Natasha nursed every two or three hours, I believed that she would stop the nighttime feedings as she no longer needed them and thus gradually begin to sleep through the night. I am a very patient person and I probably would still be waiting, but by the time she was sixteen months old, Dick had had it. He insisted that I should stop the nighttime feedings, and I reluctantly agreed. At first she slept worse, waking up every hour (or more often) and crying, screaming, throwing full tantrums. It was a very unpleasant experience. Gradually, very gradually, after the nighttime feedings were stopped, Natasha began to sleep a little better. By the time she was twenty-two months old, she would occasionally sleep through.

During her third year she probably slept all night about half the time. At first there was no apparent explanation for why she would awaken sometimes and not others. Then I began to notice a pattern. She always slept through if a baby-sitter put her to bed, she sometimes slept through if Dick put her to bed, and she never slept through when I put her to bed. Strange but true. This phenomenon lasted for several months—then faded.

We tried everything to get Natasha to sleep through the night except letting her cry. I read every article I could find and tried everything they suggested—most of which I had already tried. Most of the recommendations centered on not encouraging wakefulness by turning on lights, feeding or playing with the child, etc. I always made a conscious effort not to go to Natasha the minute she made any noise. Instead, I waited to be sure that she was awake and really crying for attention. I would then go to her (or take her back to bed, if she had wandered into our room), lay her back down, cover her up, tell her to go to sleep, then go back to bed myself. She always went right back to sleep, only to wake up again anywhere from one to four hours later. After Natasha was weaned Dick did his share of nighttime duty. This helped some, but I began to wonder if we would ever feel rested again.

Nothing worked—not even our desperation tries at yelling and spanking. Actually, sometimes these desperation efforts worked for a while but they made me feel guilty and Dick and I usually ended up arguing about it afterward. It wasn't worth it. I think that Natasha will always wake up during the night. With time, however, she is learning that she should not bother us unless it is an emergency. For those of you who are experiencing this same type of nighttime horror, have faith, things *will* get better.

There are lots of books and articles that recommend letting your child "cry it out." The theory goes that the crying gradually decreases until the third or fourth night, when it stops, and the child has been taught to sleep through the night. Well, I just can't do this. It doesn't seem right to me. I'm not saying it doesn't work. I know that you can teach a child not to cry by not responding to the crying. But I worry about what the trade-off might be.

I know that I am being manipulated by going to my child every time she cries at night, but I don't believe that manipulation is necessarily bad. A child cries because he or she needs something, even if it's only attention. I have a very unpleasant visceral response to my child's cry, and I've never talked to a mother that didn't. I believe that there is a very good reason for this strong reaction to a child's cry, and I am not willing to ignore it.

I also know that there is some point at which you cannot allow your child to manipulate you. At some point a child is old enough to understand what he or she is doing and to learn that it is okay to be alone at times, even at night. We are now working on that with Natasha.

Dick did not really disagree with me in principle, but he thought that the time had come to stop the manipulation much sooner than I did. This difference caused one of the worst arguments we have ever had.

I did let Ariana cry occasionally. She is very different from Natasha, and when she gets overly tired she needs to unwind. Crying a little seems to do this for her and helps her fall asleep. The crying begins to wind down from the first, and rarely lasts longer than five minutes. Natasha's crying never wound down. It escalated and she would become more and more agitated the longer she cried.

Natasha stopped sleeping in her crib at a very early age, sometime between eleven and thirteen months (I say thirteen, Dick says eleven). One night she became very upset when I got her anywhere near her crib, so I put her in the double bed that was in her room and she has slept there ever since. She has never fallen out of bed, but she can easily get out of bed and come into our room. I don't have any philosophical problem with having a child sleep in bed with the parents, but neither Dick nor I sleep as well when Natasha is in bed with us so we instituted a rule that she could not sleep in our bed until it was light outside. So for a long time most mornings at dawn she would come in, climb in bed with us, and go back to sleep. I may not sleep as well as if she weren't there, but it sure beats getting up with her at the crack of dawn! The number of times she comes in has gradually decreased. Now, at four years, she seldom does. In fact, she has finally begun to sleep all night more often than not. Hurray!

Although sleeping through the night was always a problem with Natasha, bedtime wasn't until she became a year old. Before that when she got tired she would come to me to nurse and fall asleep in my arms. As she got older, however, she began to go to sleep later and later. At first I didn't mind—I preferred sleeping in in the morning to having my evening free. But when at about fourteen months she was up until eleven or twelve o'clock at night and still going strong, I decided it was time to institute a bedtime. Since she was still nursing, it wasn't too difficult. Around eight o'clock I would get her into her pajamas, then let her play a little longer, and sometime between 8:30 and 9:00 I would take her to bed, read her a story, and let her nurse. At first I would sit with her until she fell asleep, but as she became more stubborn we began to tell her that it was bedtime and she must stay in bed. We would then leave the room. For a long time we had to put her back in her room many times each night, but gradually we had less trouble getting her to stay in bed.

Natasha reinvented every trick in the book to keep us with her at bedtime. She needed a drink of water; she needed a doll to sleep with; she needed a kiss; she needed a hug, first from Mommy, then from Daddy, then from Mommy again; she needed to tell me something. . . . We allowed her to carry on for a while but gradually cut off the process after fewer and fewer requests. We put an end to them by threatening to close the door if she didn't stop calling. Sometimes we actually had to close the door for a while, but usually just the threat worked and she would give up. Natasha is definitely a master at manipulation, however.

73

One night when I was being firm she stood up in her bed, stretched out her arms toward me, and said in a very pleading tone, "Mommy, I *love* you and I *need* you. *Please* stay with me for a little while." Well, what's a mother to do? There goes consistency!

Each stage passes. Sure enough, the bedtime troubles did. Now Natasha puts up only an obligatory fuss about going to bed. After one story it takes only one good-night kiss from each of us and a promise to check on her "in a few minutes," and she's asleep in no time.

While Natasha was still nursing, naps were never an issue for us. When she was tired she would fall asleep nursing and I would put her in bed. She graduated to one nap rather early. Once she was weaned, nap time became more difficult. The easiest way to get her to sleep was to be in the car at nap time; she would just drift off. But if I was at home there was frequently trouble. On the days I had a baby-sitter helping me I let the sitter put her to bed. Natasha was always better behaved for other people than she was for me, and the baby-sitter never seemed to have much difficulty putting her down for her nap. When I was on my own we invariably fought. I would read her a story and leave the room, then put her back in her room, then put her back in her room again. . . . One trick that sometimes worked was to let her sleep on the couch if she promised to go right to sleep. Other times I just didn't have the energy to fight with her. Invariably, however, when I didn't insist on a nap she would fall asleep late in the afternoon, sleep for three hours, and then be awake very late at night. It wasn't a good solution.

Just before Natasha's third birthday she had gotten to the point that it was impossible to get her to sleep before three or four in the afternoon. If I got her to stay down earlier, she didn't sleep. When she finally fell asleep she slept so long that bedtime was difficult. I tried waking her up after an hour, but that was a very big mistake; she would be impossible for several hours afterward. So I decided to give up entirely on naps. She is doing quite well without them. What a pleasure not having to fight with her over naps! We have enough to fight about.

Ariana has not been as difficult when it comes to sleeping, although there have been mornings when she was awake and ready to play at four o'clock (Natasha never did that!). Even Ariana didn't sleep through the night on a regular basis until she was about a year old, but she woke up less frequently and didn't fight as hard over bedtime. She was probably somewhat easier because we had learned something from our mistakes with Natasha, but also sleep is more important to her. On two or three occasions she has actually led one of us into her room and pointed to her bed when she was tired! How different can two children be?

When I was getting the least sleep, looking like a zombie and acting like a shrew, I read an article on the sleeplessness of parenthood which suggested that it was possible to adjust to less sleep with the right attitude. So I decided to start my day by telling myself I would feel as though I had had eight hours of uninterrupted sleep. I got out of bed, showered, dressed, and pretended to be rested. I was amazed at how well this worked. You see, there's hope. If your child doesn't let you get enough sleep, lie to yourself about it.

Chapter 5

INTO THE MOUTHS OF BABES

- Breast feeding and bottle feeding
- How soon our children were weaned
- How soon they gave up the bottle
- Introducing solids and juices
- Choking
- Letting the children eat snacks
- How we feel about sugar
- Pacifiers and thumb-sucking

Diana 🐌

When I began breast-feeding I could scarcely believe that women were able to achieve those serene expressions in the glossy magazines. It *hurt*! Everyone kept telling me that the feeding schedule should be every four hours, but Sosia was nursing every couple of hours. I learned that although nursing is as old as man, it can be difficult to get started, and there seems to be a lot of confusion on the subject. Many people I talked to felt that nursing was passé, immodest, or inconvenient.

The LaLeche League provided an enormous fund of information. I learned to relax, to prepare myself beforehand to flow into the experience, to allow the let-down reflex to happen. We have to get in tune with our bodies so that they will work effectively with our minds. We have to learn to relax, and to give that feeling of relaxation to the child.

Another important source of information was the Nursing Mothers Council. They have a more relaxed and casual attitude than LaLeche. They endorse the idea that you can have it both ways: you can nurse on demand and occasionally give the baby a bottle. They reminded me of some of the basics: to drink an enormous amount of fluid, to relax, and to nurse in a calm and relaxed atmosphere, with the baby supported.

Breast feeding was one of the nicest ways I spent time with my children. I enjoyed the quiet, intimate interaction we shared. Breast feeding was convenient, comfortable, and warm. With Sosia it was a way to share time consistently and regularly. With Benjamin it was a wonderful way for all three of us to share a quiet, peaceful moment together. We would sit on the couch and I would nurse Benjamin while Sosia snuggled up next to us with a book or blanket. That way all of us were able to enjoy the experience.

Beginning breast feeding can be a painful surprise! When I began nursing Sosia I couldn't believe that women could manage to hold out for a week or two, let alone longer. Fortunately the discomfort lasted for a very short time. Within about two weeks we had a wonderful system set up that was great for both of us. The pain was replaced by the convenience and the comfort of nursing. No bottles and messes to deal with in the middle of the night. I soon discovered the comfort and joy of nursing my baby in bed with me, then returning him to the bassinet that we kept next to the bed. I never worried about having fresh formula or forgetting a bottle. My equipment was always ready and refreshments were always at the correct temperature. If the baby was hungry, I could pull the car over to the side of the road and nurse. In a restaurant or while visiting friends a small receiving blanket made a wonderful tent that provided all the privacy I needed. Many times people didn't even realize that I was nursing at all. A loose-fitting blouse can also provide this privacy.

I nursed Sosia conveniently for about fourteen months. I was not always there to nurse Benjamin because Sosia's schedule would take me away from home more often, but I nursed him for approximately twelve months and he took supplementary bottles successfully when I was not there. I tried to express breast milk with Sosia but it proved to be an enormous bother and inconvenience. Also I was concerned about the possibility of improper sterilization and storage. So I switched to formulas that were already prepared in the bottle. Since those formulas were infrequent substitutes for breast milk, I felt it was worth my peace of mind to be certain that the milk was completely sterile.

Benjamin enjoyed substitutes of bottle formula more frequently. I tried at first to supplement the same feeding every day, but that was not always possible, and I soon found that whatever feeding I was not able to give him myself was supplemented successfully—often even more than one. It became apparent that nursing had no restrictions or minuses, just convenience and pluses.

Both children adapted easily to bottles and breast feeding. I introduced a bottle of formula as a substitute as soon as I left the baby with a sitter at about one month of age. Although they fussed occasionally, they were generally just happy for the food. After I weaned Benjamin from breast feeding he became very attached to the bottle despite all my efforts. He liked to suck on it from one side or the other so that he could watch everyone while he was drinking. It was annoying to watch, but almost impossible to get him to give up. Worse yet, when it wasn't the bottle it was a "nuk" (a pacifier). Although they are supposed to be orthodontically okay, Benjamin has developed an occlusion problem from using bottles for too long.

The dentist told me that the best way to rid a household of unwanted pacifiers was to do so with your child in a *fun* and *final* manner. For example, we attached the pacifier in question to a toy boat, said a quick good-bye, and watched it sail into oblivion. Benjamin loved the ceremony (and waved "bye-bye") and he never asked for the pacifier again!

However, bottles were still in our house. Since pacifiers had gone to the world of never-never land, the bottles gained new popularity. What to do? I called my pediatrician. He told me that there were children who needed those bottles more than Benjamin. I needed to find one. I casually forewarned Benjamin that there had been a new baby born who really needed the bottles. The bottles left one day during his nap. I thought he wouldn't believe me. I knew he would be impossible to live with. But I was wrong. He absorbed my weak story quickly and went on with the day as if he had never taken a bottle.

The two pieces of equipment that were essential to my enjoyment of nursing were a soft chair (or couch corner) and a pillow for the arm that supported the baby. With those two things at hand, I was off and happy to be nursing both my children for many happy months.

My children were introduced to solids in a very informal way. At that stage solid food is a novelty rather than a necessity. If they were curious, I would give them little tastes of food when we were eating, either by piece or by mashing something up and letting them feed themselves. It almost seemed strange to give my children table food, particularly since they were thriving on breast milk. Whenever I sat down to dinner my children would come to life and insist that they sit on one knee or in the high chair to watch. What solids to introduce became a meal-by-meal decision. There are many things on a regular dinner plate that are quite nice when chopped up for a toddler, and cooked peas or carrots are fine finger foods. I was always very cautious about what my children were eating because I was afraid of choking. Many pediatricians have lists of appropriate finger foods to give little ones. Be sure to pick one up and avoid the dangerous foods.

When I stopped nursing I purchased a supply of commercially prepared baby foods because I felt safe that the baby was getting enough protein. The little jars of food were also very convenient and traveled well. But good alternatives are in most refrigerators.

Teaching my children to drink from a cup was a bigger challenge than I had expected. Unless I had the time to sit and hold the cup, they would eventually manage to get all the liquid everywhere except in their mouths. I tried using the cups with the lids but they would pop open when they were dropped. (My children also discovered that they would explode quite effectively when thrown against the wall. Such fun.) I had better luck with a Tupperware cup that has a hole for a straw and an expanded bottom for stability. With that cup I could let go for just an instant and allow a little self-sufficiency without having to clean the kitchen floor. I still monitored drinking from the cup very carefully.

The biggest surprise about starting solids and table fluids was that now there were decisions to be made about what the baby would eat. Was he or she getting enough protein, enough milk, enough vegetable? What had too much sugar? Was baby eating the correct proportions of the appropriate foods? I worried over the food choices I made and was always certain that they had a dose of daily vitamins. Now I talk to them about their own food choices. I keep sugar products to a minimum and discourage unnecessary snacking. I read about nutrition and try to make sure that they are getting balanced meals. The choice is really theirs, so educating them and making them aware of food choices seems to be the best method to assure them continued good health.

Jan 🦆

There was never any question that I wanted to breast-feed. (And my husband was all for the idea too. . . . Was it the thought that his wife would finally have a cleavage?) The only question that ever arose was *where* to breast-feed. In front of relatives and close friends, I had no reservations. In front of acquaintances who were visiting I wasn't sure if I should ask ("Do you mind if I nurse my baby?" In my own home, I found it odd.) or if I should excuse myself to nurse in another room. I did a little of both.

After a few months nursing got to be so routine and I felt so comfortable with it, I nursed everywhere! In department stores, restaurants, the county fair, even while shopping in the super-market. I remember sitting under a tree at our local county fair and nursing when some fans of the television show I host came along and wanted to chat and look at the baby. They finally blurted out politely, "Could we see the baby?" I said, "Sure, but she's busy eating!" I guess they couldn't understand why I was holding the baby so close to me and had her partially covered with my blouse.

Blouses saved me. Sometimes I would wrap a blanket around the baby—and you really couldn't tell if she was nursing. I never bought any nursing bras, but used bras that opened in the front. As for the leaking problem, I used sanitary napkins cut in half. I just placed half the napkin in my bra and tossed it out when it was soaked.

I think nursing in public is perfectly fine if it's done discreetly. I never thought of myself as an exhibitionist, but I did nurse in public rather than return to the car (which could be blocks away) or sit in some bathroom that did not pass the white-glove test.

What really surprised me about nursing was how strong a baby's sucking can be. How can a tiny baby with such a tiny mouth cause a nipple to crack and bleed? I often wondered about this as tears sprang to my eyes when I nursed with cracked nipples (both sides!). I did all the rubbing with towels before the baby was born and used all the creams, but my nipples were still tender in the beginning and cracked and bled. I tried every suggestion offered, and the only hope I offer you is that they do heal within a couple of days. I stood over a light bulb (apparently the heat brings blood to the affected nipples and speeds healing) and didn't wear a bra as often as possible. Any moisture also slows the healing process. I kept nursing despite the pain and gallons of tears. Other women say they pumped their breasts for a few days and then resumed nursing.

I nursed each baby for about four months. When I returned to work after three months I tried to nurse mornings and eve-nings, but I found my milk supply diminished as my work schedule increased. After a few weeks I just didn't have enough to satisfy the baby. I did miss the closeness of nursing, but I found it in other ways . . . like lots of tight hugging and kissing.

Because I knew I would be returning to work, I started to supplement both babies at two weeks. (On the recommendation of my pediatrician, I used Similac with Jaclyn. I used the powder form, mixing formula every night. Powder is the least expensive, but when Jenna came along, I switched to ready-to-feed. Costs a few pennies more, but saves precious time.) I never had any problem with them taking either the breast or the bottle. Either my kids are good eaters and don't really care where the food comes from (just so it comes) or I started to supplement early enough that they easily accepted both.

Each child preferred different nipples. Jaclyn much preferred the wider, firmer Evenflo nipple. Jenna seemed to prefer the Playtex softer nipple. If you're having trouble with the bottles, try different nipples. Different children . . . different preferences. And starting so young!

At first, drinking from a cup was a novelty for Jaclyn, but when I had Jenna, Jaclyn—who was then two—wanted to continue with the bottle. Finally, when she was almost three, I suggested we give all her bottles to baby Eddie (a friend) to use. We packed them up all together, and I had Jaclyn give the package to Eddie's mom. We praised her no end. What a big girl she was now! On occasion she would ask for a bottle and we would remind her that she had given them all away.

Well, this wonderful idea lasted maybe three months, until our household went through a lot of changes and Jaclyn cried and begged for the bottle. I gave in. I felt she apparently needed the extra security and that her drinking from a bottle was only embarrassing to me, certainly not to her. My pediatrician reassures me that she will not go to college with a bottle in her mouth. I hope he's right.

Commercial baby food proved just fine by me. It was convenient and quick. Thirty seconds in the microwave and it was ready to feed! After a year I started giving both children table food, and find it a lot easier on the budget! Check with your pediatrician, but I remember everything got easier after rounding that first year. It was as if the green light came on and the babies graduated to "adult" food (cut up into wee pieces) and cow's milk (no more formula to buy!). As for juices, I gave them apple juice at three months, and today it is one of their favorites along with grape, orange, and fruit punch—all natural, of course.

This brings to mind a "natural" topic. I'm sure you've all heard of the possibility of artificial flavors, colors, and preservatives, as well as sugar, causing hyperactivity in children. I'm a believer, thanks to the late Dr. Ben Feingold, who studied hyperactive children and wrote extensively on the subject. Luckily, my children are not hyperactive, but as any concerned parent, I watch the sugar intake of my children, and I do read labels at the market. "All natural, no artificial flavors, colors, and preservatives" are keys for me.

If you'd like more information, check with your pediatrician or visit the library or bookstore. Some books you might want to read are:

Why Your Child Is Hyperactive, by Dr. Ben Feingold (1974), Random House.

Help for Hyper Children Through Diet and Love, by Janie Wall Mitchell (1984), Betterway Publications.

Improving Your Child's Behavior Chemistry, by Dr. Lendon Smith (1976), Prentice-Hall.

Feed Your Kids Right, by Dr. Lendon Smith (1979), McGraw-Hill.

Foods for Healthy Kids, by Dr. Lendon Smith (1981), McGraw-Hill.

Chocolate is my passion, and I feel guilty about admitting this after just discussing hyperactivity in children, but I really don't want my children to eat a lot of sugar. I'm not a battle-ax about it, but I feel in due time they will eat lots of sweets and I don't need to push it.

My three-year-old gets chocolate as a "treat," also known as a bribe. Two M&Ms or two chocolate-covered raisins if she goes to the potty. I never doubted that either of my kids would *love* chocolate as much as I do. They have not disappointed me yet.

The only rule that I really try to insist on is: no food upstairs in the bedrooms. Cookies and snacks are eaten in the kitchen, family room, or—the best place of all—outside! (You don't have to clean up crumbs outside!)

Neither one of my children are thumb-suckers, and neither of them took to pacifiers. I consider myself lucky. I really don't like the look of a pacifier in a child's mouth. However, when they were kicking and screaming and I wanted some quiet, I did try the pacifier; it just didn't take.

Katherine ❧

I am a big believer in nursing. I believe mother's milk is the best elixir and nourishment that money can't buy. Also, I'm one of the world's worst cooks. I couldn't face needing to remember to grocery shop, buy formulas and baby foods, wash bottles and keep them handy. With nursing I never worried about whether juices would hurt my children's teeth or whether my children would develop milk allergies or other problems.

I nursed each child for two years. I felt delighted that I always had a full, fresh, sanitized amount of milk available at any time. I fed both children on demand to our mutual satisfaction. Nursing has been a very rewarding part of motherhood to me.

Mothers' milk was practically my children's complete diet for the first six months of life. Jack and I gave them occasional bottles of commercial formula so they would be used to them and so that relatives and baby-sitters could feed them as well.

I had a few problems with leakage and sore breasts. Since I am not overly endowed, I have not worn a bra since high school, even during my years of nursing. The biggest problem I would experience was occasional leaking of milk. Suddenly without warning I would experience a tingling and swelling sensation in my breasts—the signal of the famous "let down" response that nursing mothers know—and embarrassing spots would appear on my blouse. Sometimes a child's cry (any child, anywhere) would initiate it. Other times, I would be at lunch or with a client during a regular nursing time. I learned to wear absorbent tops and cover-up jackets. After about nine months, this ceased to be a problem, although I'm not sure why.

I was happy to give my children pacifiers. A child loves to suck; not only does he or she get food and nourishment that way, it also becomes a method of achieving deep relaxation. I provided both children with pacifiers and I let them nurse on my breasts as long as they wanted, even well after all my milk was gone. They would nuzzle and peacefully fall asleep while looking so gorgeous, pink-cheeked, and contented. Although neither child sucked a thumb, that would not have bothered me because I see it as a natural pacifier. Sucking releases tension and calms them down.

I introduced solid, mashed foods to the children at six months, and finger foods took over at about nine months. Both children loved feeding themselves at early ages and felt very grown up walking around with bread sticks to gum and pieces of cheese to suck.

I had two very scary experiences with choking. The books recommended apples and carrots as great finger foods for kids, but my children choked badly on them. There is nothing more frightening than seeing your small child gasping and looking scared with a piece of apple or carrot wedged in his or her throat. My immediate response was to turn the child upside down and rap him sharply on the back. Both times this worked, and the food was dislodged and coughed up, but the fright remained with me. I promised myself I would never give either child any food until he or she had the necessary teeth and knew how to use them.

Jack and I used to love to eat gourmet deli food—remember, I dislike cooking intensely—and consequently the children ate all kinds of things in their younger days. As they got older they lost their taste for many of our more exotic favorites. I was saddened until I discovered that kids go in and out of food stages. "I want a peanut-butter sandwich," is followed a few hours later by "How could you give me peanut butter? Ugh!" Jack and I don't make a big deal out of any of this. What the children don't like today they will like later, and vice versa.

We try very hard to have only nutritious foods, snacks, and drinks around so that Deren and Alexandra can choose from wholesome foods. I like having them participate in food-planning schedules. We eat primarily fish and chicken in our house, with fresh vegetables, fruits, and salads. We started cutting out fats, oils, butter, and mayonnaise when Deren was two and my father had suffered a major heart attack. My father recovered and adopted a modified Pritikin eating plan, which made a lot of sense to our family. We have been trying to eat that way ever since. At restaurants Alexandra will look at the waiter with perfect seriousness and say "We're not a mayonnaise family."

For special treats and celebrations we bring out the cake, candy, and ice cream. Usually the kids don't want too much. (The biggest problem is with *me*.) I feel good that our kids don't get this kind of stuff habitually. They don't crave it or expect it.

Our general philosophy about food is not to make a big deal about it. I remind myself not to get excited about a particular situation. If I'm not comfortable with a certain phase, I know it will pass. Sometimes the children are hungry, sometimes they're not. Sometimes they'll eat well, sometimes they won't. I don't insist that they eat everything. I request that they take at least a bite of each thing to try it, but it's okay if they don't like it. If they're really dawdling—playing with their food or making messes—I tell them to eat three more bites of anything and then they can be excused. They can take any size bites. They also know that the kitchen is closed after dinner until breakfast.

When I get stuck in any situation, whether it is food, sleeping, or whatever, I remind myself to look at animals in nature to see how they go through the situation. Mother birds feed their babies as long as they squawk for it, mother monkeys keep their babies with them at all times, when young, on their tummies and, when older, on their backs. The mothers still swing from trees and seem to be very free. I've never seen a mother animal "forcing" a baby to eat and I'm not aware that animals in general have eating and weight problems. I know humans are different. Nonetheless, I find comfort in contemplating this aspect of nature. It reminds me not to make a big deal about any phase.

My children are sensitive, inquisitive, naughty, and delightful beings. Ever since it became clear to me that I wasn't raising two little clones to be exactly like Jack and me, I learned to celebrate their free spirits and spontaneity. I also let them know what our expectations and limits are, and somehow things usually works out.

Mary ❧

To me breast feeding is one of the most beautiful experiences nature has given to woman. It creates that special bond between mother and child right after birth. I really felt the sense of responsibility to provide Natalie with the best nutrients nature could provide.

Fortunately, it went easily with us. Sometimes the stream of milk was so overwhelming that Natalie was galloping with milk for the first couple of sucks. For the first six weeks Natalie received nothing but breast milk. I had to go to work after two months, but I did everything I could to still provide her with breast milk. I continued to pump my milk during the day in the office, but slowly that became quite a hassle. Natalie needed more milk. Pumping did not feel natural to my body. It was not like when the little baby sucked and created a need. Because of that my production of milk slowly but surely was reduced. We were very fortunate that Natalie did not refuse supplement; she was just as happy and satisfied as before. I kept breast-feeding at night and in the morning for another two months or so. I think I was the one who missed it the most. Natalie was always fascinated by the bottle and at four months she was really eager to hold her bottle in her arms.

There are many opinions about breast feeding, but I've always done what I felt was right and comfortable for me and for the baby. We are all different in our life-styles, cultures, and situations. As long as we know we've done our best, and mother and baby are happy, we must have done something right.

Natalie began to sit up at six months, so we tried giving her milk in a cup. She took it but also got wet all over. Maybe that's why she never really got used to baby cups—she preferred the good old bottle.

One day Frank found this marvelous straw especially made to

fit the eight-ounce bottle. This helped greatly, since Natalie did not have the idea about lifting up the bottle yet.

Natalie had a special love for her bottle. Even though she learned eventually to drink from a regular cup, she wanted her bottle at night and in the morning until she was at least two and a half years old.

Natalie felt more grown up as we started to give her some solid food. We started with mashed bananas, but she did not like it the first time. Then we went to rice cereal very diluted with milk and eventually some jars of Gerber vegetables, fruits, etc. We did not introduce Natalie to any sugar or salt until she was about one and a half years old. We were never too strict about it, we just did not have any sweets at home. If we go out, she may have some sweets, but she knows that when she eats too much sugar it is bad for her teeth. As soon as she was able to communicate a little, we explained to her why sweets and snacks are not that beneficial for her in a very simple way. Somehow I always felt that if I was too strict she would want to have the forbidden sweets even more. I've tried not to make a big issue about it and am very careful what I bring home to eat.

As Natalie was able to join us at dinner, we made sure we had very little salt in our food, but as she grew older I soon realized that I could not shield her from outside environmental influence, so I tried to communicate. I've always tried to answer and explain when Natalie comes up with her favorite word, "Why?"

Luckily, Natalie did not suffer much from allergies. When she was younger she got some red rashes on her face when she drank too much fruit juice, so we used to dilute her juice drinks. Somehow her body seems to be better adjusted as she has grown older.

Frank and I disagree about how much food to give Natalie. He wants to determine how much she should eat, which only gets her upset. I don't believe in forcing anything. We all need to be respected for what we desire, and we need to respect our children's desires too. Now that Natalie is three, I tell her "Daddy wants to make sure that you are not hungry because he loves you."

Thumb-sucking is still a problem. I used to encourage Natalie to find her thumb when she was a couple of weeks old. I thought it was so cute. But now she is three and a half, and her thumb-sucking has pushed her two upper front teeth forward and the two bottom teeth inward. Now I wish I had never encouraged her to suck her thumb when she was a baby. We created a game for her: every time we see her sucking her thumb, we remind her that she needs to push her teeth back instead.

For now she buys the game, but who knows what will happen tomorrow.

Susan 🐌

There has been a lot written about whether or not to breast-feed an infant. For me, the only answer was to breast-feed. As a general policy I believe that the more natural, the better, and what could be more natural than breast feeding? It was also the easiest way—nothing to remember to take along, the restaurant is always right there, and the food is always ready. An additional benefit I had not anticipated was the additional calories that I could consume without gaining weight!

Breast feeding at home was never a problem. In public it was easy for the first three or four months. I found that the best way to nurse in public and still be discreet was to wear a two-piece outfit with a loose-fitting top. As Natasha became more active and more aware of her surroundings, it was more difficult to feed her in public. She was easily distracted and would stop nursing frequently to see what was going on. I became more adept at the process, and also less concerned about being exposed for the split second it took me to react and pull my shirt down after she had quickly pulled away to look about.

One of the main drawbacks to nursing is, of course, that you can't leave your breasts with the sitter when you go out. During the first three months of Natasha's life she would take a bottle, so I expressed milk and kept bottles of breast milk in the freezer.

At about four and a half months, however, Natasha decided that she didn't like bottles. She absolutely refused to take *anything* from a bottle, and would cry if she saw one coming. This made going out without her rather difficult. Fortunately, we had little desire to be away from her. Most of the time we just took her along with us. The times when that wasn't possible (dinner works, but the theater doesn't), we just didn't stay out as late as we might have otherwise. I would feed her just as we left and we would return within four hours. We found that she could wait four hours without too much difficulty when I wasn't at home, although if I was home she would often eat more frequently.

Ariana was much easier to leave with sitters because she could go much longer between feedings and almost never balked at taking a bottle. The problem with her was that after the first few months she preferred to eat in the same place, and without any onlookers—not even her big sister. If other people were around, Ariana just wouldn't nurse. My vision of feeding Ariana while I held Natasha close to me with my other arm vanished rather quickly. Feeding Ariana in public was out of the question. The remarkable thing was that it didn't really present too much of a problem. If we were out and I couldn't find a quiet, private place that met with her approval, she would simply wait. She could easily go for six or eight hours during the day without eating. The books I read about breast feeding refer to schedules as though babies actually eat at the same time every day. They also say that the baby will gradually nurse less frequently. Well, other babies may, but not ours!

Everyone seems to wonder what happens with breast feeding once the baby has teeth. Well, that depends upon the baby. If you put your finger in your mouth and suck, you will see that your teeth really don't get in the way. The few times that Natasha started to bite a little I gently pulled away, said "No," waited a few seconds, then let her resume nursing. She soon learned not to bite. With Ariana it was a little more difficult. As she cut her first two teeth, two more were trying to come through and were obviously causing her discomfort. She was biting everything, including me. Twice she bit down rather hard. The second time she broke the skin on my nipple. It hurt! It was sore for about a week, but not so sore that I couldn't continue nursing. I think that my reaction to that bite registered, because she never bit me again.

The most unpleasant part about breast feeding was weaning. I had read that babies often wean themselves when they are ready. This sounded great to me. I expected Natasha to learn to drink from a cup and gradually nurse less and less often until she just weaned herself. I wasn't in a rush; the nursing experience was very satisfactory for me.

Before Natasha was born I expected her to be weaned somewhere around six months. When she was six months old I thought that it might happen around her first birthday. When she was one I had no idea when it would happen. Still, I wasn't concerned. It was a little inconvenient that she wouldn't take a bottle, but I really didn't want to be away from her for more than four hours at a time and I usually took her with me. I also felt that nursing was important to Natasha. She was an extremely independent child, and nursing was the only time she would come to me for nurturing. She never developed a "lovie," she never sucked her thumb, she gave up the pacifier on her own at about nine months. I was willing to let her have this one crutch for as long as she needed it. Well, not forever, but I was certain that by the time she was two she would quit on her own or be able to be talked out of nursing rather easily.

The problem was that Dick didn't have the same faith in Natasha's future change of heart, and by the time she was about sixteen months old he had had it with nursing. Until then he had been very supportive, but the inconvenience began to bother him and he felt that we were too tied down. This difference of opinion between Dick and me about weaning Natasha caused tremendous friction in our relationship. He accused me of being the one dependent upon the nursing. I accused him of not being sensitive to his daughter's needs. Tempers were hot! Finally I decided that allowing Natasha to continue to nurse wasn't worth the trouble it was causing and I agreed to gradually wean her. Five months later, when she was twenty-two months old, Natasha nursed for the last time. Approximately eight months after that she stopped asking to nurse.

I began by not letting Natasha nurse after 12 A.M. and before 6 A.M. I was rewarded with tantrums. Fortunately these lasted only a few days, and eventually she would go right back to sleep when she woke at night. It was a painful process.

About two months later I stopped letting Natasha nurse during the day. This wasn't as difficult as I had expected. The first week she asked every day. After that she gradually asked less often, but she continued to ask occasionally for about nine months!

Another month passed before I could bring myself to stop the midnight and morning feedings. I still let her nurse at bedtime, hoping to provide her some nurturing and comfort while she was withdrawing from the other feedings.

The first morning went surprisingly well. Dick got up with Natasha and gave her a snack in the kitchen. She kept asking to nurse but she didn't go crazy. The next day all hell broke loose. She threw a tantrum that lasted over an hour. She finally ate some cereal. The next few days were not fun. She would cry and ask to nurse all morning and be cranky all day. She also started waking more at night. Instead of going right back to sleep, she would ask to have someone stay with her, and she had difficulty going back to sleep.

Natasha did gradually begin to learn other ways of getting nurturing. She began to sit in my lap just to cuddle, something she had almost never done before. She also actually drank from a bottle for a few days. I didn't encourage this, but let her have the bottle while she was in my lap or in the kitchen. She quickly lost interest in it.

About one and a half months later Natasha gave up nursing at bedtime pretty much on her own. Dick put her to bed one night and she didn't ask to nurse. The next night I put her to bed. She asked but didn't seen to mind when I said no. She didn't ask again at bedtime until about one week later when she was ill. I did allow her to nurse, although I was concerned about starting something again. I let her nurse for four days, and on the fourth day at bedtime I told her that since she was feeling better, tonight would be the last night. The next night she didn't ask to nurse.

The end was difficult. Perhaps I should have stopped a little earlier, before she became so dependent upon nursing for the psychological nurturing. But when was that? I don't think I can tell even in retrospect, and I can't tell with Ariana. Each child is different. Ariana is much more interested in solid food and less dependent on nursing than Natasha, so that I hope she will be easier to wean. I don't hold out any illusions this time about her doing it herself.

Neither Natasha nor Ariana ever had any formula. By the time I weaned Natasha she had been drinking juice and water from a cup for several months. During the weaning process I added cow's milk. I plan to do the same for Ariana.

I introduced the cup to both Natasha and Ariana around the time they started eating solid food—about six months. It was quite a while before they were adept at using it. For a long time they would take a few sips, then enjoy shaking it—getting juice or water or whatever it was all over the kitchen and themselves. Some time between twelve and eighteen months they really drank enough from a cup to make a difference.

I tried using the cups with the sip lids, which are supposed to prevent spills. It's true that they prevent spills, but they make great shakers. The shaken liquid went much farther than it would have had it just been spilled. I remember at the time being quite frustrated by the mess and their apparent unwilling-ness to use a cup for its intended purpose, but looking back, that seems insignificant.

I was very nonchalant about introducing Natasha to solid food. I didn't give her any until she was six months old. At first she took a few bites, but she quickly lost interest when I wouldn't let her feed herself—that is, grab the spoon and wave it all over the place, throwing cereal or banana or whatever it was all over the room and then using her hands to rub the food into her face, hair (which she had a lot of), and all over her clothes and high chair. I wasn't thrilled with the process, and having been assured by the pediatrician that Natasha was getting a complete diet on breast milk, I decided to put off solid food until she was a little more adept at feeding herself, or until she would allow me to do it for her.

At nine months she still wasn't interested in being fed but did seem interested in food, so I began trying to come up with things that she could eat by herself. By introducing food so late, I didn't worry too much about allergies. However, I did still avoid the highly allergenic foods. When I first tried introducing food at six months, I had carefully gone through the list of foods, one at a time, suggested by her pediatrician. Thus, at nine months, I just gave her little bits of whatever we were eating, mashed up, if necessary. Some got into her mouth; most was left in the high chair and on the floor. Frozen peas worked great—she loved picking them up and the cold felt good on her gums. Perhaps I should have been more concerned about choking, but they melted into mush within seconds of her putting them into her mouth, so I didn't think that the risk was too great. Natasha was also good at eating small pieces of fruit. Grapes were her favorites. She had an amazing ability to peel fruit in her mouth and would spit out the skins.

I do not allow salt, sugar, corn syrup, honey, artificial sweeteners, and most preservatives in Natasha's diet, but I do let her eat whatever else, when, and how much she wants. I think that if I offer her good food she will determine what and how much she needs much better than I possibly could. It has worked quite well.

I have a theory, based on not much of anything, about eating habits, which is: Obesity is caused by eating when not hungry, which is caused by not paying attention to one's body hunger signals, which is in turn caused by parents enforcing strict mealtimes and not letting children eat when they are actually hungry. Only recently has Natasha begun to eat recognizable meals, with snacks in between. Before now she would snack all day long. She would sit with us at mealtime but eat very little—no more than she would eat at any one of her many snack times during the day. She still eats small meals and snacks a lot, but she is beginning to go longer between snacks without being too irritable.

Although I do let Natasha forage, I don't let her eat food everywhere. Our kitchen, dining room, and den can be closed off from the rest of the house and they have become the only rooms in the house where I allow food. This is a rule that I strictly enforce, and it does help keep some of the disaster contained.

I am a fanatic when it comes to eliminating sugar from my children's diets. Until Natasha started nursery school at two and a half, the only sugar she had was an occasionally minuscule taste of ice cream or crumb of a cookie. I didn't give her crackers or cereal or anything else that contained sugar or other sweeteners. I gave her tastes of our sweets because I didn't want her curiosity about sweets to cause her to crave sugar more than eating sugar itself would have done.

For treats I made banana smoothies, cookies, custards, and other sugar-free desserts. At first I couldn't find recipes for cooking without sugar so I invented Tasha Cookies and a few others. Since then I have found sugar-free cookbooks that have some very good ideas. I use *The Pure and Natural Cookbook*, put out by Tree Top, Inc. (1984) and *Sweet and Sugarfree* by Karen E. Baskie (1982), St. Martin's Press. There are others.

When Natasha went to birthday parties I gave her some fresh fruit or a Tasha Cookie or some other sugar-free treat to eat while the other children were eating birthday cake. Until she was about three she was perfectly happy with the substitute.

When she started school she got crackers and other snacks that had some sugar in them and I began to be less compulsive about keeping sugar away from her completely. I did, however, ask the teachers to refrain from letting her have the really sweet snacks that other parents brought in for birthdays, etc.

When Natasha reached three and a half I began to gradually let her have a little more sugar, telling her that it isn't good for her but as long as she eats "good" food it is okay if she has a few sweets. I think we would all be better off not eating sugar, but I know this isn't practical, and I don't want to put Natasha in the position of disobeying me every time she has a sweet.

Is all this worth it in the long run? I don't know, but I think so. I notice that Natasha eats a lot more fresh fruit and vegetables than most children do—she actually likes vegetables! And even if I haven't decreased her desire for refined sweets, I think that she is better off not having had any sugar during the first few years. Since babies eat so little food, it seems important to me to make every morsel count toward good nutrition.

Yes, I eat sweets—too many. I have a real sweet tooth, which probably explains my concern about sugar. Am I being hypocritical? No more so than I am by not letting her have coffee, tea, or alcohol. With all of these substances my message is the same: They aren't very good for anyone, but when you are older it is okay to have them in moderation.

It's going to be more difficult with Ariana, since she will grow up seeing Natasha have an occasional sweet. I hope that I will be able to keep her from having any sugar at least as long as I did with Natasha, but I know that it will be much harder.

Of course, a discussion of what goes into the mouths of babes is incomplete without a note on pacifiers. Natasha used a pacifier frequently during the first nine months of her life. I never went anywhere without a large supply. I kept them stashed everywhere so that I would never be without one. Whenever she fussed and didn't seem to want anything else, the pacifier seemed to quiet her. At around nine months, on her own, she stopped using them. I put them all away and they were never needed again. When Ariana arrived I purchased a new supply of pacifiers but I could never get her to use one. She, on the other hand, sucked her thumb—something that Natasha never did. I neither encouraged nor discouraged it and when Ariana was around nine months old she quit sucking her thumb. That was it. I couldn't believe how easily it happened. We hadn't even gotten to the point of suggesting that she should stop. They seem to have minds of their own from the start.

Chapter 6

TEETH/TEETHING

- Our children's teething symptoms
- Methods we used to alleviate teething discomfort
- How soon our children's teeth appeared
- Brushing baby teeth
- Visiting the dentist
- The tooth fairy

Diana ❧

Sosia was really fussy for a few days and I had no idea what was causing her discomfort. When I saw her trying to put her entire fist in her mouth, I thought, "Well, she must be teething now and probably needs something to chew on." So I began to invent things that she could chew on other than her cute little fist. My most successful teething treat was a frozen banana; it was cooling and also yummy. I also had great success with little cocktail bagels that I baked until they were hard. These were nice alternatives to high-sugar products, and Sosia and Benjamin never complained! Teething cookies were very popular, but I could never figure how to get the residue off the children's cheeks and high chairs. It finally dawned on me that oiling the child and high chair first with butter or margarine would facilitate that job nicely.

I relished the first tooth breaking through Sosia's gums. It was indeed a long-awaited event since her first tooth came in when she was about eleven months old. Benjamin's teeth came in very early. They both experienced a lot of discomfort, but often it was difficult to tell which symptoms were due to teething and which weren't. I never knew when a little bump would yield a tooth, so some of the discomforts associated with teething were blamed on colds.

Both my children have wonderful teeth. I started them brushing when they became curious about it. They would imitate me, so I took advantage of that opportunity and started them brushing on their own. Brushing teeth was particularly important for Benjamin because he was so much in love with his bottle and his pacifier. I was afraid that he would develop a mouthful of cavities. When his teeth were about fourteen months old I would help with a quick little brushing to make sure that the job was done. I let them try it in front of the mirror and I would always do mine at the same time. At least once a day I would "inspect" the teeth and give them a quick brushing while doing so. I have encouraged them to brush on their own as much as possible. Every day both of them brush at the same time I do.

I started taking the children to the pedidontist when they were three years old. He introduced them to all the mysterious machines by letting them touch and play with everything. They go twice a year, and he shows them how to brush properly and gives them both thorough checkups. I feel that it is the best way to teach them the proper care of their teeth and its importance.

A word of caution: Make sure the toothbrushes stay in the bathroom, since it's dangerous for children to walk around with things in their mouths. Also, there was a time when both my children developed a love of toothpaste. I let them have a tiny taste on their toothbrush, and kept the toothpaste on a high shelf during those episodes.

Jan ᔥ

It seemed like forever before Jaclyn got her teeth. It was actually nine months. My pediatrician kept telling me not to worry, that teeth would definitely appear in due time. But of course I worried. What if the teeth never showed up?

Finally the telltale white teeth did appear, peeking from beneath pink gums. I really didn't notice any odd behavior on Jaclyn's part. I was warned that teething can be painful for some babies, and some mothers told me that teething can be accompanied by fevers and even diarrhea. A few times Jaclyn woke at nights screaming, but I can't tell you if it was because she was having a bad dream (do babies dream?) or because she was teething. I put on some Orajel (numbs the gums) and rocked her back to sleep. One tooth (third to the left of center) did come in crooked. Is this a sign warning me to get orthodontic insurance?

Jenna got one tooth in just about nine months and had only this one tooth for a month. Of course her parents thought this was so cute! Today, at fourteen months old, Jenna has eight teeth and is in a holding pattern. No other teeth are in sight. Sometimes, it seems to this mom, growth occurs in spurts.

We've been encouraging Jaclyn to brush her teeth since she was two and a half. Her baby-sitter lets her brush her teeth while taking a bath—a great idea, since they can make any mess they want and spit as hard as they want. Of course you've got to expect that more than just their teeth will get brushed—knees, tummy, hair, walls—and you can't forget the tub!

We're talking about visiting the dentist soon, but so far haven't gone. I understand there are some dentists who care specifically for children. Your pediatrician or friends with kids can certainly recommend someone. I've got lists!

While the kids were teething I noticed them chewing on everything—toys, the crib, even fingers (mine and theirs). I bought teething biscuits but I found them to be so messy! The biscuit doesn't crumble as regular cookies might; it seems to *melt* all over hands, face, hair, and any nearby object.

Needless to say, I was not generous in passing the biscuits out. A teething toy (bought right next to the teething biscuits) worked just as well. Heck, babies don't know about a teething biscuit until we introduce them to it! And a teething toy lasts a whole lot longer than a biscuit.

I have heard that it's not a good idea to give a bottle to your child at bedtime to fall asleep with once that child has most of his teeth. The claim is that the sugary residue of the milk/juice can be harmful to teeth. I didn't pay much heed to this advice. What worked for my children (and for me) was their falling sound asleep with a bottle. I did discuss this with my pediatrician and, once again, he said to do what works. I am, but I may have to worry about paying a lot in dental bills a dozen years from now.

Katherine 🐦

Both Deren and Alexandra got their baby teeth exactly according to the pediatrician's schedule. Neither fussed too much, drooled, or had teething fevers. An extra bonus was that their teeth eventually grew in straight and even. I marveled at this because Jack's teeth are not very straight, and although mine are, I have a bad "bite." Both Jack and I should have had braces. I have kept an eagle's eye on the children's teeth to be on the lookout for potential problems. Alexandra's earliest bottom teeth looked quite crooked at first and then magically straightened out later.

Deren, now seven, has lost eight teeth. We call him Dracula and he loves it. He feels so powerful and much older. Most of his friends are in this toothless phase in the first grade, and they have a great time making jokes with each other and seeing how generous the tooth fairy has been. Deren writes the tooth fairy great letters (with my help in spelling) and tells her in great detail about all the toys he wants. We remind him that the fairy doesn't bring toys—she brings money. One night Jack and I mixed up our signals and forgot to leave 50 cents under Deren's pillow. He came into our room at about 5:30 in the morning, heartbroken and crying. We quickly made up a believable story that the tooth fairy couldn't decide whether to leave him a small gift this time or some money; she needed written instructions about this next to his tooth. It worked! That night he received both a small toy and a sweet letter to him from the fairy. He was ecstatic, and life at the Dusay family got back to "normal" (for the next hour, that is).

Both children like their toothbrushes and decide which colors they want every three to four weeks. They got used to toothbrushes because I gave them small ones when they were babies to teethe on. The bristles felt great in their gums.

When their baby teeth started coming in, I took the children with me for my cleaning visits to the dentist. They really liked the hygienist, and when it came time for their first teeth cleaning at age two, neither child was scared or uncomfortable. They had already seen me go through the procedure several times before. The children receive fluoride treatments from the hygienist, and each of us (children included) do our best to prevent cavities and tooth decay.

Mary ❧

Natalie got her first bottom teeth at four months old. Suddenly they were there. She did not even have any discomfort. Then for six months she did not get another. She was looking for anything to bite on and chew. She loved to bite fingers, and could do it for quite a long time. Fingers were more her favorite than those cold teething toys. We were quite lucky that Natalie did not have too much pain when she was teething.

When she was just a little over a year old—and eating more varieties of food—we introduced a new routine, wiping her teeth with a soft cloth diaper before she went to sleep. We started encouraging her to brush her teeth at two years old, with no toothpaste. It was a battle for a while. We had to brush our teeth at the same time. Shortly after, she wanted to have the tooth-paste, just like Mommy and Daddy did. However, she began eating it. Then she learned how to gargle, to spit the water out, etc.

Brushing teeth is quite a production in our household before bedtime. If Natalie does not want to do it, we can't force her. But when she is in the mood, we can't stop her. She goes on and on. If we leave her, it can take an hour easily—she plays with the water and cleans everything from her toothbrush to the cup and sink and mirror.

I do not have very good teeth, but Frank does. I just hope that Natalie has his instead of mine. I need to teach Natalie to be more aware about taking care of her teeth, just as much as I've made her aware of taking care of her skin.

By now Natalie is quite good at brushing her teeth before she goes to bed. She does not eat her toothpaste anymore. In the meantime I've also been encouraging her to drink more water (which she loves) after each meal.

Susan ❧

Teething generally was not a problem for Natasha. When she was three months old she started drooling and biting, but her delightfully cheerful disposition remained unchanged except for very brief periods just before each tooth peeked through the gum. All of Natasha's teeth came during the period from six to fifteen months. One day I would notice that she was fussy all day and nursing constantly for no apparent reason. The next day I would discover a tooth. I couldn't really see the tooth the first day, but I could see the break in the gum where it was coming through and I could feel the tooth with my finger or hear it on a spoon. Usually, that was all there was to it, until the next tooth arrived.

With the eyeteeth and a couple of the molars, it was a little more painful and the fussiness lasted longer. I found that the pain remedies I tried (and I tried lots) didn't work very well. I tried several brands of medication, all of which seemed worthless. I tried teething rings, but they ended up on the floor before they had done much good. Something cold to chew on did seem helpful, but keeping it in her hand so that she could put it into her mouth was a challenge. The best remedy I found was frozen peas. She liked eating them and the cold was soothing—but they don't last long. For some reason she liked holding on to a raw carrot more than throwing it on the floor, and she liked chewing on it—it would keep her quiet for longer than anything else I tried. Unfortunately, I cannot recommend this remedy to you, since children have been know to bite off pieces of carrot just the right size to choke on. Natasha was not prone to choking and I took a chance. Ariana seems to be slightly more prone to choking so I am more reluctant to give her a carrot.

Ariana was less fortunate than Natasha when it came to her teeth. From the time she was three months old you could see that the top two teeth were ready to come in. Her gums were swollen and red and obviously bothered her a lot. There were many days when her usual sunny disposition changed. She would need to be held constantly and she would bite on anything in sight. However, during a period of remission the bottom two teeth appeared. Ariana was eight months old, and I had begun to wonder if she would ever have teeth. It wasn't until she was ten months old that the top teeth, which had been causing her so much discomfort, finally appeared. What a relief!

I think that it's a myth that a fever and runny nose go along with teething, although I must admit that it's tempting to make the connection. Our pediatrician told me that it is unlikely that teething alone can cause other signs of illness. It is more likely that children are more susceptible to other illnesses while they are teething. In any event, I never attribute illness to teething. I think that it is better to be safe.

Sometime after she was a year old I started brushing Natasha's teeth. I don't remember exactly how it happened. She always watched me brush my teeth in the morning (I haven't been alone in the bathroom since Natasha was born), and one day she decided she wanted to try it. I bought a toothbrush for her and tried to brush her teeth. I was worried about her swallowing the toothpaste because I know that too much fluoride can be harmful. I have no idea how much toothpaste is too much, but I don't want to find out. So I made a big deal out of teaching her to spit and telling her not to swallow the toothpaste. She loved the idea of spitting and practiced and practiced. For a while I wished I hadn't made such a big deal out of it.

Teeth brushing quickly became part of the bedtime ritual. At first I had to fight with her to get the toothbrush away so that I could do some of the brushing. She could brush the front teeth, but didn't get the sides at all. We have reached a truce—she starts, then Dick or I finish.

Now that Natasha gets sweets occasionally, I am trying to have her brush more than once a day at bedtime. Ideally, of course, she should brush after each time she eats, but that doesn't seem realistic—especially given how often she eats!

Natasha went to the dentist for the first time when she was about two and a half. I went to get my teeth cleaned and she went along with me. After I was finished, the hygienist let her get up in the chair and ride up and down. (This was preplanned.) Natasha was also given a toothbrush, which was a real treat. I don't know what her fascination with toothbrushes is, but she does like them. After this visit we talked about the fact that next time she would get to have her teeth cleaned too. I made it sound like it would be fun and she seemed anxious to give it a try. When she was three she did have her teeth cleaned and treated with fluoride. I had my teeth cleaned at the same time and I gave her the option of going first or second. She decided to go second, but then kept asking if it was her turn yet. I expected her to be a little hesitant, but when it was her turn she opened her mouth with almost no coaxing and kept it open. Her eyes were wide but she did not seem frightened or intimidated by all the equipment. She followed directions and sat still through the whole process, including the fluoride treatment. I was impressed. And the good news—no cavities!

Ariana has four teeth and is already taking an interest in brushing them. She is often in the bathroom when I brush Natasha's teeth. One night she kept reaching up to the sink and fussing. I handed her a toothbrush and she took it, chewed on it for a while, then stood in front of me, handed me the toothbrush, and opened her mouth. How could I refuse? I brushed her four little teeth (with no toothpaste) and then handed the toothbrush back to her, and she played with it until I was finished with Natasha's teeth. This is just one more example of how eager Ariana is to be a part of everything that Natasha is doing. Sometimes it is easy to include her; other times, it is more difficult.

Chapter 7

BABY CLOTHES AS
BABY GROWS

- How our children ranked according to the pediatrician's height/ weight charts
- Growth spurts and slow spells
- Buying practical clothes and shoes
- Determining the correct size for your growing child
- Where to find 100 percent cotton clothes
- Putting together a toddler wardrobe

Diana ❧

Both of my children were big—around eight and a half pounds—when they were born, and they gained a respectable amount of weight during the first few weeks. When Sosia was about one year old she developed into quite a rotund little figure. This worried me a little bit because I did not want her to develop into a rotund person. The pediatrician assured me that just before children begin to walk they can put on quite a bit of weight, which they promptly "walk off" when they begin moving around more. As soon as Sosia began walking she slimmed down quickly. It also seemed to me that the children put on a little weight just before they went into a growth spurt.

My children were bigger than the clothes that were supposed to fit their age range. I was always one of the tallest in my school classes, but now have turned out to be of average height, so I just assumed that somewhere in their little bodies they had some large genes. As it has turned out, although they are relatively big babies, they now fit quite nicely into the median.

When they were newborns I found the most useful piece of clothing (other than a diaper) was the stretch knit body suit. Natural fibers were the best choice for comfort and durability but I occasionally used the ones in other fibers I had received as gifts because there just never were enough of them. The body suits worked well for a long time. They provided warmth for the whole body, packed very easily, were easy to care for, and provided full mobility. Best of all, the baby could move everything all at once and the little suits would stay on.

Each one of the children had a "nice" outfit that included a nice blanket, a fancy baby outfit and baby shoes, but they were strictly for show-and-tell. Dresses were a novelty; Sosia and I never found them comfortable for everyday use. Her little legs would seem cold, and when she began to crawl the dresses impeded her progress.

When they started toddling I dressed them in little overalls. The overalls were great because they could be rolled up at the cuffs and the straps could be let down.

I found that if I decided on one particular color scheme—for instance, all primary colors—I could mix and match with ease. You'll find that various parts of outfits become soiled at different times during the day, and a complementary color scheme can save changing entire outfits all day long.

I didn't buy any real shoes for my babies until they could walk. I had heard that putting shoes on an infant is like taking part of their tactile abilities and covering them up. If you watch your baby's toes, they have such expression! I decided to let the toes be out there experiencing life to the fullest. If the weather was warm enough, I let the children go barefoot. On cool days I added little socks. When they begin standing I bought little leather booties that would give them some traction but still allow them to feel things. When they started running in the park I bought little tennis shoes.

Once my children were walking I preferred little sweat pants or elastic-waist pants for everyday use. They suit the weather in San Francisco and they allow a certain amount of self-sufficiency (no buttons or zippers). They are easy to get on and off and they permit a full range of easy movement.

Allowing my children to be comfortable and self-reliant on a daily basis is very important to me. Sensible clothing that they can handle gives them a sense of control. It also makes getting them dressed up even more fun—it becomes something exciting and different. When they are dressed up they *act* dressed up, and it's fun.

Jan ❧

Of course you compare your child with others. You know you shouldn't. You know that every child grows and develops at his or her own pace. But you still compare.

Jaclyn was our chubby one. John called her our "mini sumo wrestler." On the growth chart she was right on target in height, slightly chubbette on weight. If you've got a chubby child, don't worry, for, true to my pediatrician's prediction, she did slim down when she started walking.

Jenna is our petite one. She's a good eater, but just never developed the chubby arms and legs one often sees on babies. She was barely twenty pounds on her first birthday.

Since I've got girls, I much prefer them to be slim rather than chubby, but every child is different. A friend of mine brought her two-year-old son over to play, and he's so huge for his age, he looks like a four-year-old.

When the child is two you can usually predict how tall your child will grow up to be. You simply multiply his or her height at two years by two. Jaclyn will be around five feet six. I don't know how accurate this is, but check with me in sixteen years and I'll let you know.

As for clothing, I have always found that my children exactly fit the size on the label, but I usually buy things a size or two larger. It is astounding how quickly they outgrow their clothes and shoes. But goodness . . . we want them to grow!

Snaps at the crotch on overalls and outfits for baby are a must. It makes it so much easier to change diapers. The European designs for baby tend to look wonderful, but most don't have the snap closures. If I have to choose, I'll take practicality over trendsetting design any day.

I much prefer all-cotton clothes for my babes. It just *feels* good, feels like quality, and seems to be durable too. I often sought out an all-cotton clothing line for children called Sprouts. It was designed and developed by a mom whose young daughter was allergic to synthetic fabrics. The designs are often whimsical . . . stars, clouds, or bright red lips silk-screened on cotton. I love them.

If you're wondering exactly what you might need at the new-born stage, check with your local children's store. They often provide you with a layette list, free! The following list is from one of my favorite stores. Besides diapers and blankets, I found snap-front T-shirts and gowns that tied at the bottom to be necessities. These gowns were so convenient to change baby, since in the first few weeks your child seems to mess his or her diapers a dozen times a day.

SIZE CHART

3 Mos.	Birth to 13 lbs	Small	Birth to 13 lbs
6 Mos.	14 to 18 lbs.	Medium	14 to 18 lbs.
1 Yr.	19 to 22 lbs.		
18 Mos.	23 to 28 lbs.	Large	19 to 24 lbs.

BASIC CLOTHING

- ☐ 4–6 Undershirts
- ☐ 4–6 Night Gowns
- ☐ 2–4 Sacque Sets
- ☐ 3–4 Sleepers
- ☐ 1 Sweater Set
- ☐ 2–3 Pairs of Booties/Socks
- ☐ 2–4 Bibs
- ☐ 2–3 Blanket Sleepers

SLEEP AND BEDDING

- ☐ Bassinet, Cradle, or Moses Basket
- ☐ Bassinet Liner
- ☐ Bassinet or Cradle Sheets
- ☐ Bassinet or Cradle Bumper Guards
- ☐ Portacrib
- ☐ Portacrib Bumper Guards
- ☐ Portacrib Sheets
- ☐ Six-Year Crib
- ☐ Six-Year Crib Mattress
- ☐ Mattress Protector
- ☐ Crib Bumper Guards
- ☐ 3–4 Crib Sheets
- ☐ 2–3 Waterproof Pads
- ☐ 3–6 Lap Pads
- ☐ 2 Quilted Crib Pads
- ☐ 2–3 Crib Blankets
- ☐ 4–6 Receiving Blankets
- ☐ Dust Ruffle
- ☐ Canopy

ADDITIONAL NURSERY FURNITURE AND EQUIPMENT

- ☐ Infant Seat
- ☐ Car Seat
- ☐ Highchair
- ☐ Playpen
- ☐ Lamp
- ☐ Crib Mobile
- ☐ Chest of Drawers or Chifforobe
- ☐ Dressing Table or Bathinette
- ☐ Clothes Hamper
- ☐ Stroller
- ☐ Carriage
- ☐ Adult Rocking Chair
- ☐ Cloth Baby Carrier
- ☐ Swing
- ☐ Jump Seat
- ☐ Walker
- ☐ Diaper Stacker
- ☐ Diaper Bag

SAFETY EQUIPMENT

- ☐ Gates
- ☐ Electric Plug Ups
- ☐ Shock Guards
- ☐ Door Locks
- ☐ Safety Doorknobs
- ☐ Cabinet Locks
- ☐ Drawer Stops
- ☐ Zippered Harness
- ☐ Net Crib Retainer
- ☐ Window Safety Locks
- ☐ Child Safety and Emergency Book

BATHING, DIAPERING AND TOILETRIES
- [ ] Bathtub
- [ ] 4–6 Baby Washcloths
- [ ] 2–3 Baby Towels
- [ ] Cotton Swabs
- [ ] Safety Manicure Scissors
- [ ] Baby Soap, Oil, Lotion
- [ ] Baby Shampoo
- [ ] Brush and Comb
- [ ] Infant Fever Thermometer
- [ ] 4–6 Dozen Diapers
- [ ] 1 Box Diaper Liners
- [ ] 3–4 Waterproof Pants
- [ ] Diaper Pail and Deodorizer
- [ ] Premoistened Disposable Wipes
- [ ] 6 Diaper Pins
- [ ] Baby Scale
- [ ] Hot Water Bottle
- [ ] Vaporizer/Humidifier

FEEDING
Bottle Feeding
- [ ] 6–8 8 oz. Bottles, Glass, or Plastic
- [ ] 2–4 4 oz. Bottles, Glass, or Plastic
- [ ] 2–4 Extra Nipples
- [ ] Bottle Brush
- [ ] Nipple Brush
- [ ] Sterilizer
- [ ] Gizmo for Dishwasher
- [ ] Tongs
- [ ] Bottle Warmer
- [ ] Food Grinder
- [ ] 1 Food Nurser
- [ ] 1 Disposable Bottle Kit
- [ ] 2 Extra Rolls of Disposable Bottles

Breast Feeding
- [ ] 1 Box Disposable Nursing Pads
- [ ] 1 Breast Pump
- [ ] 2–4 4 oz. Bottles for Water or Juice

List Reprinted Courtesy of: Lullaby Lane, 556 San Mateo Avenue, San Bruno, California, 94066

Katherine ❧

I'm a mother who goes by what "looks right" or "feels right." I thought each of my children looked fine at birth. Deren had a fairly large head, which caused some difficulty during his birth, but each child "looked right." Since Deren was our firstborn I took him to the pediatrician for well-baby visits each month. There he would be measured, weighed, examined, and evaluated. One month his weight would be in the 50 percent percentile and his height in the 75 percent percentile. The next visit all this would change. These measurements and growth spurts became fairly irrelevant to me because Deren looked fine, was nursing well, and appeared perfectly healthy.

I was far more lax about taking Alexandra in for regular pediatric checkups. The medical rules had changed by then and the pediatrician said that fewer visits were required for healthy babies in their first year of life.

Deren has had some tremendous growth spurts. Now that he is seven, he pays attention to his body and teeth. He enjoys seeing how long his feet are; he compares his hand size to mine. He's one of the taller kids in his class and loves to test his body and what he can do. At the park he is quickly up the tallest slide (the wrong way up); he dangles from monkey bars and trees to see how far he can jump and the maximum to which his body will stretch.

Alexandra was a tiny baby, and on the small side as a child for her first two years. Since she nursed well, was happy and healthy, I wasn't concerned about her size. My parsimonious spirit would say, "Great! She can continue to wear these wonderful baby clothes longer!" She would wear six-month sizes when she was nine months old, and some of her nightgowns until she was nearly two years old. Alexandra has remained slim and nicely proportioned to this day.

I would not even consider weighing them or measuring their heights. This was unimportant to me because they continued to "look right." Jack occasionally plunked them on a scale, when he'd think of it, and each year he makes height marks on a special wall to commemorate their birthdays and compare them from past years. Alexandra is taller at three than Deren was. He has become more chunky and solid.

Because each child grows out of shoes, shirts, or pants nearly every six months, I buy clothes that coordinate easily. I love mix-and-match colors. Deren looks fabulous in bright colors such as navy, white, and red. He wears various versions of these colors and is able to easily dress himself in colors that go together. We throw in burgundy, beige, and green as well. Meanwhile, Alexandra is a knockout in pastels. She's loaded with pinks and baby blues. She's recently been able to wear red and a few stronger colors, but pale pink is exquisite on her.

I shop the sales at my favorite baby stores and often buy two sizes larger to put away for the next season. This works wonderfully. The clothes they really seem to go for are sweat suits, tennis shoes with Velcro fasteners, and the types of things they can easily put on themselves.

Mary ಇ

Surprisingly enough, Natalie was twenty-one inches long when she was born, and she has stayed tall. She weighed only six pounds at birth and has a petite build, but she's long. She must have gotten Frank's height, because I am only five feet two and a half inches.

When she was an infant it was very interesting to see her grow. She went a little plump, then skinny, then a little plump, and again long and thin. Now at three and a half years old, Natalie is long, but she can still wear undershirts of eighteen months size, except they are too short.

Every child is born with a certain build. As long as we know we give them ample nutrition and they are healthy, why worry?

Natalie was so little when she was born that infant clothes were too big for her. Not until she reached one month old did she start to fill up her clothes. We used to buy her clothes at least six months bigger until she started to wear dresses and walk. Then we started to buy one-year-older-size clothes. I really enjoy having a little girl. There are so many cute shoes and clothes available now and she loves them too.

Because Natalie sweats so much and develops skin rashes very easily, 100 percent cotton underwear is important to us. All her sleepwear is cotton—first with snaps in the crotch, then with zippers, and now two-piece pajamas so she can lower the pants easily and go to the toilet herself.

Cotton clothes can be hard to find. Here are several excellent mail order sources: Garnet Hill, P.O. Box 262, Franconia, NH 03580; After the Stork, 3002 Monte Vista NE, Albuquerque, NM 27106; Hanna Andersson, 5565 S.W. Hewett Boulevard, Portland, OR 97221.

Susan ❧

I loved going to the doctor to find out how much Natasha had grown. She was in the ninetieth percentile for both her height and weight for the first nine months of her life. After nine months she stopped growing at such a dramatic rate. In fact, she actually lost three ounces over a two-month period. I debated with myself whether or not I should be concerned, but decided that she was obviously a very healthy child. I attributed the drop in her weight to her recent burst of energetic activity. Three months later she had gained one pound four ounces and she has continued to be quite normal in her growth rate, although no longer in the ninetieth percentile.

Ariana has also been fun to watch. She was off the chart for about the first nine months; now, at one year, she has dropped down to the fiftieth percentile and we have stopped being concerned that we had a giant on our hands.

The amazing thing to me about watching them grow is how difficult it is to remember what they looked like just a short time ago. Somehow it seems as if they have always been just as they are today. When I see new babies I can't believe that either Natasha or Ariana were ever that small. Impossible!

I know they were, however, because they both wore Newborn-size clothes for a few weeks. For us, the method of sizing infants clothing turned out to be rather absurd. At six months Natasha was wearing size nine months; Ariana, size twelve months. At two years Natasha was wearing size toddler three. Why don't they just tell you the height and weight range that will fit into a particular garment?

Natasha and Ariana outgrew their clothes rapidly. I usually purchased clothes one size larger than the perfect fit so they would last longer. Now that Natasha is in school she often ruins an outfit before she outgrows it.

At first the most useful articles of clothing were stretchies or sleepers—those one-piece knit outfits. My children lived in them for the first six months of their lives. Dresses were impractical for everyday use. Once the children were walking, I preferred the protection of long pants. I seldom put Natasha in a dress until she started school; then she absolutely refused to wear anything but dresses. I let her wear what she wanted to wear, but I absolutely insisted on shoes suitable for running and climbing (no fancy shoes). For me, that was worth making an issue about. Ariana has not yet expressed any opinions about what she wears and is still wearing overalls and sweat suits.

During the first year—or at least until they were walking more often than they were being carried, I found that one-piece outfits were more practical than two-piece. One-piece outfits stayed in place; two-piece outfits pulled apart and exposed their little tummies. I liked snaps in the crotch for the first year or so because it made diapering much easier. Some mothers I talked to didn't like them, however, because they tend to come unfastened, particularly when the child gets really active.

Until Natasha and Ariana walked they never wore shoes. Once they started to walk they wore moccasins called Petti Bears, made out of washable fabric that looked like suede. It was almost like having no shoes on at all but gave them the protection they needed. They had adjustable laces so that the children didn't outgrow them too fast. They wore these until the shoes were no longer available in their size and then they graduated to rubber-soled shoes.

The most exciting part of having children is watching them develop. They begin their lives unable to do much of anything and in a remarkably short period of time they are walking, talking, talking back, reasoning, and learning unbelievably complex things. If it weren't for all the work involved, I would keep having babies just to keep watching this remarkable process! Natasha developed at an unusually rapid rate, doing everything early. When Ariana arrived, however, she was slower to develop than Natasha by a substantial margin. At first I was concerned that this would be a problem for Ariana, that we would always compare and find her lacking. I worried for nothing. Yes, Ariana has developed more slowly, but it hasn't been any less fascinating to watch. We haven't been any less amazed at the process and we certainly don't find Ariana wanting in any way. She has her own wonderful traits and has captured our hearts just as completely! It's fun to watch and compare, but in fact how each child compares to the norms is of little significance. When you watch your child develop some new ability, it is always a wonder to behold.

Chapter 8

TOILET TRAINING

- How soon our children were potty trained
- What we did (or didn't do) to encourage them
- Potty chairs and toilet seats
- Introducing training pants and underwear
- Nighttime diapering
- Using public bathrooms

Diana 🦢

I have a friend who takes a great deal of pride in how soon her children give up diapers. She considers it a point of importance and prestige. We have children of the same age, so for months I listened to detailed accounts of where all of these critical events occurred—as I continued to change diapers. It wasn't my children's fault. Here in San Francisco you need a letter of recommendation to use a public bathroom. Diapers are just more convenient if you or your children are at all spontaneous. Some people are very creative about taking the potty chair along in the back of the car and some of my friends used little cup potties effectively, but I was paralyzed with the fear that we would be in some public place and no bathrooms would be available to us. I hoped that my children would wear diapers for a long time, thereby eliminating my worries of where and how and what we would do if the inevitable occurred.

Now my children are potty trained, and we are able to use public toilets because we know when we must wait a little bit. My mind is at ease. How did I do it? I purchased little potty chairs and put them in strategic places around the house. My children were accustomed to them and began to tell me when it had just happened. Then we progressed to when it was about to happen. From there we became great successes at getting everything together and using the potty chairs. Sosia finally came to me and told me that she was a big girl and she would need to wear only panties. I made sure that she had little panties, and pants with elastic waists, that allowed her to essentially take care of herself. She would just call me for the wiping parts. Of course there were times when it didn't work out so well, but generally Sosia was perfectly toilet trained by the time she was two and a half. I didn't use too much praise or too many rewards. It never became an issue between us. I was happy that I was not in a hurry to toilet train her. It was just a natural progression of things.

When Benjamin was born (Sosia was two years, nine months), Sosia lapsed back into diapers sporadically for about two or three weeks. We took almost no notice of her mishaps and simply encouraged her to remember next time. For about two years I kept a rubber sheet on both of their beds for safety. But except for rare occasions they were unnecessary. When they were becoming toilet trained it was just a matter of a week or two before day and night success was met. After a few nights of dry diapers we moved them into pants at night too.

I'd heard that boys are different, and Benjamin was. He was much more mature and verbal when eventually he decided that he was going to use the toilet. We carried on big conversations about it. "So, Benjamin, when are you going to use the toilet and stop wearing these diapers?" "Oh, maybe next Wednesday." "Why next Wednesday?" "Oh, because then I will have some panties."

They are both very much in control of the situation now, well adjusted and normal, and I think that my easy attitude played in my favor here immensely.

Jan 🐤

It's no wonder books (and lots of them!) are written on this subject. I don't want to write another book, I just want Jaclyn to be potty trained!

I really thought it would be easy. What is the big deal about showing a child how to use the toilet? I had heard all the stories from other mothers about how they trained their child in one day. The stories never bothered me—until now.

Jaclyn, now three, understands all about going to the potty "just like a big girl," but still much prefers wearing a diaper. We have talked and talked and *talked* about how big girls wear pretty panties and how proud we are when she uses the potty, but she insists on wearing a diaper—because, she says, she is a baby, just like her baby sister, Jenna.

We have gone to the store and picked out some pretty panties— Grandma from Hawaii has sent pretty panties, so has Aunt Linda. Her drawer is full of pretty panties! Every morning we ask her to pick out the panties she'd like to wear, and for a while she thought it was quite a novelty, but lately the novelty seems to have worn off, and it's back to diapers!

We always try to be very positive and full of praise when she goes to the potty. "Mommy is so proud of you!" is a favorite of mine. (Once when I sat on the potty Jaclyn came to me and said, "Mommy, I'm so proud of you!")

We are progressing, though. She will always do number two in the potty. But we accomplished this only after much bribery. We made a deal: If she pooped in the potty, she would get a treat (usually two M&Ms). It worked. We're still working on number one.

To help this training along, we've got step stools (really a great tool) to help her climb onto the potty herself, a potty chair, and a potty seat with a horse on it that squeaks. Anything to accomplish the task! We've always given her the choice as to what she'd like to use. To be perfectly honest though, the toilet, plain and simple, without any horses that squeak, is my preference. No cleaning up to do. When Jenna gets ready for the toilet, that's exactly what I'm planning to train her on.

We bought a book called *Once Upon a Potty* by Alona Frankel to help Jaclyn along with this experience. It's a cute book, and little Prudence was a character Jaclyn loved. The book is about how Prudence gets a present—a potty—and how she learns to use it. We must have read this book hundreds—no, make that thousands—of times. I'll never forget how Prudence sat and sat and sat and sat and sat and sat until . . . success!

What really is amazing is how long these little bodies can hold their urine. Jaclyn will go for hours and sometimes the entire morning before she'll either go to the potty or pee in her diaper. You can ask a hundred times, and you can see that she needs to go, but of course she refuses. And of course we've had accidents. What is so funny is that she will come and tell you exactly where she peed, knowing quite well it was *not* in the potty.

My patient pediatrician assures me Jaclyn *will* be potty trained, and he warns not to push too hard. If you do, they will rebel in one way or another. He says that one day something just clicks in their little brains, and presto! Potty trained!

Katherine 🐦

This is a very easy topic for me. After buying two different toilet seats that Deren refused to use, I began to start some logical thinking about toilet training. He was about two and a half when he showed a fleeting interest in peeing in the toilet. This was only occasionally, and it wasn't worth continually asking him if he had to pee, or putting him on a potty chair. He was still drinking from his bottle and this was a great comfort for him. I personally enjoyed changing his diapers and wondered how he would toilet train. I was in no hurry to take on that project.

One day I casually asked him when he was going to pee in the potty and give up his bottle. He looked me directly in the eye and in all seriousness stated, "On my third birthday." That sounded reasonable enough to me, so I said, "That's a deal! I won't bug you about either your bottle or the toilet." After that, life was a breeze. Deren and I never had words about potties or bottles again. On the day of his third birthday he gave me all his bottles (so I could give them to poor babies whose moms might not be able to afford bottles). Together we gathered them all up and they filled up a big paper bag. Later that day Deren voluntarily used the big toilet, and with a little practice and help from Daddy, his aim got better. (Even though he is seven at this writing, his aim is still not great.)

Alexandra has been quite different. The summer she turned two Jack and I had to make a business trip to Europe, which turned out to be the very first time in our lives that we would be away from our children for more than one night.

We had a wonderful French exchange student living with us at the time, and she and the children went to stay with my parents, who live in the country, for the two weeks we were gone. They had a great time swimming, riding tricycles, seeing their grandparents, playing with Sugar and Spice (their honey-colored cocker spaniels). Alexandra wore only diapers because of the hot summer days. By the time we came back from Europe she was *completely* and happily potty trained and has been ever since. I think she enjoyed watching her brother pee on the bushes and at other times sit on the toilet. She's such a happy copy cat, and she seemed to breeze through the phases much quicker than her brother. This taught me that what you buy for one child that doesn't "work" may ultimately be used by another child. This concept appeals to my frugal spirit, because having a baby and going through all these stages can be expensive.

Mary 🦢

I've always heard that forcing your child to be toilet trained can have some serious effects later. However, introducing them to toilet training early and backing it up with consistency and without force or anger can be okay too. That is what they do in many other countries, especially in Asia, where most children are toilet trained between one and two years old.

Being consistent is the biggest problem in our society, since most of the time Mother works or does not have enough time because of no help. I found that waiting until Natalie was ready to be toilet trained was no problem. We had gotten used to the convenience of diapers anyway; having to take her to a public toilet is a new hassle.

When my mother came for a visit from Holland and Natalie was almost two years old, my mom decided that it would do no harm to introduce Natalie to toilet training. My mother had lots of patience. She would sit and read Natalie a book and sing with her while Natalie was sitting on her little potty chair. They did this mostly in the morning and before Natalie went to bed. She got such a surprise when she did it that eventually she always praised herself, too, by saying "good girl" as soon as she heard the sound of her urine dripping into the pot. Then she loved to empty her little pot and flush the toilet herself. By the time we came home, Natalie needed no diapers during the day.

Two months went by. Unfortunately Grandma went home, and consistency was lacking. I was back to work, and we changed baby-sitters. That time was very difficult. Natalie went back to diapers, although once in a while she went potty.

Then, when Natalie was two and a half years old, we got a new and excellent baby-sitter. She had much patience and was able to give Natalie a new consistency. Within another two months Natalie was toilet trained during the day. She was very proud of herself and did not want to wear diapers at night. We did go through some accidents at first and needed the pad under the sheet to protect the mattress. By three years old Natalie was totally toilet trained. She gets up at night if necessary to go potty.

The only accidents she sometimes still has are at school. If we put on a complicated outfit for her, such as pants with belts, she cannot get undressed fast enough and she wets the pants instead. An advantage of going to school, however, was that Natalie met classmates who already used the toilet. Now we are all glad not to have to carry diapers around. We have a new routine for Natalie if we go to public toilets. We want Natalie to recognize the difference between trusted, clean places and the uncertain hygiene of public toilets, and we've taught her not to sit directly on public toilet seats.

All in all, toilet training was not too bad. Now Natalie feels very grown-up in this matter and is very proud about it. I did talk with friends about their methods of toilet training, but I never forced Natalie in my way. We were encouraging. Natalie likes the idea, and we backed it up with consistency.

Susan

Toilet training is an issue that concerns some people a great deal. People started asking me whether or not I had started to "train" Natasha when she was just six months old. I would just smile and say "No, not yet," and leave it at that. There are many books written on toilet training, but I didn't read any of them. Quite frankly, I don't see what all the fuss is about. There are two premises on the matter that make sense to me: (1) when children are ready to be toilet trained, they will train themselves (the correlator of this is that children cannot be trained before they are ready), and (2) that one shouldn't get into a conflict with a child over toilet training because in this matter (as with eating) the child has all the power. Armed with these beliefs, I did nothing other than follow Natasha's lead. I admit that it might have been harder to do this if she had started later, but I would have tried.

When Natasha was about eighteen months old she began to show an interest in the toilet for something other than water play. I told her that when she was a big girl she would poop and pee in the toilet and she wouldn't need to wear diapers anymore. I bought a potty chair—a very inexpensive one from the Sears catalog—and put it beside the toilet. There were no bells or whistles. Somehow all the fancy models (some actually play a tune when used) seemed a bit ridiculous to me.

Some time after eighteen months Natasha began to use the potty chair. Gradually she used it more and more frequently. When it got to be too much trouble to keep taking her diaper off and on, I purchased training pants for her. When she was twenty-three months old I stopped putting a diaper on her during the daytime and began to remind her to "go potty." She still wet her pants occasionally, but usually not if I remembered to remind her to go to the bathroom every few hours. By the

124

time Natasha was two and a half years old she almost never needed to be reminded to go to the toilet.

Whenever Natasha wet her pants I would gently remind her to please try to not wait so long next time. I tried not to get angry with her, but I must admit that there were times when it was difficult—especially when I had just asked her if she had to go to the toilet, she had replied no, and then *immediately* (within seconds) wet her pants.

Just because I didn't push doesn't mean that I wasn't proud. She seemed so grown up to be wearing panties. But soon after she was out of diapers, I wished she were back in them. I could change a wet diaper at my convenience no matter where I was, but when she had to go potty, *she had to go.* (I learned where lots of toilets are—especially in grocery stores.) Fortunately her ability to wait for a more convenient time and place increased until now, at three and a half, it is never an issue.

Natasha continued to wear a diaper at night for several months. I mentioned to her a few times that when her diaper was dry in the morning she could sleep without one. She didn't seem very interested. Since it's much easier to change a wet diaper in the morning than it is to change a wet bed during the night, I wasn't in a hurry. Then, just before Natasha's third birthday, a baby-sitter forgot to diaper Natasha when she put her to bed. Natasha woke up in the morning and went to the toilet. Her bed was dry. That was the end of diapers. I put a rubber sheet on the bed—just in case.

Part Two

YOUR CHILD'S HEALTH AND WELL-BEING

Introduction 🐣

As new moms we have all struggled with issues concerning our children's health and well-being. We each had different experiences with illnesses, different ideas about childproofing, different preferences about equipment, different energy levels for involvement in groups and lessons, and many different ideas about the most helpful resources. This is what Part II is about.

In Chapter 9 we talk about selecting a pediatrician (when and how) and when and how often we called and visited their offices. Between us we have experienced a variety of illnesses, some more serious than others. We relate what it was like to go through these times and what helped us cope. We also talk about whether or not our work and social life came to a halt when our babies were ill.

Chapter 10 deals with childproofing. Is there such a thing? Most of us made all-out efforts in this area, but few of us felt secure in the results. What did we do? What worked? What didn't work? We made changes in our own houses and in our yards, but what about other people's homes? A lot of changes occur in a house with the arrival of a new baby—not just as a result of childproofing. We relate how much our houses changed to meet the needs of our children and how much we expected our children to adjust to an adult environment.

All of us had different ideas about what equipment was essential and what was useless. In Chapter 11 we tell you about our experiences in this area. Many of us felt we wasted money on toys our children didn't play with. We hope that our experiences can save you some money. And we tell you about how we handled the impact all this equipment had on our once uncluttered existences.

129

INTRODUCTION

Even the most reluctant of us found that group activities for new moms and babies were valuable. Chapter 12 deals with these activities. Which ones did we find most helpful and why? If you are feeling isolated, perhaps you will find some ideas for activities you can try. If this isn't possible, we hope that the information in this book will help you feel a little less alone.

Chapter 9

HEALTH AND SICKNESS

- Selecting a pediatrician
- Calling the doctor at night
- How often our children got sick and some of the ailments they had
- Going to work when your child is ill
- Serious illness
- Medical equipment and supplies to have on hand

Diana 🐾

Selecting a pediatrician is one of the most important decisions that you will ever make. You will need to talk to this person about everything and at all hours of the day or night, and sometimes on holidays. It was important to me to select a pediatrician during my pregnancy. I wanted to make sure my concerns and philosophies had been discussed before we met in the hospital, since the pediatrician takes over the minute the umbilical cord is cut. I asked my obstetrician for a list of names of pediatricians that he recommended. I then asked friends who they used. When a name appeared on both lists I made an appointment with the pediatrician for a visit. I was able to find out a lot about the pediatricians by looking at their office surroundings. I also asked about their feelings about antibiotics, immunizations, and breast feeding. One pediatrician smoked throughout my entire visit, an easy elimination.

The pediatrician I chose was an enormous source of information, support, and comfort. I called him with questions about pacifiers, diaper rash, and toilet training. I also called him to ask about fevers that were scaring me to death and stuffed noses that barely allowed breathing. The office had a call hour set aside every day for questions.

There is something to be said for your intuition as a mother. You see your little child every day. You are the one who can best assess how he or she is—whether the child is just feeling a bit under the weather or really at odds with the world. A pediatrician who believes in mothers' intuition is the most valuable ally you can ever hope for. Never, never listen to anybody who questions your opinion about anything that relates to the health of your children. A doctor may be the best in the world, but he or she is not in the house all day with a sick baby—we are. We see the changes that occur. We notice when a simple sore throat turns into a serious illness. It is up to us to communicate our fears to the pediatrician so that he or she can make an evaluation. We know when something isn't right and needs attention. Be willing to recognize that intuition and act on it when necessary.

Sosia was a healthy baby. She saw the doctor mostly for regular checkups and vaccinations and rarely had to undergo anything too traumatic. Suddenly she developed an illness in which she began to vomit. She had several unexpected little occurrences that were a surprise at first. We soon became frustrated by them, and I finally got scared. The episodes seemed unprovoked and failed to follow a pattern. Food didn't seem to make any difference. I called the doctor and explained the situation. The doctor who was on call explained the procedure for treating the flu: Take the temperature and withhold food for an hour, then keep the child on ice chips and clear fluids for a few hours, then slowly move on to bland solids. No problem. I launched into the plan full force. First I gave Sosia ice chips, then some Seven-Up that was flat. I planned to give her a little chicken noodle soup and unbuttered toast. Sosia never made it past the ice chips.

This lasted for three days. Through the night and during the day her temperature would soar and then suddenly she would vomit. I called the doctor several times during the next three days as I watched with horror and panic as Sosia seemed to become sicker and weaker. She lost a lot of weight as I continued to withhold solids according to the doctor's instructions. Finally something in me clicked, and I realized that although I was following instructions religiously, something else was wrong. I called the doctor and told him that this was not the flu and I needed to have Sosia seen. We went to the office, and within the hour test results showed that Sosia had a urinary tract infection rather than the flu. A quick dose of antibiotics and she was on the road to recovery in a matter of hours. The improvement was dramatic and immediate.

What did I learn? What every mother learns. The doctors have expertise; their skills are wonderful. But they cannot know your child as you do. Trust your instincts. Go with what you feel is the best. If you feel that your child needs to see the doctor, then make sure that your child sees the doctor. If your child is not improving according to plan, then make sure that your child is given proper attention.

When Benjamin came along we had an entirely different experience. He was hand-delivered any number of viruses at regular intervals, courtesy of Sosia's preschool. I learned to take a temperature properly, because Benjamin gave me plenty of opportunities to practice. Within a week of his birth Benjamin had Hemophilus influenza delivered to him by Sosia. From there we went steadily downhill to the point that Benjamin didn't need any regular checkups because he was already seeing the doctor so regularly. On three consecutive Christmas Eves we visited the doctor with ailments that included ear infections, the flu, and strep throat. Benjamin considered anything in the same neighborhood as the doctor with grave suspicion. He had tests that scared him and hurt him. He is still very frightened of the doctor. The good news is that children outgrow a lot of the germs that seem to float about three feet off the ground and hit anyone in that size range.

When my children were sick an automatic alarm seemed to go off in my head at regular two-hour intervals and I would give the little one a quick check. If you don't wake up on your own when the children are experiencing a difficult cold or illness, you may want to consider getting a small alarm clock or sleeping on a futon in their room. Yogi and I usually moved the sick child in with us for the night. It made everyone a little more comfortable.

I found that because Benjamin got sick so frequently and for such long periods, I began to take his illnesses very seriously. At the first sign of a runny nose I would give him extra fluids and more rest. If he got sick, I tried to cancel my appointments whenever possible. I dropped in more frequently during the day to check on him when the baby-sitter was taking care of him. When he became seriously ill (not often, thank goodness) I canceled everything. When my children were sick their fragility was so obvious that I would get frightened. I would not be able to concentrate on anything other than them anyway, so it was best to be with them.

Jan 🐦

"Who's your pediatrician?" is a question I'm often asked—and a question I often ask. After two babies, I know how important it is to choose a good pediatrician.

Everyone has his or her own criteria in selecting a doctor. I looked for someone who was progressive, supportive of women who work, and who had a kind and comforting manner. Dr. Harry Verby of San Mateo, California, is all of that and more. He has become more than a healer. He is a friend, comforter, and adviser in all matters pertaining to health. I am not in any way hesitant (well, maybe just a little) to call with a question or to request a recommendation for a school, dentist, whatever. I hope you are as comfortable with your pediatrician. If not, have the strength to ask your friends for their recommendations and begin your search—again.

When I asked for recommendations, Dr. Verby's name headed the list. I made an appointment to meet with him *before* the baby was born. He was more than happy to meet with me and we had a good, long talk about children, work, and what to expect in the first year of a baby's life.

My older sister warned me that in the first year I'd be seeing the pediatrician a lot. She was right. When Jaclyn was six days old she went in for her first visit. She had infant jaundice (a common ailment I have since found out—both my babies had it), and since then she's had her share of fevers, colds, measles, ear infections, throat infections, and even that broken arm.

When Jaclyn got her first cold at about three months, I bought a humidifier. Personally I now believe that although there are medications that give some relief, the only thing that really cures a cold is *time*. Of course with both of us working, who takes the child to the doctor? Mother. By agreement. I know that my husband is concerned, but my concern spills over into big-time worry. If one of my babies is sick and I don't know why, I find myself unable to concentrate at work. If she is *really* sick, I've postponed my workday to take her into the doctor. Luckily this has rarely happened.

But there was the time when Jaclyn had a bad case of diarrhea for several weeks. She was about a year and a half old, and I remember being baffled by it all since, although she had an inflamed throat, she was active, eating and drinking well. She never ran a fever and never complained of any tummyaches. She just had diarrhea.

Dr. Verby suspected immediately that the antibiotic she was taking (amoxicillin) for her sore throat was causing the loose stool. This was complicated by whole milk and other milk products such as cheese and ice cream. We took her immediately off the medication and milk and milk products. We got her stabilized. Then we put her back on whole milk, but the diarrhea started again! Apparently her system had lost its ability to digest the sugar (lactose) of whole milk. Why? We can only guess. In one week she was teething, had an inflamed throat, and was taking an antibiotic. Perhaps she had a genetic predisposition to what is known as lactose intolerance. Perhaps a combination of these factors caused it. In place of whole milk, she is drinking low-fat acidophilus milk. It looks like a scary word—I had never heard of it—but you can find it alongside whole milk at the supermarket dairy counter. It looks like low-fat milk and tastes like it too. And it worked! (But what the heck is acidophilus, you ask? Apparently this milk contains the bacteria—sounds awful, but they are good bacteria, I'm told—lactobacillus, which help to digest milk and other food.)

I only bring this up to alert parents. We hope that Jaclyn will be able to digest milk again, although, almost two years later, she is still on acidophilus.

There seems to be a growing debate about childhood vaccinations. My pediatrician *asked* me if I wanted to give my kids the childhood vaccinations. I rather liked this approach. I never felt pressured, nor was I led to believe that vaccinations were simply routine. I did choose to inoculate my children. Before each shot we discussed the vaccination (what it was and why) and all side effects. Be sure to ask about side effects. Both my children broke out in a mild case of measles three weeks after their shots. Since this was a *delayed* reaction to the measles shot (normal reaction is within ten days), I took each child in to make sure that, indeed, this was a reaction and not some new, wild, exotic disease!

If you'd like to compare, these are the shots that my children had: 1. DPT: diphtheria, pertussis, tetanus. This is a bacterial vaccine and all three are combined in one shot. It's a series of five shots taken at about two, four, six, eighteen months and at five years. 2. Oral polio virus. Taken as drops on the tongue. A series taken four times: two, four, and eighteen months and again at five years. 3. Measles, mumps, and rubella. This is combined in one shot and taken at fifteen months. 4. Hemophilus B. One shot taken about two years old. Taken to prevent meningitis.

Katherine 🙿

I interviewed several pediatric groups when I was pregnant with Deren. I wanted doctors whose philosophies and developmental theories matched mine. I eliminated several doctors for various reasons—messy, unwholesome-appearing waiting rooms, unprofessional or unfriendly nursing and reception staffs, the doctor smoked, and other reasons.

The group I chose was highly regarded by my obstetrician, and I was happily impressed with them. There are four doctors in this practice, and they continue to add more pediatricians because their business is so good. I talked with each of them personally and they in turn exhibited certain strengths and personalities that were different from one another, yet compatible with mine.

I have been very pleased. We have our primary pediatrician, but the others are fully available and we have used them all.

I don't take my children into the office very often for "well baby" visits because I know that many sick children pass through those doors, and I don't want my healthy kids to pick up a virus or an illness. This may be a personal quirk of mine, but I would just as soon keep them away from the office unless they need shots or medical care.

Alexandra has never had a serious illness or injury. Deren, on the other hand, has had stitches in his head in four different places from four different accidents, and once broke his arm skiing. He was also hospitalized for a week.

When Deren was fourteen months old and still nursing regularly, Jack and I decided to accept an invitation to present an international seminar in Mexico City for three days. We decided to take Deren and to take an extra week to vacation on the resort island of Cozumel after the meeting. We were careful about what Deren ate, and everything went smoothly until our flight back home. Deren developed a high fever and had diarrhea for the entire trip. I ran out of diapers somewhere over Los Angeles and had to use towels and napkins from the bathroom. Deren got sicker and sicker and I tried to get him to nurse more, hoping that maybe there were still some antibodies in my milk.

When we finally got home I tucked Deren into bed with us and we all had a fitful night. He continued to nurse and was very weak. I called my pediatrician early and he told us to bring Deren right in, which we did. The doctor suggested we do a BM culture for the lab and continue to give Deren lots of liquids, including Pedialyte, which contains the right electrolyte balance for a child who is losing lots of bodily fluids. Deren refused to take any of it and he looked like a poor limp washcloth. I called the doctor three times that day; he said if Deren did not begin to improve we would have to hospitalize him.

A little later Deren refused to nurse and I knew we were in big trouble. I was panicked. He had never refused breast milk! I asked Jack to call the doctor and have him meet us at the emergency room. When we arrived the emergency staff agreed Deren's condition was serious and immediately hooked him up to an IV to get more fluids into him. Then they took him upstairs to an isolation room in intensive care. Our pediatrician joined us, and Jack and I immediately donned hospital gowns and masks and scrubbed up. They allowed us to enter the room and observe while Deren was given a spinal tap and his vital signals were evaluated. My heart was racing as I squeezed Deren's hand and Jack's hand alternately. "Dear God," I silently begged, "please, please let Deren get better right away!" The doctors agreed he had to be admitted on the spot and I said, "You must admit me, too, because I will not leave his side." This was a bit unusual for the staff, although they were just starting a "room in" policy. I kept crying and kissing Deren, and Jack stood strong right next to me. We spent the rest of the day there. Jack went home to see evening patients and packed me a little bag with a robe, nightie, and toothbrush. He included a few toys for Deren.

Deren was placed in a huge crib with big metal bars. When the staff wasn't looking I put on my nightgown and slipped into bed with him. He was noticeably pleased as he looked at me with questioning eyes.

Nona, our office manager, canceled my appointments for a week and people began to send flowers. I remembered the joy we felt when Deren was born in the same hospital. We had been so thrilled to receive the beautiful flower arrangements on that occasion. Now friends phoned anxiously. I would not leave my sick baby's side.

The entire night was scary and uncomfortable. I didn't sleep a wink. Deren would sleep and cry and be restless. I tried to nurse him a few times and he would put his feeble mouth to my breast. He wasn't strong enough to take a drink.

Jack was there first thing in the morning. He had jogged over and Deren was happy to see him. The doctors did their morning rounds and saw some improvements. They had to wait two more days before the results of the bowel-movement culture would be in. Their guess was that Deren was suffering from some type of salmonella.

Deren started to improve dramatically on his second day in the hospital. The entire staff was thrilled. I began to look around at the other child patients and felt mortally sad for many of them. One child with blond hair and dimples looked like Deren's twin brother. His parents were there continuously and would cry and look morose. The poor boy had an enormous tumor as large as a basketball on his stomach, and hope was running out for him. Sometimes a nurse would walk by our room and see Deren and exclaim, "He's better! He looks wonderful!" She wouldn't immediately realize that this was Deren rather than the little boy with the tumor. Even doctors made this mistake.

Deren continued to thrive. Our nanny, Minnie, would come over for several hours each day to hold Deren and relieve me so I could get a little food and fresh air.

The diagnosis came in: a rare form of salmonella B, usually contracted from contaminated food or drink. Jack and I both said, "How?" And then we remembered that on our last day at the hotel in Cozumel, Jack had taken Deren in the big swimming pool, which contained only water from the ocean. Later that day when Jack went snorkeling, he'd noticed a big pipe spewing gallons of waste into the ocean, which in turn was being pumped into the hotel's swimming pool! We decided it must have contained raw sewage that was contaminated with salmonella.

What I learned from this experience is that never again would I take a baby or a young child to a country that has questionable health standards or outbreaks of diseases that are dangerous, whether I was breast-feeding the child or not. This experience, although it had a happy ending, was far too scary and continued to haunt me for many months.

Fortunately, Deren contracted this condition on the last day of our trip or we would have been faced with the big problem of where to hospitalize him in a fairly remote vacation spot. I shudder to think about these possibilities. The emotional experience of going through health problems is devastating. It was reassuring to have already chosen my pediatricians in advance and to have been clear about their policies and medical viewpoints ahead of time.

Mary 🐦

I did not interview pediatricians before Natalie was born. Lots of my friends, however, do go around and talk to several doctors before deciding on one. My cultural background just did not allow me to be comfortable doing this—and besides, I would not have known what to ask. My choice of pediatrician for Natalie was based on the recommendation of friends who lived in my area. I thought, "If I am not satisfied with his services, I can always look for another doctor, and at that point I will have a better idea of what we want."

We were fortunate that Natalie had very few problems even after each of her vaccinations. I remember the first time she got a cold and had a little temperature. I called the doctor at 7 A.M. for consultation. He had a special hour put aside every morning to answer any questions parents might have about their children. During Natalie's infancy I often called the pediatrician for some advice. I wanted to make sure I did everything I could for every little sign Natalie gave me.

One of the most frightening experiences was when Natalie got a skin rash all over her body and face, starting from her buttocks. We took her to the doctor early in the morning. Apparently it was the way her body reacted to the fever she had had a couple of days before that. Luckily, so far we have never had that experience again.

As Natalie grew older our confidence in knowing what our daughter needed grew too. We developed much better communication with the doctor.

Being a working mother, it is very important that I have someone reliable I can leave Natalie with at home. But when she is sick I always make my schedule flexible for her needs, especially if she has to go to the doctor. One of us—either Frank or I—is always with her.

Susan ❧

I had some very definite ideas about what I wanted in a pediatrician, so I was glad that the custom was to interview doctors before making a selection. I wanted a doctor who was up to date and who would give me the information I needed to make decisions for my child rather than try to make decisions for me. I also wanted someone my children would like and, since I prefer to let nature take its course when possible, someone who would not be too quick to suggest medical intervention. Some doctors assume that if a mother brings her child in to see them, she wants some treatment prescribed. I often take in my children because I am concerned, but I always hope that no treatment will be necessary.

When Dick and I started interviewing doctors I wasn't sure that I would be able to find what I was looking for. The first doctor we talked to heightened my concern. Neither of us liked him at all. But the second one pleased us so much, we stopped looking. Not only did Dr. Smith meet all our criteria, but his office was five minutes from our home.

I enjoy the "well-baby" visits because Natasha and Ariana have always been basically healthy. It's like getting a pat on the back for a job well done. I don't use these visits to ask many questions about normal growth and development since I rely more upon my reading (see Chapter 12) and instinct when it comes to the millions of little decisions we make about the children's care and nurturing. I ask questions when I am concerned that something may be wrong or if I am having trouble with a particular problem, such as tantrums.

One of the things that I like very much about Dr. Smith is that he is not only open to my questions, but also very informative. He doesn't usually offer information unsolicited, but he answers questions with everything anyone ever wanted to know about the subject. Every answer is an opportunity for learning. For me, the more information I get, the better I feel. Fortunately, both Natasha and Ariana also like Dr. Smith very much.

Even before the current debate about the pertussis vaccine, Dick and I questioned Dr. Smith about the advisability of having our children inoculated against the common childhood diseases. We had heard that the immunity one gets from certain diseases is somehow better than the immunity acquired from a vaccine. I don't recall Dr. Smith's entire explanation now, but we discussed it at some length and Dick and I decided that the vaccines were advisable. When it came time for each of Natasha's and Ariana's DPT vaccines, Dr. Smith went over with us the potential risks and the benefits of giving the pertussis vaccine. We decided that for Natasha and Ariana, who had no preexisting condition that we were aware of that might make the risk greater than normal, the risk was worth taking.

One of the problems with being so comfortable with Dr. Smith is that it is disappointing when he is not available. Often when I call after hours he is not on call. Often the other two doctors in the same office, whom I also respect, aren't either. I invariably get another doctor who is taking calls for "our" doctors. I understand the need for this, but I wish that Natasha and Ariana would get sick when Dr. Smith is on call! When either of them gets sick, it is invariably after office hours. I don't like calling the doctor after office hours, but I sometimes do if I'm afraid the condition will worsen during the night.

I'll never forget the first time I found it necessary to call the doctor in the middle of the night. Natasha had been perfectly healthy during the day except that she had a minor cold. About three o'clock I awoke to her crying. I stumbled out of bed thinking that something did not sound exactly right. When I reached her room I noticed her breathing was very labored. It seemed as if each breath took every ounce of energy she had. I sat with her for a few minutes trying to calm her and letting her nurse, which she did without much difficulty. As she nursed I tried to decide what to do. I considered waking Dick up, but decided not to because then there would be two of us awake in the middle of the night feeling helpless. I debated whether or not to call the doctor. Natasha finished nursing and was resting in my arms. She was less agitated, but her breathing did not improve. I decided to call the doctor.

If this had happened during the daytime, I would have telephoned the doctor's office without any hesitation at all. But these things never seem to happen during the day. Or do things just *seem* worse during the night?

Once I had made the decision to call, it was easy. I told the doctor (not Dr. Smith, of course) what was wrong and tried to answer his questions objectively. He could hear Natasha breathing over the telephone and said she had croup. He explained that normally croup in babies was not serious, and as far as he could determine Natasha did not have a life-threatening condition. He told me what to watch for. Since I didn't have a vaporizer, he suggested that I take her into the bathroom, turn on the hot shower, fill the room with steam, and sit with her until her breathing improved. He told me to be sure to call him back if she did not improve or if any of the more serious symptoms he had mentioned developed.

In the steam-filled bathroom, Natasha's breathing did improve some, but not dramatically. By the time we ran out of hot water, Natasha had fallen asleep in my arms and seemed to be okay, although her breathing still sounded terrible. The next time she woke up I nursed her in the steam-filled bathroom. She still sounded terrible but she had not gotten any worse. This time she slept until eight or nine o'clock. When she got up she acted as if nothing was wrong. After she had been out of bed for a short time, the croup disappeared and she sounded like any other child with a cold. It was amazing. Had I imagined the night before?

143

Later in the day I spoke with Dr. Smith and he assured me that this was normal. He suggested that I purchase a vaporizer because Natasha's croup would probably return each night for the next few nights and she would probably have it again in the future because some children are prone to croup. When I went to the drugstore to purchase the vaporizer I was confronted with a choice between a vaporizer and a humidifier. I didn't even know the difference. I learned that vaporizers emit hot moist air while humidifiers emit cool moist air. I almost bought the humidifier because I was concerned about the possible danger from the heating process. I called the doctor, who told me that it was the vaporizer we needed. The water molecules emitted from the vaporizer are smaller and thus penetrate where needed. He explained that the new vaporizers are not as dangerous as they were years ago because the new models don't heat the reservoir of water and the heating coil has a protective casing around it. I purchased the vaporizer and have used it a great deal since, for croup has become quite commonplace in our household. I always position it out of Natasha's reach—the steam is hot as it comes out.

When Ariana was born I assumed that I was a pro. No more calls to doctors in the middle of the night because of croup. I knew what to do. But of course Ariana never gets croup. Her colds center in her sinuses and she gets so congested that she can't breathe through her nose and therefore has trouble nursing.

It seems so tragic when children, expecially babies, are ill. When your own child is sick it is almost unbearable. I was amazed at my inability to be rational. Whether or not to call the doctor becomes a major issue. A friend of mine once listed me as one of the people she would most like to be with in an emergency. I was flattered, but she obviously doesn't know how helpless I feel when my children are sick.

When Natasha was an infant the world stopped when she was sick. I canceled appointments, refused to go out in the evening, and was grateful I could stay at home with her. Even after she began to improve, if she was on any medication, I made sure that I was available to give her each dose. People to whom I entrusted the total care of my precious child now somehow seemed incapable of administering a teaspoon of syrup. When Ariana was ill the first few times I felt the urge to cancel everything, just as I had done with Natasha, but I decided that it really wasn't necessary. I do keep appointments now, but I feel guilty doing so. I still try to be at home when either of them is really feeling miserable, but I think that I have become a little more objective about just when this is.

Medical Equipment and Supplies

Following is a list of items we found useful. Remember to keep some of these in the car or, when traveling, to pack them in your suitcase, but carefully away from little hands!

Vaporizer
The moisture will remove all the wallpaper and make you feel like you spent the night in a jungle, but it will let your baby sleep and you will get some much-needed rest as well.

Diarrhea medicine (check with your pediatrician)

Children's aspirin substitute (such as Tylenol or Liquiprin)

Syrup of ipecac

Children's nose drops (such as Neo-Synephrine)

Children's decongestant (such as Sudafed)

Children's antihistamine (such as Benadryl)

Syringe (for accurately measuring medications)

Thermometers
The digital thermometers are fast and easier to read and well worth the expense. Also, there's no risk of glass shards or mercury should the thermometer break.

Hydrogen peroxide (for washing cuts and scrapes)

Band-Aids (for their placebo effect)

Antibiotic cream

Good reference books

Remember to check with your doctor before using any of these drugs—especially when your children are under two years.

10

CHILDPROOFING

- How we created safe play space indoors
- Whether or not we transformed our houses because of our children
- Is there such a thing as "childproof"?
- Safe alternatives to the crib
- Childproofing the yard
- How vigilant we felt we had to be

Diana 🐤

When we knew that Sosia was on the way we thought it would be a good idea to buy her a crib and changing table. Believe me, she was not the least bit impressed. She didn't want to sleep anywhere, especially in the bed we had bought for her. Thank goodness Benjamin liked to sleep or the crib would have received no use!

My friend Mary had the same problem with her little tyke that I had with Sosia: Logan hated his crib. Mary decided that what Logan really hated was being confined to such a small space. She went to the foam shop and bought a queen-size mattress and laid it on the floor of Logan's room with little throw pillows all around it. She very carefully childproofed the room with everything there was available for the electrical outlets and the windows and the doorknobs and made the room *totally* safe for Logan. All his toys were put in big laundry baskets. Anything that was the least bit questionable was stored in the closet with a childproof knob on the door. Thus Logan found freedom in his room and—you guessed it—he started sleeping through the night. When he did wake up at wee hours of the morning he would play quietly for a little while. Mary became a very happy mommy after her brilliant change, and I always admired her ingenuity.

Another woman in my play group had a similar brilliant idea. Her tiny studio apartment had virtually no unused space, but in the hall was a sizable closet. She cleaned out everything inside, bought a foam mattress of the same dimensions as the floor space, and bought a childproof gate for a doorway (mesh, not accordion, gates). She wallpapered the closet in a darling bright wallpaper, and that became the baby's space for sleeping and playing. When her little guy became old enough to roam, she vigorously childproofed the apartment and let him roam a bit in the morning, allowing Mom and Dad a little bit of extra sleep.

I took childproofing very seriously with Sosia. Almost everything in our house moved or changed places. All the outlets were covered with little plastic covers that I could not remove on a bet but Sosia could remove in an instant. (There are superior covers available now that screw on.) I also spent a great deal of time teaching her that it was not okay to play with those things. But it was Benjamin who taught me the meaning of childproofing. While Sosia seemed to have an innate sense of self-preservation, Benjamin lived by Murphy's law: If it could happen, it did happen to Benjamin. He climbed where Sosia had never ventured. He found things behind the stove, under the refrigerator, and in the dog dish that had never interested Sosia in the least. We childproofed with a new vengeance and instructed Sosia and ourselves again and again to put things away after we used them. We removed everything that could be pulled off tables, any plants that could be eaten, and everything else that could be remotely harmful to help Benjamin preserve himself. Fireplaces were just not used for several years. Once again Mary came up with a grand solution: She wired her fireplace cover to the sides of her fireplace. Another couple I know turned their fireplace into a planter with safe plants in it.

Jan 🐜

I don't want to appear like a total nutcase, but there is no place that I feel my children are completely safe. Their rooms are fairly safe, but there are lamps and outlets. I have tried to put plastic inserts in the electrical outlets, but those brilliant minds work those tiny fingers, and both kids have easily taken them out.

It is amazing, though, what the magic word *NO!* can do. Jaclyn went ahead and did whatever it was anyway. Jenna, our second, *usually* refrained. I really feel there is a difference when you say "NO!" for their safety. Sometimes it's tough, because they really are just being curious.

One Christmas a thoughtful friend (and a mother of four) gave me several packages of child safety latches. They were much appreciated. These latches for kitchen drawers, cabinets, and cupboards prevent toddlers from opening them while parents can unlatch them fairly easily. I didn't put latches on every drawer or cupboard, just the ones that held potentially dangerous objects and substances such as knives, cleaners, and detergents.

I kept one unlatched cupboard filled with plastic containers and covers that Jaclyn loved to play with. Another friend kept a drawer filled with "safe" kitchen items such as a rubber spatula, plastic cookie cutters, etc.

We bought three gates to put at stairways but never put them up. They were the accordion-type gates and I was told that

hands and heads can get caught, often severely. The gates recommended today are made of netting. My kiddies just learned to
be careful around the stairs, and to descend (at our insistence)
s-l-o-w-l-y. Kids can learn (didn't we?) but it's often the hard way.
We've had our share of tumbles down the stairs, but not until
after they could walk! Learning can be so tough. Especially on
our own babies.

Katherine 🦢

The house stayed exactly the same for five months after Deren
was born. He could only sit up, roll over, and push up. Then he
learned to crawl. Disaster struck that day in his fifth month and I
was panicked! Oh dear! I need to cover every electrical outlet,
get rid of glass tables and tipsy vases and plants. I need to
conceal phone wires and electrical cords. I need baby gates for
the stairs and to put in front of the fireplaces. I need to be
constantly alert for pins and buttons on the floor. I must make
sure that the long windows have Lucite guards in front of them
so they won't break when the toys go flying. I need latches on
the kitchen cupboards, etc., etc. The tasks to babyproof the
house seemed nearly overwhelming.

We went from a lovely tranquil home with a peacefully sleeping immobile baby to a graduate course in babyproofing the
house. Jack and I examined the house everywhere from the
floor to twelve inches up in order to make sure Deren would not
mortally harm himself. The bathrooms and kitchen seemed to be
the prime battlefields where our son might get hurt.

What a shock to have to transform a house we had happily
lived in for so many years into a different place in twenty-four
hours. We learned quickly enough that twelve inches high did
not mean a thing. This little explorer was learning how to pull

himself up. I began to get pretty upset because that meant that nothing was safe or sacred—except maybe the chandeliers!

All of the knickknacks on the tables, the candlesticks, the precious gifts from good friends that we had attractively displayed on coffee tables and end tables through the years had to disappear quickly.

I mentioned to Jack that we might consider locking up our home for five years and rent a small, bare apartment with wall-to-wall carpeting instead of shiny hardwood floors where Deren was going to receive his share of bumps.

Since Jack had raised two children from a previous marriage, he began to reassure me that this phase wouldn't last long and that our child (or children) could happily co-exist with—or live without—collectibles and pretty antiques. I calmed down and realized that Deren would be under constant supervision during these early ages anyway, and we could wonderfully childproof his room, our room, and the kitchen and bathroom. For the time being, we could put extra baby gates across the unsafe rooms. Deren didn't need an entire house at his disposal for the time being.

At Christmastime I found an enormous circular baby gate that fit perfectly around the big tree and presents. This way we weren't concerned with everything being unwrapped prematurely or with little fingers pulling down ornaments or electric lights.

Mary ❧

Our house easily accommodated an additional family member, but the house and its surroundings are not designed for leaving children unattended. Our house is multilevel, with many compartments for different rooms. As I've mentioned, the first thing we had to teach Natalie was how to crawl up and down the stairs.

Surprisingly, we did not childproof our house, except for covering the electrical outlets. The most dangerous furniture is in the living room, where we hardly spend any time except when we have company. Natalie seldom goes there and she is a pretty careful child. She also needs constant company—she loves to be where the people are! The only place she sometimes is on her own is her bedroom, I guess because all her favorite things are in there. We do have to watch where we leave our things, such as drinking glasses or little notes. Small items can easily end up in the garbage can, since Natalie loves to throw things in it.

We live on a hill, so outdoors we have only a portion of flat garden with grass and a swimming pool on the other end. Because of the pool I never felt I could leave Natalie unattended outside. She loves water. One day she even plunged into our fish pond! As she was looking down at the fish, she tipped over. Fortunately, Frank was there with her, since the pond is over two feet deep. She told me later that she wanted to swim with the fish.

Basically childproofing depends on the people who live in the house, how active a family they are, and how the children behave. We all seem to adjust accordingly.

Susan 🐌

As Natasha started moving around, I began the difficult task of trying to childproof our house. I had no idea how many devices were available for this until I started shopping. The list is endless and the devices are available from many sources. I found them in baby-clothing and furniture stores, from the Sears catalogue, and from mail-order houses that I found listed in the little advertisements at the backs of magazines for parents. F & H Safety Products (Box 2228, Evansville, Indiana 47714) seemed to have the most complete stock.

There have been lots of articles written about how to child-proof a house. I read every one I see. But I believe the term "childproofing" is a misnomer. Children will find a way to get into things that are dangerous no matter how carefully you put them out of reach, so you still have to watch the little devils every second. Childproofing is essential, but it doesn't create a child-proof environment.

I have done a fairly complete job of childproofing, but the house is not entirely safe and I check on Natasha and Ariana frequently if they aren't in the same room with me. They are absolutely not allowed in the laundry room, since that is where we store all of the cleaning supplies. The door is locked with a childproof doorknob cover.

Some things just seem to defy childproofing. Besides the toilets and water faucets (I've turned down the water heater but I'm not willing to turn off the water!) I find that electrical cords are impossible to childproof. There are all kinds of devices for the outlets, but when you have something plugged in, the cord is invariably on the floor and thus very available and irresistible to a teething child. Sharp edges on furniture are also difficult. There are devices available that attach to the corners of furniture with suction cups but babies learn to take these off and chew on them before they are mobile enough to worry about the sharp edges. What's a mother to do? Supervise closely and hope for good luck!

The childproofing that we did inside was relatively predictable and inexpensive. Outside was another matter. Until Natasha could let herself outside I did not worry much; I just made sure that I was always with her when she was outside. But we live on a very busy street and have a pool in the backyard, so when Natasha could get outside without assistance—even though she was good about not doing so—I was nervous. We spent a fortune putting a gate in the front yard and covering the pool (an adult can walk on the cover safely). Our yard is now a fairly safe place to play and the girls can be outside without constant supervision. Another possible solution to the outside door problem is to add locks. A simple hook positioned high enough to be out of reach will work for a while.

After we childproofed our home I found that I had to remind myself that other places we visited were *not* childproof. I've read that the most common accidental poisonings in children occur at grandparents' homes. When we visit other homes or stay in rented rooms, I try to identify danger spots and make them off limits for the girls; I also try to be extra vigilant. The Fourth of July incident that I related in Chapter 3 made me even more aware of how important it is to be extra careful when away from home.

Another problem for which I have not found a satisfactory solution is how to childproof once the second child arrives. With one child it is fairly easy to keep small choke-size items off the floor and away from little mouths. When Ariana arrived I had a terrible time trying to get Natasha to keep her toys out of Ariana's reach. None of the articles I have read on childproofing even mentions this problem. I guess no one else has found a solution to this one either. I constantly reminded Natasha about the danger to Ariana and instituted a rule that toys with small parts were to be used only while Ariana was napping. This helped but was by no means foolproof.

Chapter 11

EQUIPMENT

- Whether we used cloth or disposable diapers
- What baby equipment we found useful—and what was a waste of money
- Buying tips
- Selecting children's toys
- Decorating the nursery
- Dealing with clutter

Diana 🐥

I am not going to surprise you when I tell you that there are a lot of things available for babies. Making your selections can be difficult, and organizing all of your purchases is no easy feat.

Although at first it seemed redundant to have both a crib and a bassinet, I discovered both were essential. I didn't have a bassinet for Sosia, but made sure that Benjamin had one. It was wonderful to be able to put him in an infant-sized bassinet to sleep when he was tiny. It also moved easily from room to room so that he could be near me and comfortable.

I enjoyed the little chairs that babies can sit in. They are easily moved about and provide a different position that is comfortable for the baby.

I used cloth diapers for Sosia. I felt they were more ecological and better for the baby. But I decided that my small contribution to ecology was a tremendous hassle for me! Benjamin was a disposable-diaper baby, and I was a very happy mom.

A diaper bag is an absolute necessity, preferably washable, since it will get crumbs, juices, and other unmentionables all over it all the time. Also, in a pinch a nice cloth diaper bag can serve as a changing pad or a pillow.

A front pack and backpack were essential for us. My children literally lived in them for a year. A baby pack frees both hands and is a very secure place for the baby. I used the backpack whenever Sosia had separation anxiety. I just carried her around all the time everywhere, whether I was doing the dishes or the laundry, and she was happier being with me.

We purchased a playpen for Sosia and it came in handy a couple of times when I just had to take a shower or something and I wanted to be sure she was confined. But she did not like it, and the controversy over whether it is bad or good kept me wondering. I kept it just in case and used it for a toy box.

I thought the umbrella strollers looked very convenient at first, but they are a pretty rough ride if you are going over anything bumpier than carpeting. I found a wonderful stroller that folded up compactly and had nice rubber wheels that gave the baby a soft ride. Make sure that you can steer a stroller easily before buying it, and check to see if the height is comfortable for you.

Our high chair was great because it had a nice big tray that extended partially around the baby. That helped eliminate spills to either side, and it was washable, *everywhere*.

Car seats are rated on their safety. They must all meet government standards. There are some that are easy to put into the car and take out again. That is a wonderful plus for a baby who falls asleep in the car or is taken to restaurants. Check how well the seat fits your car before purchasing. Some are not designed for foreign-car seats; others require complicated installations.

The indoor swing was a secondary consideration that, as it happened, I couldn't have lived without. When Sosia was distressed, either the swing or I settled her down. Sometimes the swing was worth everything.

A rocking chair is a must. Mine had a soft seat with a high back and soft arms. When the baby is sick or nursing you deserve to be wonderfully comfortable. You will spend a lot of time in the rocking chair, so comfort comes before design.

There are beautiful toys available for tiny babies. Many of the toys are wonderful to look at, delightful to hold, and of absolutely no use to anybody. I found that I bought too many toys. The children outgrew them really fast, especially the ones that hang over the crib. Crib mobiles can't be used for anything after the baby starts moving, and personally I wonder how much the baby ever enjoyed them anyway. Be smart, have fun, buy *one*.

The toys that we go back to again and again are our blocks, balls, crayons, paper, dress-ups, musical toys, imagination props, glue, paints, Play-Doh and clay, Tupperware bowls, spoons, measuring cups, and pans. Many of our best toys came from the kitchen.

I tried to buy toys that had more purpose to them than just shaking or watching. Children need to work out roles and feelings, and the toys they play with are tools that they use to learn about their environment. I tried to find toys appropriate to the developmental stage the children were going through, activities that helped them optimize their development at any point.

I found toys and swings and other big bulky baby things to be very distracting; however, their usefulness far outweighed the inconvenience of having all that stuff around, so Yogi and I agreed that the equipment would be there for a certain period and then it would be put away. I developed a kitchen drawer filled with toys that turned out to be a godsend in many ways. If someone dropped by unannounced I just opened the drawer and dumped in everything in less than sixty seconds. On the other hand, if I needed a quiet moment, I just pulled the drawer open and the baby had wonderful toys to play with right on hand.

If we spent a lot of time in one specific area of the house, we kept toys there for the children. It was wonderful to be able to have them happy too. And it left other areas relatively neat.

Babies need so many things—furniture and toys and clothes and diapers and wipes. I decided along the way that life just needed some streamlining. I could not be running up and down stairs for every little thing that I needed. In addition to keeping toys in different areas, I made several little stations around the house in strategic locations and stocked them with diapers, wipes, and burping cloths. It saved many a trip to the changing table and made life a lot easier.

Jan 🦢

Let's hear it for modern-day conveniences. Whoever invented the disposable diaper (was this person a mom?) had great intelligence and probably wanted to save time. There are some moms and dads who swear by cloth diapers (and diaper service), but I knew from the start, disposable was the way to go. And I was not disappointed. I don't believe that disposable diapers gave my daughters more rash problems or infections than cloth diapers would have. As for cost, I had a friend who calculated the costs for cloth (diaper service) and disposable and found they cost about the same. When both my children were in diapers I easily spent $30 a week on them.

Car seats are required in California. I shopped and shopped until I found what I thought was the most convenient and safe seat. Some models had so many straps that I was afraid we would tend not to use them because they take forever to buckle and unbuckle. I found a seat that really is a one-step safety seat. The straps and a padded bar come over the head and snap between the legs. It's called Safe and Sound and it's made by Collier. It costs around $50 and will go from newborn to four years or forty pounds.

There are many great fold-up strollers available. I selected the Aprica stroller that folds for travel and storage. When my second child was born I looked for a double stroller, because Jaclyn at two still wanted to ride (Jaclyn at three still wants to ride). I found that a lot of double strollers were not safe; they tipped if one child was in the front and no child in back (or vice versa). I also didn't want the children facing each other (I didn't want to encourage any potential fighting and I wanted both to look forward, truly!). I finally found a British-made stroller called the McLaren that does a great job as a double stroller and folds compactly too.

I hate to admit this, but I bought a high chair that went with the color scheme of my kitchen. It works fine and converts to a desk later if you wish. I'm not sure I would recommend it or buy it again. There's an excellent Fisher-Price high chair on the market that has a wide, almost wraparound tray that can be easily cleaned. I have also found that the seats that slip on to tables are great for traveling; mine works well as a high chair and was inexpensive.

As for walkers, swings, jumpers, backpacks and frontpacks, I got them all but really rarely used them. You might want to borrow one from a friend to see if your child really takes to it. I borrowed a playpen for a week and knew it wasn't for me. Jaclyn hated it and I couldn't stand the thought of a child confined to a small play area.

As for toys, there are so many on the market, it's difficult to decide which to get. Ironically, my children have loved simple, familiar toys—the telephone, clock, tea sets, and books. And I'm constantly surprised how much fun my children can have with a paper bag or a discarded box!

There was (and still is) something oddly appealing to me about seeing toys, dolls, blocks, and tricycles in our house. You may think I've gone cuckoo, but it warms me to see tricycles and sandbox toys in our yard as I pull into the driveway after work. It says to me that there are little kiddies here . . . and they are mine! Sound crazy? Probably, but since I'm away from them during the day, any glimpse of the angels can be warming.

Of course I find myself constantly picking up toys and stuffed animals and pieces of Mrs. Potato Head. We try to confine all toys to the family room and stuffed animals to the bedrooms. This is easier said than done.

Katherine 🦢

I have unfortunately bought many baby things that were useless or unneeded. It's a trial-and-error process, and if that isn't enough to drive a new parent bonkers, I have discovered that what worked with one baby didn't work for the other.

There were certain pieces of equipment I bought that were real hits. Both children, for example, thrived in bassinets as their first beds. I repainted an old forlorn wicker bassinet white and a girlfriend helped make a pretty white eyelet dust ruffle. I tied blue bows on it for Deren and changed them to pink for Alexandra. Other good investments that both of them used were a crib, infant seats, walkers, baby gates for staircases, drawer locks, car seats, a high chair with a huge tray, a baby swing, electrical outlet covers, and a portable fold-up stroller.

The items that became big mistakes in our family were playpens, a changing table (too narrow—I used the bed or the floor), front/back carriers, heat-up food dishes, jump-up-and-down swings, a huge deluxe stroller, an antique high chair, a baby bath. These items gathered dust and I eventually gave them away.

Some of the toys they loved and felt pleased with were plastic books with wipe-clean pages, soft cuddly animals, colorful mobiles with music, bath toys, crayons and coloring books, big bedroom slide, an activity-center game for the crib, and, later on, Lego blocks.

The toys that were relegated to the unplayed-with pile were things with too many parts, puzzles with lots of pieces, and fragile things.

EQUIPMENT

One thing I really check out at day-care centers, nursery schools, and elementary schools are the types of equipment and toys they have. There are many items I wouldn't consider buying the children (too big, too messy, or too expensive) and I like to make sure that the schools have the swing sets, slides, sandboxes, art easels, and giant block-building sets. Geodesic climbing structures are a plus as well as extensive children's libraries, clay, and finger painting. I love it that both children can involve themselves in these activities each day—and I don't need to keep these things on hand.

Mary 🐚

We have gotten a lot of mileage out of our high chair from Silver Cross. It can be a high chair or a low one with a bigger table. As Natalie grew bigger, she preferred to sit low. It's easier for her to climb into and she has a bigger table she can use to write or play.

The automatic baby swing was also wonderful. Natalie fell asleep many times while swinging. Anytime she was fussy or we happened to be occupied and could not keep an eye on her, we put her in the swing. In the summertime we moved the swing outdoors and it was lots of fun. It is good for about a year and a half.

One piece of equipment we did not use so much was our Prego stroller. It is more designed for infants and is rather bulky. We bought a second stroller that was lighter and cheaper. Natalie sat more comfortably too.

Another item I find very useful is a booster car seat. We use it if we take another toddler in the car, and also for Natalie in a second car. Natalie's car seat is practically bolted to one car, so it is wonderful to have this additional booster seat. Sometimes if she goes out with her grandparents we just take the booster seat. She sits higher, and the seat belt can protect her better too.

Generally we just decorated the baby room minimally. I must have had the feeling that I wouldn't live in this house for a long time and I wanted the baby room to stay pretty neutral for the next owner. Frank painted a chest of drawers and he also made shelves for books and toys, both in white and yellow. Everything was neat and uncluttered, fresh in colors. Well, all that did not last very long. Before we knew it a neat baby room looked unreal. Toys and stuffed animals are all over the place, but slowly I have learned to love it. There are signs of life in there. However, it could easily get out of hand. I have to make a point of picking up Natalie's toys after she finishes playing, and at the end of the day everything is in its place again—except whatever she is still busy with. Clutter used to drive me bananas. I have compromised by allowing some of Natalie's toys to be used as part of the decoration in the family room, where we spend most of our time. Even our bedroom manages to have some of her books and bears.

Toys do accumulate so easily. We feel we need a warehouse for unused toys, since Natalie might be interested in them again in the future. As much as our daughter loves to visit Toys "Я" Us, I must admit I do too. There are so many wonderful educational toys available these days, even a sophisticated computer for toddlers. The only toys that are useless in our house are the dolls. Except for one ugly bear, which has been Natalie's favorite for years, she does not play with dolls.

Susan 🙶

I found both the front pack and backpack extremely useful. They go where strollers won't and they are easy to take when traveling. For the first six months I used the front pack rather than the stroller. I preferred having Natasha and Ariana close to me. I think that they slept better and when awake they could see the world around them from a better vantage point. If I had to give up something, I would give up the stroller rather than the packs.

Another item I would not like to be without is our little table seat. It fits on to almost any table and we have used it in many restaurants, at Grandma's house, and in hotel rooms. It folds flat for easy packing and can also be used at home. Again, if I were to give something up, it would be the high chair, not the table seat—and the seat was much less expensive than the high chair.

A diaper bag is, of course, essential if you are planning to take the baby out of the house. I found that diaper bags were not as useful as a simple Le Sac nylon bag, which I purchased in the handbag department of a large department store. It is extremely lightweight and virtually indestructible. It carries everything I have ever needed, and will also be useful in the future for lots of other things. It has already doubled as an overnight bag for Natasha.

Many people (especially those who sell them) would consider toys to be essential equipment. I found none to be indispensable. In fact, most of them were useless. I wish I'd saved my money, at least for the first two or three years. I bought some toys for Natasha and Ariana, and they were given many others, but they preferred the things that they found around the house. There is one exception. They love any toy that makes lots of noise. In our house, however, we veto all toys that make a lot of noise!

It seemed to me that a crib must be a very boring place, so when Natasha was an infant I bought crib toys, hung mobiles, and filled her room with all the stimulating things that I could find. She wasn't interested. She was so anxious to get out of the crib as soon as she was awake, I doubt that she even noticed all those things hanging over her. She wanted to be where the action was. She watched people and what they did, not mobiles. I followed her lead and made sure that she was in a position to see what was going on around her. I took her everywhere with me.

All the money I spent on crib toys was not a total waste. Ariana loved them. On many occasions she woke up in the morning and didn't call to be picked up but instead played with the stuffed animals in her crib, pulled the cord on the music box (or whatever else was hanging there), and talked happily to herself.

As an infant Natasha preferred brightly colored plastic toys she could put in her mouth. As she got to the point where she was grabbing for things (around three months), she would hold on to a toy or two occasionally if I put it within her reach, but for the most part her toys were things she noticed around her that *she* decided she wanted to play with. My earrings, my necklace, the spoon on the table (she would have played with the fork and knife, too, if I had let her), my keys, or just about anything that was within reach—especially if I didn't want her to have it. Ariana liked those things and also one or two very soft cuddly stuffed animals.

As toddlers some of their favorite store-bought toys were the "doughnuts" on a spool; a ball with various shaped blocks that fit into shaped holes; blocks (of any kind) that could be built up and knocked down; crayons; clay or Play-Doh; and balls. Natasha and Ariana seemed to prefer very large beach balls or very small balls that bounce very high (and were thus lost almost immediately).

During this stage, as others, most of their time was spent with toys *they* discovered. Some of their favorites included plastic storage containers, kitchen utensils, keys, paper bags, cardboard boxes, sheets, anything with lids, pots and pans, etc. A favorite place of theirs was the kitchen, where they were allowed to get into some of the cupboards. For a while they would only take things out of the cupboards; later they liked to put them back in, too, but never where they belonged. Both girls went through a stage when they loved taking the silverware out of the dishwasher as I was trying to put in the dishes. They would then walk away and hide the silverware. Some of it they brought back, but some I found later in the strangest places. Their all-time favorite "toy" was (and still is) water. They will play in the bathtub or at the kitchen sink with the water running longer than they will stay with any other activity. On more than one occasion when I needed a break, I put them in the bathtub and sat beside them with a magazine or newspaper. (I never used a ring seat in the bathtub. Until they could sit up I used an infant bath, holding them myself, and I never left them unattended in the bathtub until they were well past the age where the ring would have been useful.)

In general, the children decide what they want to play with. I just observe. I can take credit only for arranging my cupboards (mainly in the kitchen) so that they are free to explore, and for

163

not saying no when they get into things and make a mess. In truth, I found it was much easier to clean up the mess than to put up with a child who was fussing because she was bored and I was too busy to play with her.

I draw the line in the bathroom, where my makeup would have been lots of fun. This mess I am not willing to deal with, so I keep a drawer in the bathroom filled with toys, the kind you buy that are guaranteed to captivate your child's interest and teach them everything they need to know—the kind Natasha and Ariana are not the least bit interested in. Both girls find Tampax fascinating when I'm in a pinch (they discovered this on their own too!).

Starting around two and a half or three years, Natasha's favorites have been all types of art supplies. Everything from crayons, watercolors, marking pens, colored pencils, glue, scissors, tape, and Play-Doh. I received a great recipe for a Play-Doh substitute from Natasha's preschool teacher, Ginger. Not only is it cheaper, but Natasha loves to help make it.

Mix 1 cup flour with 1/3 cup salt and 1 teaspoon cream of tartar. Set aside. To 1 cup water add 1 tablespoon oil and several drops of food coloring. Mix liquid and dry ingredients together. Place over low heat. Stir often until the dough is the consistency of mashed potatoes. Turn onto foil and let dough cool. Store in airtight container.

Although toys take over your house, there are other important pieces of equipment. One very important item is the camera. Take out stock in your favorite film company. You are going to buy a lot of film and you might as well get a piece of the action.

I bought a playpen out of desperation one day when Natasha was at that stage where she could get places rapidly and could not be trusted alone for even a second. I couldn't figure out how to get the groceries in from the car without somehow confining her. But in general I don't like playpens. I wanted my children to feel free to explore their world. For all the times I used the playpen (with both children) it wasn't worth the expense. With Ariana I could have used the crib for those moments when I needed her to be confined. Natasha had such an aversion to her crib, however, that I'm not sure that would have worked.

I have never been a particularly good housekeeper (Dick would tell you that is an understatement). I find housework to be extremely thankless, a task when once done is immediately undone. But even when our house wasn't very clean, it was neat. That is, before children. Now, no matter how many hours I spend straightening up the house, it always looks like a disaster area. There is a rule I have noticed: Once played with, a toy will stay in the middle of the floor, never to be played with again, until Mom puts it away, at which time it will again be played with—just long enough to get it back into the middle of the floor.

I'm amazed at how accepting both Dick and I are about the changes that have come over our house. I grumble about how much time I have to spend picking up the mess, and about the fact that I don't notice Dick helping much, and Dick grumbles from time to time himself but we both put up with a lot more than we thought we could.

The mess didn't start right away, of course. When Natasha first arrived we added only a cradle in our bedroom and a crib and changing table in the spare bedroom—which was to be Natasha's bedroom when she moved from ours. I didn't do any decorating, not only because I'm a lousy decorator but also because we were planning an addition to our house and expected Natasha to change rooms before she would be old enough to notice any decorating that I might have done. There were a few other things around the house, such as diapers, blankets, etc., but they stayed where I put them and were rather unobtrusive. When Natasha began to crawl and then walk, however, she distributed her toys around the house and began to leave them there to trip anyone who happened by.

We have not been particularly restrictive about where Natasha and Ariana may play. They like to play wherever we are and we like having them around. As a result, toys end up just about every-where in the house. I try to keep most of them put away in the toy closet (this used to be a linen closet) and just keep a few in the den and our bedroom and bathroom. But so far teaching Natasha to put her things away when she is finished seems hopeless.

Our house is no longer our own. But we couldn't be happier. It has been taken over by the two most wonderful kids in the world and the mess is a very small price to pay.

Equipment

You won't need all of these items at once, and you won't need some of them at all, but here is a list of equipment to consider as you make your plans—and prepare your budget!

Bassinet or cradle

Crib and mattress—also crib bumpers, sheets, comforter or quilt, and mattress pad or rubber sheet

Changing table and mattress with mattress cover

Dresser

Lamp with dimmer switch

Diaper bag

Trash can and/or diaper pail

Infant seat with cover

Car seat with cover

Front pack and/or backpack

Baby carriage, stroller, umbrella stroller

High chair with cover

Toy chest and/or toy shelves

Table seat

Booster seat

Baby bath with sponge liner

Indoor swing

Jumper

Walker

Playpen

Portable crib

Smoke alarm

Fire extinguisher

Intercom

Potty chair and/or toilet-seat insert

Rocking chair

Changing supplies—diapers, wipes, lotions, ointments

Feeding supplies—spoon, cup, bowl, bottles, nipples, bottle liners

Childproofing items—safety caps, locks, guards, plugs, gates

Medical supplies (see Chapter 9)

Toys

Camera and film

Decorations, mobiles

12

GROUPS, LESSONS, AND RESOURCES

- The importance of children seeing other children—and mothers seeing other mothers
- Participating in play groups
- Other group activities our children enjoyed
- How soon we enrolled our children in classes
- Lessons they have taken
- Are we encouraging or pushing?
- Books and magazines that we found helpful

Diana 🙢

When I brought Sosia home I was certainly shocked to realize that she was there all the time. We needed to establish things that we could do and enjoy together. Friends can be a major source of information and support, but if you are the first one on your block to bring home a new baby, knowledgeable friends can be in short supply. That will mean it is time to make new friends.

A little research on your part will uncover all types of classes and groups that form around new mothers. There are often "parenting classes" offered through the hospital where you delivered. For the first several weeks postpartum you and your baby go back to the hospital to share your wonderful mixed-up feelings and emotions with other new parents.

I attended a Baby Gym Class that met at the Jewish Community Center. It was wonderful to see so many other new mothers and to share my amazement and delight and frustration at being a new mom.

Another excellent class was Child Observation, set up through the Community Colleges in San Francisco. In other areas similar classes are called Gymboree, Side by Side, Parent Education, etc. The class included a trained Parent Education teacher who led the class and decided what equipment would be available to the children. There might be exercise mats for them and structures to climb on, balls or big pillows filled with foam blocks. The mothers would sit and talk about issues that they found interesting or bothersome. The teacher would lead a discussion or speak to us privately, giving us answers and information. As the children grew and changed, our discussions and printed handouts would reflect those changes. The class was an oasis for me. I had access to an expert who was available to me on a weekly basis. If you have trouble locating a Parent Education class in your area, check with your child-care switchboards, parent hot lines, or your pediatrician.

The first several months of Sosia's life taught me that it was a very long day with the baby. There were many times when I really wanted to have other mothers to share things with. Fortunately I was blessed with a guardian angel somewhere out there who recognized that I was in a real quandary. When Sosia was about six months old I found a wonderful play group. We are nine moms with children who have met once a week for about four years. At first we met in each of our living rooms and watched our tiny infants squirm or sleep. We talked about everything and we praised each other on the wonderful job we were all doing as mothers. We had no set schedule of topics, although someone would be assigned to make coffee and bring a snack. We exchanged everything from recipes to political points of view. The variety among us was immense and, most important, our various points of view were respected. While Mary insisted that Logan eat only brown rice, Chris didn't feel that an occasional bit of chocolate would do Alexis any permanent damage. Ana impressed us with her tremendous skills in organization, and I would forget to bring a diaper. Was it the pediatrician that I called first? No, it was probably Ana. From there she would help me decide who in the group had something similar or some friend with a similar situation from whom we could get the needed information. I was able to extend my family into a multi-religious, multi-cultural and multi-purpose group. Our children played and enjoyed each other and became the closest thing to cousins outside of cousins.

We formed by approaching each other in different classes and through our friends. We established a basic guideline of how we would meet and we then let the group mold itself as it moved along. We tried to share different ideas and suggestions from all our sources. We discussed information we had on temper tantrums. We pooled information about preschools, restaurants that catered to families, and activities to do with children. We went to the parks and zoos on outings together. We became incredibly good friends. We learned together, and we learned that a group of women can provide tremendous support.

I have heard of a number of ways to start and structure a play group, such as asking a few people that you meet in different classes, placing ads in local newspapers, inviting friends of friends. Some play groups have discussion schedules; others are strictly set up to expose children to children. Some are set up around baby-sitting co-ops where the children play while the mothers have free time that they exchange. Some meet only in parks while others meet in homes. If you are interested in being in a play group but you haven't found one, then *form your own.*

There are several newspapers in the Bay Area specifically related to parenting. These newspapers share ideas about parenting and resources, and they point out different places and activities that may be enjoyable for families. I found many wonderful ideas in the local publications.

170

I also enjoyed reading *American Baby Magazine* and *Parents*. Both are wonderful magazines that address the specific issues of parenting. Many articles came at the precise moment I needed them. It's nice to get a magazine when you are very busy and may not have time to check out books to read.

There were many books on the subject of parenting that I enjoyed. T. Berry Brazelton's books, *Infants and Mothers* and *Toddlers and Parents,* give a wide range of information on a variety of different types of children and babies from quiet to active. Brazelton shows the wide range of completely normal development while giving wonderful parenting suggestions. Louise Bates Ames and Frances L. Ilg have a series of books: *Your One Year Old, Your Two Year Old,* etc. Unfortunately I didn't discover them for a long time, but once I did I found them invaluable. You can imagine my relief when they told me to expect my children to say "I hate you" as part of their normal development! Johnson & Johnson puts out a series of books on children. *Your Toddler* and *Your Preschooler* are still wonderful sources of countless different types of parenting information.

I resented the books that tracked the babies' every effort from birth to twelve months. Although my children measure up admirably on anyone's development scales, keeping track left me frazzled and feeling pushed. I didn't want to feel like a failure if I forgot to write down when Sosia first hinted that she might turn over. The comparisons these kinds of books evoked made me feel that parenting was nothing more than a game of who has the fastest or the most modern model! Those types of books quickly got lost somewhere and fortunately I haven't located them again.

Jan ❧

I felt it would be important for Jaclyn and Jenna to interact with other children. But with no visible small children in our neighborhood, I signed Jaclyn up at three months for Gymboree. Gymboree is now a franchised individual and group activity for children from three months to five years of age. It was started by a mother who was looking for some sort of stimulating physical activity for her growing child. At Gymboree parents and children sing, explore, discover, and play. I think it's a good program, and have now signed up Jenna. If you're interested, look in the phone book. Perhaps there is such an activity near you. An added bonus is the opportunity to talk with other parents— and finding that their frustrations (a child not sleeping through the night, pinching/biting a sibling, refusing to be potty trained) are the same as yours.

At Gymboree we met other parents interested in having their child interact with others. I invited all of Jaclyn's classmates at Gymboree and their parents over to my home to discuss the possibility of starting a play group. We did start one, and three years later, are still meeting once a week at parks, pizza parlors, pumpkin patches, and homes.

We meet once a week at 10 A.M. on Wednesday. One mother is responsible for the activity each week. We've been to the zoo, fire station, and lots of parks. Once when it was my turn I arranged to have all the children fingerprinted and records made for each of them (the only copy going to the parent). With the growing number of kidnappings, I am a firm believer in this. If you're interested in doing this, contact your local police department. They can probably lead you to a group or show you how to do it yourself. I worked with a nonprofit group interested in locating missing and abused children.

Having been born and raised in Hawaii, I really wanted my

children to learn to swim. I enrolled Jaclyn when she was eight months, and Jenna started the day she turned three months. They don't really *learn* to swim at such an early age, but it's great exercise and they have no fear of water. The particular program I have the children in teaches them to swim to the side of the pool and pull themselves up, the idea being that should they fall in, they won't panic but will be able to take care of themselves. Some studies have shown that babies (three to four months) literally hold their breath underwater, eyes open, and "swim." My kids never did "swim" after their first lesson, but after two and a half years of swimming lessons Jaclyn now can swim across the pool and pull herself up the side. Both girls love the water, and both as tiny babies literally walked into pools. Reason enough for me to give them swimming lessons. Reason enough for my pocket book. (You can call your local YMCA or YWCA for swimming lessons or look them up in the Yellow Pages of your phone book. That's exactly where I found the Peninsula Swim School for my kids.)

I enrolled Jaclyn in gymnastics when she was two. She loves it and still attends once a week. I tried both of them in a music class. Jenna at ten months loved it and sang all the time. Jaclyn at three was totally disinterested and had to be reprimanded by the teacher for wandering about. Today, Jenna attends once a week, Jaclyn does not.

Involving my children in different activities seems to be important to me. Why couldn't I just let them play in the sandbox? I could, I guess, but there are so many other things to try! As a working mom I can't take my children to all their activities—activities that fall during the workday. But I feel strongly that my working shouldn't prevent my children from attending different activities. Call it the working mom's guilt syndrome, but I have it.

The children's care-giver chauffeurs them to school, swimming lessons, gymnastics, play-group functions, and music lessons. The way I "participate" is at night, talking to the children and their care-giver. I love to hear every little detail. It's not as personal as being there myself, but second best is hearing about it.

And every now and then I will call an instructor or a play-group parent just to see how things are going and to assure the instructors and other parents that just because I'm not there doesn't mean I'm not concerned.

I must admit I didn't read any books on parenting or on children growing up. I relied on friends, our pediatrician, and maternal instinct for advice, hope, solace, comparison, compassion, and general all-around "Help!" Sometimes it's tough to see the right answer, but so many times your own gut-level feeling about anything from diaper rash to the right school is correct. Whoever came up with "woman's intuition" wasn't kidding. Ladies, let's give ourselves credit for knowing, believing, and doing—even if the book doesn't say so or our friends don't agree.

Katherine &

I really craved having contact with other mothers and babies when Deren was small. I found a church play group for six-month-olds and their mothers. We would sing the kids songs and observe them in free play both indoors and out. I loved this group. We parents compared notes and developmental traits in our children, discussed baby-sitters, husbands, jobs, homemaking shortcuts, nursery schools, and beneficial ways to structure days. We would sip our coffee and eat pastries that one of us mothers donated. This was a nice casual atmosphere in which to watch our children interact.

Because this group met only once a week, I looked into other mother/baby activities. The Jewish Community Center offered Kindergym—which we called "diapergym"—and infant/parent swimming lessons. I promptly signed Deren and myself up for these activities. We greatly enjoyed them together and I looked forward to seeing the other babies and their parents. We would laugh and enjoy our babies for the structured one-hour program and then stroll our babies to a nearby restaurant or a cafe that welcomed children.

I would also take Deren to the park each day, since we live right across the street. We would stroll to baby stores, book-stores, and toy stores. The stroller wheels wobbled terribly after the thousands of miles we put on them (or so it seemed).

After Alexandra was born it didn't seem as important to me to take her to the child observation or "diapergym" groups. I had already observed a child's natural development with my firstborn and I felt quite comfortable with what I was offering Alexandra. She also had Deren to interact with. Instead, I took her to my twice-weekly exercise group at Danielle's house. She loved that. Many of the other moms brought their babies to this group, and they enjoyed each other thoroughly.

Since Deren had already started a morning nursery school, I savored the special time that Alexandra and I would have together—just the two of us. I took a more leisurely approach with her and did not try to hurry any of her phases. She did her infant swimming during the summer at a regular pool instead of the outdoor heated pool during the winter at the Jewish Com-munity Center. I relaxed more with Alexandra. Perhaps she is a more relaxed type of child too!

After a certain point I didn't read child-development books unless I began to intuit that something wasn't quite right or there seemed to be a problem. Then I would look up the topic in one of my medical books. The most well-worn chapters in my Dr. Spock book were entitled "Colic" and "Sleep." I was quite upset when my papeback edition began to disintegrate from repeated contact with the hot steam from my bubble baths. I saved those precious pages. I have them still, because those subjects made such an impression on my life. Spock couldn't solve our colic and sleep problems, but I felt reassured that I wasn't alone in my quest for information and solutions, and that someone was truly trying to help.

There's a fine array of baby books on the market today and it becomes an exciting adventure to go to the childhood section of the local bookstore or library. I also enjoy the abundance of baby and parenting magazines. I admire the Dr. T. Berry Brazelton and Penelope Leach books, among others.

Mary ❧

Children need to interact with other children. There is a big difference between having one child and having two or more children. With more than one, they learn so much from each other. Natalie is very lonely. There are no children in our neighborhood, except one family where both parents also work. Everyone seems to mind their own business these days.

Fortunately we have a wonderful community center, which provides many programs, including play groups, for children and adults. When Natalie was slightly over a year old we enrolled her in several activities with our baby-sitter. On some occasions Frank went with Natalie, since his time was more flexible than mine. Then Natalie joined the Kindergym. She went twice a week, basically to have some interaction with other children her age as well as to explore, climb, jump, and swing. Apparently she was doing a lot of watching rather than participating. It was not until she was two that she started to participate and was willing to try different things on her own. Eventually Natalie entered a preschool at two years and three months. It is one of the best decisions we ever made for her. It has changed her attitude toward other children immensely. She is no longer shy about others. She is very straightforward, even to strangers, and feels very confident.

Natalie loves music lessons. Unfortunately we have not had the time to take her more often. She loves to sing and dance. Now that she is almost four years old, I hope we will have time to take some classes more seriously. For over a year now Natalie has been willing to entertain anyone, anywhere, and at any time with her songs.

Swimming is another activity she loves. We enrolled her in swimming classes for safety reasons also, since we have a pool outside. Unfortunately we were not able to follow through because of lack of time and the fact that I have to commute thirty minutes each way every day. Our house is so secluded that it is not even convenient to pick up groceries.

Well, life is full of imperfections. As much as we want to provide the best of everything for our children, there are sometimes reasons that will make us unable to do so. As long as we know we do our best, I don't think we need to punish ourselves for all those unfortunate imperfections.

My best resources have always been my clients, my friends, and family. There is much information available on all sorts of topics, but it is impossible for us to find all of it ourselves. I do enjoy reading *Parents* magazine. Reading about what other mothers go through is like having a friend sharing her experiences with me.

Susan 🦢

When I first heard mothers mentioning play groups they conjured up in my mind a horrible scene—uninteresting moms sitting around gossiping as they watched their little brats pull each other's hair. Not for me! My vision changed as my experience increased. Today I think that such groups are a valuable part of a new mother's schedule.

When Natasha was about nine months old I attended a parenting workshop. As the moms talked the babies played. I noticed how much Natasha loved being around other children and began to think about the importance of group activities. I grew up in a neighborhood where I made friends with other children on the block, but where we live now few neighbors know each other, and it isn't safe for the children to walk next door because of the traffic. If Natasha was going to have other children to play with, I was going to have to make an effort to arrange it. So I began to seek out activities for Natasha, not really knowing where to begin.

It was about this same time that I began to look around for swimming lessons for her. I did this in part because she liked the water so much but also because we have a swimming pool and I was anxious for her to become water-safe as early as possible. I don't think that young children are ever truly water-safe, no matter how well they swim, but I wanted to increase Natasha's chances of survival in the event of an accident. My search for swimming lessons led me to the Marin Jewish Community Center (MJCC), which turned out to have the best infant-toddler program around and was where I later found many other great activities for Natasha and Ariana. Natasha loved her lessons. I never had to encourage her to go. The problem was dealing with the disappointment on the days there were no lessons! The program teaches the parent to teach their child to swim. It was a fun time for both Natasha and myself. Now, at three and a half, Natasha is able to swim across the pool and climb out by herself, and she can tread water for an extended period of time. (I've never timed it, but I'm amazed how long she keeps it up.) Fortunately, she also has a healthy respect for the water. We have strict pool rules, which she follows to the letter!

As a result of the swimming lessons I discovered the MJCC Kindergym. Classes met once a week for forty-five minutes and provided lots of equipment for free play, then a short circle time with songs and parachute play. The length of the circle time increases with children's attention spans. Natasha loved the equipment (things we couldn't afford and didn't have room for at home) and she especially enjoyed being around the other children. I enjoyed watching her play and learned things from the other mothers.

Later came Side-by-Side, also at the MJCC, a wonderful pre-preschool program for toddlers eighteen months to three years. Sessions met once a week for ninety minutes. They are set up like a preschool, but moms (or dads) stay. When you first arrive the kids circulate through various stations where they have creative things to do—Play-Doh, coloring, painting, puzzles, books, play house, and a special art project each week. There are also a few activities such as playing on a minitrampoline and a slide. Next there is a snack, then outdoor play with balls, climbing apparatus, and a sandbox. Last is circle time, with songs, puppets, and stories. Again, the length of the circle time increases gradually.

The degree of participation by the parents varied greatly, depending on the need of their child. I was pretty much ignored by Natasha, so I spent my time talking with the instructor and other moms. Not only was it an excellent opportunity to talk with other mothers about problems and joys of parenting, but the teachers were well trained and offered wonderful advice. It was also wonderful watching the kids really enjoy themselves. Natasha and I attended Side-by-Side (she called it "Bye-by-Side") until she started preschool at two and a half. By now my vision of play groups and other mothers was completely different and I gladly joined one started by some of the Side-by-Side moms.

I still spend a lot of time talking about children with other parents. I rely on them for information and ideas. I learn that the obnoxious behavior that my child is exhibiting is not abnormal and is likely to pass. I am reassured that I have not made some grievous error in handling Natasha and Ariana. I also get lots of ideas about methods of discipline, activities to try, etc. No one can tell me what will work for my children, but by listening to what has worked for other children I pick up lots of ideas I may want to try.

I solicit the advice of friends and the parents of my children's friends, but I have also gotten a lot of unsolicited advice from well-meaning (I'll give them the benefit of the doubt) strangers in public places. Most of it I wished the person had kept to himself or herself because it usually came out as criticism. But I really appreciated one woman in an airport who, observing my frustration with Natasha's unwillingness to stay in sight, and thus my difficulty with gathering luggage, advised me to remember that every stage passes quickly. She was right!

Once Natasha started preschool she was frequently around other children her own age. The more she was around other children, the more important it seemed to be to her. So I began inviting her school friends over to play. At first this was another opportunity for moms to chat, but it progressed into a way of getting Natasha off my hands for a while, even at home. I discovered that when she had a friend over, Natasha would play without interrupting me for extended periods of time. I was ecstatic! I started inviting her friends over and offering their mothers the time off. And when they reciprocated it was heavenly!

Ariana has just recently reached the age of really enjoying other children, but she has the advantage of having an older sister and built-in playmate. She loves playing with Natasha. I'm amazed at how well they play together now. Natasha can still be a little rough at times and often too domineering, but Ariana takes most of this in stride and the balance is definitely tilted toward enjoyment and away from torture. When Natasha has friends over Ariana tends to get left out of the play, but she watches intently and doesn't seem to mind the exclusion.

Ariana is also taking swimming lessons. She loves the water, but seems a little slower at actually learning to swim. I suspect that this is because I am less religious in my efforts to teach her. I haven't had time for Kindergym for Ariana but we will begin Side-by-Side as soon as she's old enough.

When your child is driving you to distraction, the only really useful resource is someone who will take the little monster off your hands for a while. For this reason, among others, Dick is high on my list of essential resources. It is true that most of the day-to-day responsibility for taking care of Natasha and Ariana falls on my shoulders. However, I would not like to change places for a moment with the many moms who are doing the job alone. Just knowing that if I really cannot cope I can count on Dick to step in makes it easier. When I am just about at my wit's end, he senses this fact (I guess it's pretty obvious) and steps in and takes over. I almost never even need to ask, he just seems to appear. In the same vein, I consider occasional baby-sitting, from paid care-givers, friends, or relatives, to be an absolutely essential resource.

For me other important resources have been those that add to my knowledge of what is normal developmental behavior. Understanding my children's behavior helps me to deal with them more effectively—and to maintain my sanity! I took a course in developmental psychology in college that gave me a good foundation. After Natasha was born I read a variety of books and magazine articles on children.

I did not approach this reading in any systematic way. During the first year I read more for fun than out of necessity. Now when I become particularly frustrated by Natasha's behavior

Benjamin, Diana, and Sosia Bert.

Grandpa Jim Telford, Sosia, and
Benjamin enjoy a day at the
San Francisco Zoo and
the playground.

Yogi and Sosia discover the joys and thrills of sleigh-riding.
(Photo courtesy John W. Telford)

Sosia and Benjamin in one of their long mornings of play.

Yogi and Benjamin share a hug.

Jaclyn, Mom, and Jenna Yanehiro.
(Photo credit: Michael Jang)

Daddy and one of his "angels."
Jenna at Halloween as an angel.

So proud as flower girls!
Katie Okamoto, 4 (left), and Jaclyn, 3 (right).
(Photo credit: Steve Okamoto)

Three sisters:
Jenna, 1; Laura, 14; and Jaclyn, 3.

Jenna and Jaclyn: Two babies, two bottles, one broken arm.

Peek-a-boo! Can you see who's under the hat? Alexandra, 4.

Jack and Katherine with Deren, 6, and Alexandra, 3,
truck down the Truckee River.

Dressed up for the holidays with
the Dusays: Jack, Katherine, Deren, 7,
and Alexandra, 4; San Francisco.

Katherine and Alexandra, 2,
admire the view at Squaw Valley.

Jack, Katherine, and Deren, 6, get ready to
attack the ski hill at Squaw Valley, California.

Natalie and Mom, Mary Oei.

Natalie with Uncle Hans in Holland, spring 1985.

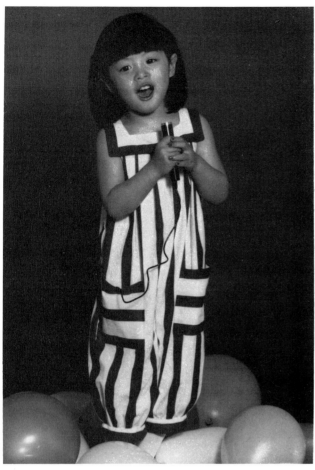

Natalie loves to sing.

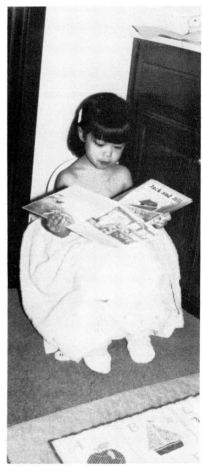

See how comfortable I am on my little toilet?

Natalie loves the water (1½ years old).

Natasha, 2½ years.

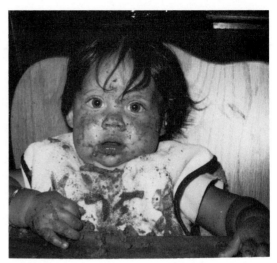

I can do it myself! Natasha, age 6 mos.

I still love my baby sister! Natasha, 3½ years, and Ariana, 1 year.

I love my baby sister. Natasha, 2½ years, and Ariana, 2 days.

The only way to travel at the Keels' house! Natasha (8 mos.) with Dad.

(and thus rather intolerant and ineffective), I look for a book to help me. In this search I will discover (or be reminded) that her behavior is normal. Almost like magic I become more tolerant, less frustrated, and more effective. The books usually suggest methods of dealing with the behavior, but for me the most important thing seems to be knowing that it is normal.

Here are some of the books that I found to be the most helpful:

Frank Caplan, ed., *The First Twelve Months of Life* (New York: Bantam Books, 1978)

Stella Chess et al., *Your Child Is a Person* (New York: Penguin Books, 1977)

Louise B. Ames and Francis L. Ilg, *Your Three Year Old* (New York: Dell Publishing Co., 1980)

Louise B. Ames and Francis L. Ilg, *Your Four Year Old* (New York: Dell Publishing Co., 1980)

Selma H. Fraiberg, *The Magic Years* (New York: Charles Scribner's Sons, 1984)

Part Three

SOCIAL SKILLS

Introduction 🦢

Our infants became social creatures so quickly. Part III covers the acquisition of social skills; how our children did it, how we helped or hindered the process, and how we reacted to the wondrous event.

Communication skills are important social skills; infants seem to fly from nonverbal to verbal communication. Chapter 13 tracks our children's progress in this area and covers such issues as correcting speech, using baby talk, naming body parts, use of bad language, talking to strangers, talking on the telephone, and that so important but sometimes so difficult skill of *listening* to our children. Both our philosophies and our experiences varied greatly here.

Education is the topic of Chapter 14. What does that mean for an infant, toddler, and preschool child? We talk about reading to our children, taking them on outings, playing learning games, and involving them in preschools and lessons. We approached these things with different degrees of energy and advance planning. How important did we think these things were and why did we do what we did?

One of the ways we help our children acquire social skills is through discipline. We discuss this in Chapter 15. Our philosophies varied immensely. We differed on such things as types of discipline, whether or not to use corporal punishment, consistency, and on whether or not we thought warnings were appropriate before action. We tried to tell you just what our philosophies are, and what seemed to work best for us. For some of us it was hard to discipline; for some it was hard to watch the other parent be the disciplinarian. Some of us talk about how it differed the second time around.

We found that our children began to exert their independence at remarkably early ages. How we reacted to this is the subject of Chapter 16: Did we encourage independence? How soon? How did we handle regressive behavior? What about interacting with strangers?

13

COMMUNICATION

- Nonverbal communication
- How soon our children started to talk
- How we encouraged them
- Baby talk
- Naming body parts
- Bad language
- Using the telephone
- Talking to strangers
- Listening to what our children have to say

Diana 🐎

I love to talk. From the day they arrived I talked to both my children as though they were little relatives visiting. Babies communicate in ways that are hard to explain. When they are tiny it is usually just with cries. But long before they start saying "bye-bye" they are asking and pointing. I always answered.

Yogi works a lot with babies, even little preemies, and he tells me that they are calm and receptive to his explanations of what he is doing. He feels that babies can understand much more than we think they can; they just can't respond clearly because they don't have the motor coordination. Babies learn a great deal from the voices and communication directed toward them.

So I talked. We talked about when I was going to bathe them and where we were going to go that day. I told them everything that was going to happen. Although others may have charted words and counted the exact vocabulary of their children, I related to the flow of everyday life—although it was more like the tide rolling in. At one point I realized that Sosia or Benjamin had added verbs or adjectives to their vocabularies and were speaking in sentences. Then they started using words with four syllables. They were communicating with us by means of *words* rather than gestures!

I made a point of providing the children with information about what word went in which place. Rather than forcing them to speak by making them call for milk by name, I would just hand them the milk and say, "Here is your milk." They learned to talk in a simple, day-to-day way. They are both wonderful talkers now. Now that they are speaking completely we may correct tense or pronunciation, but when they were learning to talk we just let it happen.

Along with verbal development came a most interesting phenomenon. Words that I just couldn't have uttered in the presence of my children! Was it the park, the playground, or possibly overheard in the car? I didn't know from whence they came, but did decide that certain words were allowed in the bathroom only. They are usually okay there. Some words are best left unsaid.

I always used distinct and clear language and complete sentences. My children have inherited my love of talking. They both talk clearly and they like to talk all the time. Sometimes we all go crazy talking all the time. I love it.

Jan 🦢

We both agree that Jaclyn's first intelligible word was "da-da" —which my husband immediately took to mean him. Of course I wish it had been "ma-ma," but the "m" sound is not easy for babies.

In all honesty, I don't really think that Jaclyn meant her daddy when she said "da-da," because she was later da-da-ing all over the place. But it's awfully fun to speculate.

I'm not one of those parents who note every moment (significant and otherwise) of my child's development. I wish I were. I can't remember exactly when Jaclyn started to talk. Jenna, now one year old, is still babbling unintelligently although we swear she calls her favorite stuffed bunny "ba-ba."

Jaclyn was a relatively slow talker. She understood everything we said, but just didn't respond in complete sentences, with the adjective, verb, and noun in their proper places. But when Jaclyn was about two and a half, I remember her putting together her first sentence while taking a bath. She said, "I (pause) love (longer pause) Mommy!" It could have been "Daddy," but I swear it was "Mommy."

I praised her to no end, and after that she simply took off. She seemed to marvel at herself for putting together words and making sentences. She can say everything from the state she lives in (California) to the type of milk she drinks (acidophilus).

Baby talk was something I promised myself I would never do, but I did. Sometimes I found I couldn't help responding in that high-falsetto-cutesy sort of way to my babies. My husband and I did not "goo-goo" and "ga-ga," but we do talk to the children differently than we would to a college student. A bruise or a cut is a "boo-boo"; the children "pee" and "poop" instead of urinating and moving their bowels. Her baby-sitter has taught her to say "I fluffed" when she lets out gas, and her anus is her

189

"bottom," but I've insisted that she refer to her vagina as just that. At this age (three years) she is very interested in her private parts. It seems to fascinate her to have such folds and crevices. I'm told this is natural, and that we as parents should deal with this openly and honestly so as not to let children think their private parts are "bad."

It's always interesting to hear how Jaclyn repeats what she heard. One night we were watching *The Wizard of Oz* on television. The next day she said she'd like to watch what sounded like "the river of yours." When I repeated in bewilderment, "You'd like 'the river of yours'?" she answered, "No!" and said it again. I tried substituting all sorts of words—liver, yards, liver pâté, deliver yours, your *what?*—and finally, after twenty frustrating minutes, we got it! *"Wizard of Oz!"* You can be saying the words *exactly* as they're saying them and be wrong. They seem to hear it correctly, but can't get it off their tongues the same way they hear it.

Katherine 🦢

As a psychotherapist, I know the value of people effectively communicating with one another and understanding each other. The most exceptional communication I remember with both children was right after each was born. I immediately wanted to look at each of them, eye to eye, and make our first loving connection. After all, we had waited patiently nine months to finally face each other. The wait was truly worth it! Jack and I requested that the doctors delay putting the required eye drops in the children's eyes because we wanted a special uninterrupted thirty minutes to develop eye contact and bond. I wish we could have had hours for this interchange because the eyedrops blurred their vision and interrupted this primal greeting ritual.

Communication to me means far more than words. I like to "read" faces and bodily expressions as well as listen to the words.

190

I couldn't wait for Deren and Alexandra to learn words and sentences because I was very curious about what they would want to talk about. I wondered what went on in their heads. It tickled me to imagine that someday both Deren and Alexandra would be verbally relating their own thoughts, stories, and comments. Deren talked wonderfully by the age of two, and Alexandra was using full sentences at twenty months.

As a baby and toddler, Deren would intently study people's faces. I would get comments like "He looks so serious." I know now that he was watching people talk so he could copy them. Deren and Alexandra frequently comment on all types of "common" things that I usually overlook because of more pressing "important" things (such as going to the cleaners or loading the dishwasher). They eagerly reflect on an ant, a rock, a flower. How refreshing it has been for me to have children and talk to them. They provide an instant way to get out of a mundane situation. Their enthusiasm and laughter is contagious.

Our son Deren learned various "four-letter words" here and there. He promptly made sure his little sister learned them with the exact pronunciation. He had a big experience on this subject during his first week of kindergarten (I remember how we had held our breaths and crossed our fingers, hoping he would get into this wonderful school that is literally across the street). The children were each assigned a specific letter of the alphabet and were instructed to make the sound of that letter and then form a word. For instance "c" would be "cat" and "d" would be "dog." Deren got the letter "f." He went "f-f-f" and then looked around happily and blurted out "f - - -!" He truly thought everyone would laugh uproariously and he would be on his way to a career as a comedian. Instead, there was a shocked silence from the kids and the teacher. The teacher asked him to apologize to the children and Deren was embarrassed and proceeded to act sillier. She took him to the principal's office to calm down. The teacher said, "I know you're not allowed to use those words at home." Deren promptly replied, "Oh yes, we talk like that all the time!" The teacher said he wouldn't be able to talk like that at school. The school called us at work and said it wasn't an emergency, but we needed a parent-teacher conference. The incident came and went. I kept hoping that in the future Deren would not blurt out four-letter words and not be asked to leave the school we tried so hard to get him into. He became happier every day and would occasionally disobey other rules like other children. He loves to test people and things.

Alexandra, our curly-haired, blond, blue-eyed angel has learned from her big brother a vocabulary that would make even a sailor blush. We simply ignore her and she doesn't get a big excited payoff from us about foul language. She has dropped much of it for the most part. However, when her grandfather came to visit she called him a "f - - - ing idiot" and we were mortified. Fortunately, Grandpa is a bit hard of hearing. On occasion she will say "I don't say 'goddammit,' 's - - -,' 'f - - -,' or 'stupid idiot' anymore." She thinks "stupid idiot" is in the same classification as the other words and we don't tell her it isn't because when she wants to come out with a naughty expression, chances are it'll be "stupid idiot" and that won't offend anyone nearly as much as the others.

My children are not self-conscious at speaking and copy whatever they hear. They also make up words as necessary. Alexandra says "drawler," which means to color and draw at the same time. Their communication reminds me of their innocence and creativity, and I continue to cherish their expressions as I slow my world down to see life through their eyes.

Mary 🦆

I really believe that there is a very special communication between mother and child, especially during infant and toddler periods, or until the child is able to fully express himself to everyone. I spent many intimate moments with my daughter, studying all her movements, expressions, and characteristics. These moments slowly developed into an understanding that no one, even Natalie's father, can replace.

To me communication is a very important part of Natalie's

growth and development. Besides just showing affection, I can tell her how much I love her and how much I care. I believe this will help her develop her self-esteem for later, to grow as a happy human being. Frank and I always try to talk normally to Natalie, but we can't help using a higher pitch in our voices.

Natalie's verbal development is rather slow. This is probably due to the several baby-sitters of different nationality we have had. She has been exposed to so many languages that it has been rather confusing for her.

One morning when Natalie was nine months old she was in bed with us and started rattling, "da, da, da, da." After a couple of weeks she was able to say, "dada . . . dada. . . ." It was not until she was one year old that she was able to say "daddy" and "mommy." Other words came after she was two.

Teaching our daughter to talk was the next step. At dinnertime we would tell her to say "please" for everything she liked to get to eat. She used to say "pease" in a sweet manner, bending her head and putting her hands on her chest. If you did not know better, you would think that she has excellent manners. "Pease" was Natalie's favorite for a long time because she realized that it was the way to get almost everything she needed.

Natalie started to communicate in sentences at around three years old—still not perfect, of course. She still mixes up "his" and "hers," "he" and "she." But it is fun listening to her and hearing all the words she creates herself. The word "kitchen" was so difficult for her that she used to say "chicken" for a long time.

Natalie loves to talk now, whether or not it is in perfect English. She approaches and talks to strangers, which I have to watch for. She has the ability to create a conversation with total strangers at the supermarket, on the street, or wherever. But with my friends she is always somewhat shy in the beginning. As soon as she feels she has to be extra friendly to someone, she backs off.

On one Sunday morning I took her to have breakfast with a friend in a coffeeshop. An older lady came in after we did and adored Natalie. They had a nice chat. When Natalie came back to our table she had earned $1.00. I told her to give the money back to the lady, but she said, "No, she gave it to me, it's mine!" I guessed she was right. Going out with Natalie is a wonderful way to meet and talk to people. She attracts them, and before we know it we start talking to strangers too.

Susan ❧

As an infant Natasha had no difficulty communicating her needs to me. Before experiencing it, this communication seemed a mystery. But what's so complicated about responding to an infant's cry? For me it was automatic. The first thing I did was to pick her up and hold her, and with Natasha, more often than not, that was exactly what she wanted. She was, and is, very social, likes lots of attention, and wants to be where the action is. If she still cried, I would nurse her. She rarely wanted anything else. I did change her diapers, but that was because *I* didn't like her to be wet or messy—she never seemed to mind. Ariana would cry when she was tired or overstimulated, but Natasha seldom did. If Natasha was tired, she simply fell asleep. Overstimulation was *never* a problem for her!

That's all there was to it for the first three months or so. It was very time-consuming, but not very difficult.

Beginning around three months, Natasha found lots of other ways of communicating. Smiling and laughing communicated a lot about what she enjoyed. If she wanted something she would grab for it, or point to it as if to say "Give that to me." If she wanted to be held, she would hold out her arms. As she was learning to walk she would crawl over, pull herself up, and hold out her hand for us to take and walk with her. There were lots of other ways that she got her point across, and again I was amazed at how easily I understood what she wanted or needed. Still, crying was her most effective method of making her needs known.

The progression from nonverbal to verbal communication is as fascinating to watch as the progression from immobility to mobility. From the first moment Natasha and Ariana made wonderful cooing noises. These progressed to various animal sounds (my favorite was the porpoise) and then to syllables. Natasha said "mama" several times very early, then went on to "dada" and didn't come back to "mama" for some time. At ten months she would say "mama" on demand, but I don't think that she understood the meaning until she had been talking for a while.

Sometimes during this progression from sounds to words, Natasha would talk gibberish. I'll never forget one afternoon at my mother's house when Natasha stood facing the wall and talked gibberish in full paragraphs, complete with gestures and inflection, as though the wall could understand her strange language. I wonder whether she knew what she was saying. It truly seemed as if she did!

I always talked to Natasha as though she could understand every word I said, and I don't use baby talk. After the first few months, when I'm sure Natasha didn't understand a word I said, I was never sure just how much she understood, and I was always amazed that she understood more than I expected.

I kept notes on when Natasha said her first words, sentences, and paragraphs, but I never made any notes about her ability to understand and follow simple commands. I suppose it is less obvious exactly when these events occur and thus they are harder to chronicle. One night when Natasha was about ten or eleven months old, Dick was at home with her while I was out. When it was time to put her to bed, Dick said to her—not really expecting her to comply—"Go get your pajamas." Natasha left the room, went into her bedroom, got her pajamas from her drawer, and returned to where Dick was watching television. She loved complying with our requests, especially when we asked her to do things such as clear the table. (Unfortunately that compliance was short-lived.)

At first Natasha obviously understood a lot just from the inflection of our voices. She would nod her head to whatever question you would ask. She understood the concept of a question even if she didn't understand the actual question. We had fun asking her bizarre questions like "Are you a monkey?" to which she would enthusiastically nod her head yes. I don't know who enjoyed the game more.

Natasha uttered her first words at twelve months. Remarkably enough, "no" was not Natasha's first word. I was sure that it would be because we said it to her so often. I was so certain I could never forget her first word, I didn't write it down. Now all I remember is what it wasn't.

By thirteen months Natasha was using words such as "cheese," "banana," and "down," and by fourteen months she had over a fifteen-word vocabulary. One of her favorite words was "mine."

One of the things that amazed me the most about her beginning language skills was the fact that she pronounced most words correctly from the first time she used them. If she didn't get it right the very first time, I would correct her once or twice and that would be it. We wondered if this had anything to do with the fact that we didn't use baby talk with her. Apparently not. Ariana has difficulty saying certain sounds and mispronounces many words continually. Although Ariana's language skills have developed more slowly than Natasha's, I am no less in love with listening to her talk.

Natasha made an enormous leap in her vocabulary just before fifteen months as she began to repeat just about any word we would give her. Soon she had words for most objects in her world. She learned the words for all the objects in her little picture books, which she loved to "read."

By eighteen months Natasha started putting words together in simple sentences and then gradually longer and more complex sentences. She seemed to have an insatiable desire to learn words, and by the time she was two years old she was talking in paragraphs. To this day she wakes up in the morning talking and goes to bed at night talking and rarely stops talking all day long. Her energy is endless, but for me it's exhausting!

Again Ariana is different. She began to say "up" around twelve months but didn't learn any other words until around sixteen months. Of course Natasha never stopped talking long enough for Ariana to even try to talk!

The questions started at around twenty-one months. First, Natasha asked what certain objects were called. She would point to an object and say "What's this?" Rapidly the questions progressed to the more difficult "Why?" questions, which I suppose never stop. I know that it's wonderful that she is so curious, but I do get tired of trying to come up with answers to all her questions! I try to answer and try not to say "just because," which I often have the urge to do! I don't want to stifle her curiosity, though it sometimes seems relentless.

The progression in her language skills did not go evenly but seemed to make quantum leaps overnight. Then there would be weeks with no apparent change. Dick and I would ask each other "Did you notice the change?" I suppose there was a bit of a contest there, to see who noticed a particular change first, but it was always a good-natured contest. Natasha's language skills are so advanced for her age that I have to remind myself at times that she is still a little girl and I shouldn't expect too much of her in other ways.

It's hard not to want to show off your child, and I found myself wanting to show off Natasha the most when she started to talk. During one visit to the pediatrician, Dr. Brown advised that it was not a good idea to push a child too much to show off because even very precocious children sometimes stop progressing if they are constantly under pressure. I try not to push, but I think it is natural to want to show off your child's newly acquired skills.

Natasha is a very outgoing child and likes to perform for others, but even she talks less when other people are around than she does when we are at home alone.

Natasha loved telephones. Soon after she began talking she would carry on conversations into her play telephone. With the real thing she was less predictable. Sometimes she would say a few words for Grandma, other times she would just smile at the telephone as though the person on the other end could see her. At three she began answering the telephone. She usually forgets to say "Hello" and just says "Who is it, please?" then gives me the telephone—often with no information about who is on the other end. She now carries on fairly lengthy conversations with grandparents and friends on the telephone, but she still seems to think that she can be seen because she will gesture and nod or shake her head.

14

EDUCATION

- Whether or not we engaged in formal early teaching at home
- Encouraging receptiveness and curiosity
- What children learn at different ages
- Projects and expeditions that were successful for us
- Reading
- Selecting a preschool

Diana ~

At our house we try to look at our little ones as complete people. We strive to create children who can handle life's challenges. Educating them means talking to them about how to speak for themselves.

We did no formal education at home. We did absolutely no reading preparation or flash cards. We were thanked by Sosia's kindergarten teacher for not trying to educate her at home. It meant that she did not have to undo anything that we had done wrong. Sosia went into the kindergarten room like a fresh, clean slate. She had been exposed to swings and scissors and physical activities so that her body was developed enough to meet her mind.

In planning activities I researched what things were appropriate to learn when, and I had some guidelines from the Child Observation teachers about how to introduce new pursuits to my children. Much of my information came from seeing how my friends interacted with their children. My children and I learned and pursued interests together. When they became involved and interested in something, I did everything I could to learn more and to expose them further. Ask me anything about trucks or bugs!

I was delighted that a lot of regular daily activities were also considered basics of learning. Pushing young children to learn to read is not as important as making sure they can do physical things like pedal tricycles, climb, and jump. These are the basis of all the learning that follows.

This isn't to say reading is unimportant. We read books all the time. I got hold of books from everywhere and about everything. I read to both my children religiously, beginning when they were about six months old. I would read every night. It was harder to read for Benjamin because Sosia preferred more advanced stories, and if it was a picture book, she liked to tell us what the picture was before anyone else could. But we managed to reach a happy medium by combining reading time with one story for Sosia and one story for Benjamin. They both benefited greatly by having the different levels exposed to them. We always talked about the stories and would guess what was going to happen next. We often read stories fifty or sixty times. *Curious George* was a memorization project for Benjamin when he suddenly decided he was going to learn to "read."

We planned many outings. We went to the bug zoo and to dinosaur exhibits. We went swimming and ice-skating. I allowed the children to absorb things at their own pace and at their own speed, and I allowed them time to think about the things we saw. We also talked a lot about the things we did so that they would learn the vocabulary to discuss it. I exposed my children to different elements and allowed them to manipulate things on their own. I tried to stretch their imaginations and to look everywhere for new media and possibilities. We used cotton balls, toilet-paper rolls, Kleenex boxes, and Styrofoam trays to create and mold and paint numerous different projects.

We played a lot of learning games. When we were waiting somewhere we played a game of feeling things through a scarf or blanket. I would put my keys or the baby's bottle under the blanket and we would feel it and guess what it was. We would listen for different sounds and guess what they were—doors closing, a fire truck, a dog barking. And we talked about all the things that we were doing. When we were waiting to see the doctor we would talk about what we were going to do. I found that my children understood me completely long before they were able to respond. I felt it was important to speak to them in good English and to help them with vocabulary when we played our talking games. If I couldn't understand what they were telling me, I would ask them to take me to what they wanted or show it to me. That was one way to increase their knowledge and their vocabulary in a natural way without putting undue pressure on them to perform or respond.

I made my entire home an environment where my children could learn. I tried to orient as much of my home as possible to my children's skills. We had stools that allowed them to turn on the water by themselves and therefore wash their own hands. I let them wash dishes with me and let them serve themselves at the table whenever it was possible. I let them touch everything they could, even if it made a mess or seemed strange. I let them play with many things in the kitchen. By exposing your child to the everyday things in your home, even the tastes or sounds of things, you are allowing them to learn and experience without formal or goal-oriented education. It is a natural process to let a child explore his environment and pique his curiosity. When he drops something from the high chair, it becomes a natural learning game. Where did it go? Let him wonder, and then point to it before you retrieve it.

As a parent I try to grasp opportunities to teach all different things all during the day. By keeping a constant flow of conversation my children have learned the vocabulary for things that amaze me. They are ready for information and they are excited about being exposed to many different things. We do not have to bring out workbooks or reading primers. We can teach them things all day every day and still have a wonderful time with them.

When Sosia turned two I found a wonderful school with twelve children and two or three adults that met twice a week for two and a half hours a session. Although two is tiny, Sosia was ready and happy to go off into her own world to play and explore with her peers. It also coincided with Benjamin's birth and gave her a needed sense of maturity while providing me free time for Benjamin. Later she attended a three-year nursery school and that has been followed by kindergarten. The process of entering schools varies from location to location. But I was surprised that in our area we were expected to wait-list our children within a few weeks of their birth. I did, even though school seemed eons away.

Benjamin has followed his sister's lead and is currently applying to his own kindergarten.

Jan ﻉ

I have always been a believer in learning because one *wants* to, rather than because one *has* to. There are new methods these days in teaching *infants* to read, count, even learn a second language. I have done reports on this for our television program, yet I feel reluctant to have my own children follow these methods. Maybe I'm basically lazy, because they do require a lot of commitment from the parents. But I believe a child should be allowed to romp and play and generally be a kid. There's time enough for school.

Of course we bought books and lots of educational toys. Many were gifts (I was thankful someone else had done the shopping!)

Jaclyn has absolutely no interest in some toys or books and simply loves others. I thought this was odd until I learned about the Montessori school of thought, which holds that a child knows instinctively what to play with, given a number of choices. Jaclyn starts Montessori preschool this fall at three. (She could have started at two and a half years, had she been potty trained.)

Selecting this particular Montessori school was easy. I asked (once again) my pediatrician (his kids went to this school) and some friends and neighbors. The school is about four blocks from our home, a convenient factor.

A good idea is to visit the school with your child. You may have one opinion of the school, but it is your child who will attend. You know your child best—watch for cues that he or she may give, such as smiles and reactions to activities and teachers. Call ahead for an appointment and let them know you'd like to bring your child. How receptive they are will tell you a lot about the school.

Jaclyn and I visited her school twice. Even though Jaclyn was a visitor, I felt the teacher tried hard to make her feel a part of the class. At our first visit she was acting very shy (normal, they say; surprising, we say), so the teacher asked one of the students to take Jaclyn's hand and bring her into the circle to sit.

Jaclyn was also encouraged by a teacher to try one of the "jobs," a Montessori word for an individual activity such as working on a puzzle, stringing beads together, pouring water into a cup. All the "jobs" are designed to enhance hand-eye coordination, organizational skills, and so on. For Jaclyn *and* me, this school is perfect.

Reading books is a favorite activity of Jaclyn's, and we hope will be for Jenna too. This may be because we started reading to her at an early age and did it consistently. Maybe it's simply because she likes the activity. Whatever, it's such a nice activity to like, especially at bedtime.

I've learned to allow my children to pick their own books. They often will select the same book several nights in a row. Although it may be boring to read after several (two, to be exact) nights, repetition is a way to learn. The only salvation in reading the same book night after night is, you can close your eyes and read the pages. This helps, especially after a long, tiring day.

Recently our care-giver has been taking the children to the

library. They are learning to select books, take care of them at home, and return them before the due date. It's a great and free activity—teaches responsibility, something one is never too young to learn. I must credit Gwenda Williams, our care-giver, for this activity. The children love it!

Katherine 🦢

Just being a member of a household is an educational experience for both parents and children. When Deren and Alexandra were little I brought home educational toys, rattles, books, and mobiles. They enjoyed these things, at least temporarily. However, the biggest educational opportunities they enjoyed were being with us, going to the park, taking a stroll and examining everything they would find on the sidewalk.

When Deren was a preschooler of about two I was working more hours and signed him up in a child-care program. I drove him every day from home to across town. There were five children between two and four who became Deren's everyday playmates, and two full-time adults who supervised and played with the children. Deren took several months to adjust because he wanted to be with me at every moment. He'd cry when I'd walk him in. Usually, out of guilt and curiosity after I had pulled the car away, I would park and peek through the day care's curtains. Deren would be laughing and having a great time. I felt enormous relief and still I would ask myself the same questions over and over. Is this what I should be doing—working? Or should I be a full-time, stay-at-home mom? When he'd cry I figured I must be doing the wrong thing. I'd then rationalize and say, "He cries at home with me, too, and I'm not all that stimulating with kids." My thoughts would go around and around. This center was the best environment I could find for him, and the two directors provided nurturing and educational experiences. Deren attended this home day-care facility for almost a year, and then he was old enough to go to a regular nursery school in our neighborhood. I was thrilled when he entered and he seemed to be quite sure of himself compared to many of the three-year-olds who were leaving home for the first time.

Sometimes I feel twinges of guilt about having sent Deren off to a day-care center instead of keeping him home. However, I've learned that at nearly any age many children will go through some separation anxiety. Since I had to return to work, I believed he would be far more stimulated being with teachers and other children than having a full-time baby-sitter.

The decisions we parents must make at every age and each stage are unending. Alexandra stayed at home with our live-in baby-sitter until she was about two and a half. Then she started the same nursery school our son attended previously and she thrived.

At this writing Deren is in the first grade and goes to a grammar school right across the street. No more carpools for him! We wave at each other when he plays on the roof playground each day. He enjoys learning and is thrilled that he can read simple sentences and books. One day he came home all excited because he thought he got a love note from his teacher when she wrote, "Dear Deren, please rewrite this." He said, "She called me 'dear,' and said I could take as much extra work as I wanted from the homework box at school."

Alexandra is enchanted with her nursery school. She learns how to paint, do puzzles, glue and cut. She also learns about gardening and vegetables. They pick fresh ones to eat for snacks each day. She dresses up in costumes and builds enormous structures with her blocks.

If at any point I noticed that the learning institutions that they attend change or are no longer positive environments for the children, I will evaluate my options carefully and make the necessary changes. To me education needs to be a balance between interesting and stimulating subjects and must have a human element in that each child has a unique blend of personality traits.

Before I enrolled the children in day care and preschools, I talked to many parents to get the specific information I wanted.

Some of my questions were: "Do the teachers touch and relate to the children? How do they handle discipline? What does the school look like? What is the preschool philosophy?" After I got recommendations I would make appointments to visit the schools and observe the teachers and the students. I would evaluate the physical structure and the manipulatives. My husband and I selected the Jewish Nursery School because of its warm, nurturing environment. An added advantage was that it was very close to where we live!

As for grammar schools, Jack and I were in agreement that we wanted a school that stressed academics and learning and provided a structured day for the child with a nice balance between activities that develop the child's intellect, physical coordination and fitness, and personality.

I believe it's important to visit many schools and talk to other parents, teachers, and the students. Since Deren has a strong drive to acquire knowledge and move at a fast pace, it was important that he go to a school with an academic environment that continually challenged his eager mind.

Alexandra will probably attend an elementary school that provides some choices within a structured framework. She loves music, art, physical movement, and reading stories and has a fine imagination. I want these qualities preserved and will select a school for her on that basis.

Mary ❧

Parents have always wanted to teach their babies to eat, reach, crawl, turn, sit, and eventually walk and talk. These are the first steps to becoming an independent little human being. For generations parents have done the same thing over and over again, but there are much fancier toys available, with bright colors, different shapes, and sounds. We always try to have them all for our babies. It's very exciting to think how many educational toys and books and programs on television are available, but it is also very easy for the parents to overdo spending on their children these days.

Then, too, we live in a competitive world, and our generation certainly is aware of all the subjects our babies are supposed to learn. It seems overwhelming at times.

Our type of education for Natalie's first year was mostly centered on giving her as much love as possible. We wanted to make her feel how much she is wanted. We also did all the other regular activities parents do to help their infant reach the first step of human independence. Now that she is older, our responsibilities are more philosophical—teaching her good manners, to communicate, etc. Now she is aware of everything we do, why we do it, and how we do it.

We enrolled Natalie in a few classes for toddlers (see Chapter 12). Children go to school younger and younger. I remember I used to cry when my parents took me to school when I was four years old. Natalie started preschool when she was two years and three months old and she loved it. She did not even cry when I left her for the first time alone.

Natalie attends a Montessori school about eight miles away. We are lucky not to live in San Francisco, since there it's very difficult to find a good preschool unless you book your baby as soon as he or she is born. What I love about this school is that the class environment is very peaceful and calm, yet a little bit structured. I had tears in my eyes when I went to watch these little toddlers in the class, busy doing their little projects. They are so adorable. In the school Natalie learns how to share, respecting other children and learning how to play with them. She loves school so much.

We started Natalie going to school three half-days a week. One year later we decided to enroll her for five half-days a week, and she is in day care until 5 P.M. three days a week. I felt rather sorry for her being left at school for so long when she was only three years old. But I was wrong.

Natalie happened to love school. She is very independent now and very spontaneous. She has so much freedom to do all kinds of creative artwork all day. Activities are already available for her little mind to explore. She is no longer the shy little girl she used to be. She is very comfortable with herself when she interacts with other people. She just does not like to be alone.

For us, as parents who work sometimes six days a week and for long hours, enrolling Natalie in a preschool has been very beneficial. We do not have time for play groups or for walking in the parks or playgrounds. The school replaces all that and we know she is in good hands.

At home our focus is family. We do not force Natalie to learn academically. I feel she is too young for that. Unless she insists on learning, we just enjoy being together, singing, talking, learning about manners or whatever.

Susan ❧

Infants learn an incredible amount. I'm not sure that we have much to do with what they learn or when they learn it, but we are surrounded by newspaper articles and advertisements telling us how important it is to have the right environment for our infants (and toddlers and preschoolers and . . .). I figured the right environment certainly couldn't hurt, and tried to introduce the children to stimulating activities.

Dick and I feel our role is to provide the children with lots of love and nurturing. We smother them with affection and let them know that they're terrific. We don't do this to make them good students but because we love them and get personal pleasure from showing our affection. I do believe that feeling loved is the basis for feeling secure and happy, and a happy, secure child is more receptive to learning. In addition to setting the mood, we expose Natasha and Ariana to the world around them and encourage them when they show an interest in anything. Dick and I make a great cheering section.

As you read in Chapter 12, Natasha and I went to swimming lessons, Kindergym, and Side-by-Side when she was little. I didn't take Natasha to these activities because they were educational, but she did learn a lot—including how to interact with other children and to wait her turn. It was a fun way to expose her to a lot of things that I couldn't afford to have in our home and to get her around other children. And it was a great escape for me, too. Natasha could turn her focus away from me, but I could be there and observe. And I found that the opportunity to talk to other moms and the instructors, who were trained in child development, was really helpful in coping with the various stages of Natasha's development.

When Natasha was a toddler, I talked to her all the time, trying to answer her endless questions and expose her to as much as possible. I tried to encourage her in her interests, and I tried not to get bored when she wanted to do the same thing over and over. The fun part was getting to observe the incredible process of a baby turning into a little girl. It happens right before your very eyes. It really is magic.

During this period Natasha spent a lot of time manipulating things. She got a lot of practice in the kitchen. I let her help with food preparation as much as I could. I tried to let her do things (like pour and mix) even when I knew a mess was inevitable. The messes, however, were amazingly few. She was constantly surprising me with how well she could do things. There *were* messes, and lots of times when I would have preferred not to have her "help," but most of the time I took a deep breath and let her do it.

Books became important now too. Before she learned how to handle books carefully I tried to find indestructible ones. She didn't like cloth and plastic books but was satisfied with cardboard books so we used those. Soon after her first birthday Natasha started learning the names of objects and our "reading" consisted of looking at pictures and naming the objects. Gradually she became more interested in having me read the words in her books. Her favorite books were the ones with few words. She would have me read the same book time after time, as many times as I would, until she had the book memorized. Then she would "read" it to me. Bedtime stories have now become a ritual. Unfortunately, it is often the only time I read to her. Gradually the length of the story that she will listen to has increased, and our library has grown too.

When she was about two years old I bought *Dr. Seuss's ABC*. It immediately became her favorite book and within a remarkably short period of time she knew the alphabet and began to point out letters to me on signs, in books, and everywhere around us. It seemed to me that the next step would be to learn to recognize words. I pointed to words printed in large print in her books as I read, but it was apparent that she wasn't particularly interested, so I haven't pushed it. She'll let me know when she's ready.

Ariana's interest in books has developed differently. By the time she arrived bedtime stories were already a ritual and she just naturally became a part of it. At first we would read two books: a picture book for Ariana, which we "read" first, then a storybook for Natasha. As Ariana's attention span has increased she has stayed interested in more and more of Natasha's stories.

I have tried very hard not to push Natasha and Ariana and simply to encourage them to do the things they are interested in. It seems to me that childhood is a time to have fun and learn through good times and play. I want my children to see that learning is fun. One sure way to turn them off to the learning experience is to push them too hard too early. But sometimes the line between encouraging and pushing is difficult to find.

At two and a half, Natasha was more than ready for preschool. I shopped around for a school that had a philosophy close to my own—that is, no emphasis on academics, but a warm, friendly, fun environment where children play together and where there are lots of materials available for learning when the child is ready. I also wanted the school to be close to my home. I found a wonderful school five minutes from our house. One thing that turned out to be important, though I didn't consider it when I was looking, is the after-school child-care program. Preschool is over at 11:30 A.M., and you have the option of picking up your child after school or at 1:30, 3:30, or 5:30. I don't have to commit to child care in advance, but can let the school know by 9:00 A.M. the same morning. This allows lots of flexibility, which is important in my ever-changing schedule.

I knew that Natasha would adjust well to school, but I did expect her to at least look back once on the first day. I should have known better. I planned my day so that I could stay around for a while to give her time to adjust. As I walked in the door with her she made a beeline for one of the puzzles on the table and never looked back. I stayed for a few minutes and decided that I might as well leave. I was concerned about causing a problem by telling her that I was leaving, but I didn't want to just disappear, so I chose my words very carefully: "Natasha, I'm going to do a few errands and I'll pick you up after I'm through." She replied, without looking up, "I know, Mommy." That was the end of it. It's wonderful to have such an independent child— but she could at least have said that she would miss me! (That incident wasn't nearly as ego-shattering as the occasion later in the year when she threw a tantrum because I was taking her home from school. Or the time in the summer when she woke up feeling sad one morning because she missed her school and her teachers!)

Natasha started piano lessons and gymnastics soon after she entered preschool. I know this sounds like I'm violating my rule about not pushing, but I don't think that I am. Natasha has always been enthusiastic. With her the problem is not having enough activities.

One day Natasha didn't want to go to her piano lesson. I talked to her teacher about it and told her that I didn't want to push her into something she didn't want to do at such an early age. The teacher made a suggestion that I agreed to. I told Natasha that she didn't have to stay for her lesson, but that we would go and tell her teacher that she didn't want to stay. By the time we got there she had forgotten she didn't want to go and proceeded to march up to the door with her usual enthusiasm and have a great time.

Natasha's activities are fun for her, and they also provide some time during the week when someone else has to deal with her energy level. I can just sit back and enjoy watching my little ball of fire have fun.

15

DISCIPLINE

- How soon we started to discipline our babies
- Saying no
- Time-outs
- Physical punishment
- Recognizing what is age-appropriate behavior
- Threats versus direct action
- How we dealt with tantrums and scenes
- When parents disagree about discipline
- Disciplining more than one child

Diana ❧

Discipline is a way of teaching your child how to live in the world among other people. Discipline also helps the child develop internal limits. It is a day-to-day process. At first I was very interested in being a perfect disciplinarian—to always say no when the baby crawled in a particular direction or yes when the baby smiled in a certain way. Each day that became more complicated. What works on the bus is totally impractical in the kitchen. What works in my living room is perfectly unacceptable at Grandma's house. A Cheerio that found its way under the kitchen table may not pose imminent harm, while something found at the park may provide a full set of dangers.

I started feeling that my grip on my role as a disciplinarian was falling into a vague realm that I really didn't like. I asked the instructor at my Child Observation class what form of discipline was correct and how I could best bring about the child of my dreams. She said that the word "discipline" is difficult. For many people it conjures images of domination over another person. That is not what I want to achieve. I want children who are capable of making judgments on their own. She told me the best way to create secure, well-disciplined children is to say and do things that are honest—to focus not on consistency in discipline but on consistency in being honest. Each event warrants a different behavior. A different day may bring a different response. You may not care if the baby hides his shoes on a day when you have nowhere pressing to go, but on a day when you are meeting a friend you may feel quite differently. Breakfast is altogether different on a day when everyone has overslept. The important thing is to be honest with the emotions of that particular day. The honest feelings are what always come through.

Discipline is an area where many people will offer their opinions. Some of my friends felt that I should not have fed Sosia whenever she cried. After all, wasn't I setting a dangerous precedent, letting her call the shots all the time? Nonsense! There was only one way that Sosia could convey that she was hungry. If it was spoiling her to answer her when she cried and to feed her when she was hungry, then I am guilty of spoiling her. She and my let-down reflex seemed to work together.

People told me that I should let my children "cry it out." They told me not to pick them up whenever they cried. I say, if you are able to pick them up, then pick them up. They are asking for a basic need. They are asking to be close to you. How can you deny that basic urge and expect them to trust you later on? I often felt that somewhere along the line life had become twisted. Our biological urges were to be denied on account of the thought processes of someone in history.

Believe me, there were times when Yogi and I debated in earnest the pros and cons of letting children cry, of letting them sleep with us, or letting our children "get away with" a certain thing. The needs of the children invariably won out, and I do not regret it now. For the first two years, just teaching the children that I can be depended on for their needs and their care should be enough.

People have different values that will come into play. Your children may not meet their standards. A stranger may not feel that your child is behaving in a socially appropriate way. But the basic values of the golden rule—do unto others—are where I found myself sitting with regard to discipline. Could my children throw sand in the park? Not on your life. And the same goes for a child that might throw sand at my children.

If I were a little baby in a big crib in a room down the hall from the people I loved and wanted to see, would I want them to come down the hall if I cried? Maybe even give me a little hug? You bet I would. This is what Yogi and I did, and I would again, tired or not.

In assembling my ideas about discipline I depended on the best experts I knew—my own mother and father, who were super, and my two wonderful parents-in-law Joel and Kita Bert, who are so wonderfully mellow that they cut all the disciplinary problems down to size by saying things like "Well, maybe they need to see what you do during the night before they will understand what you want them to do."

I also follow the principle of loving my children because of who they are, no matter what they did, and hating *what they did*. I let them know if what they did was wrong, but they are always loved and appreciated. I always let them know I love them even if I didn't like what they were doing or how they were acting. I give Sosia and Benjamin "time-outs" where they sit in their rooms or on a chair until they have an opportunity to think about what they did and to change their behavior. Then I give them a big hug and tell them I'm happy that they're going to behave better and that I love them. My "time-outs" are immediate. I do not threaten; I stop the behavior as it is occurring and remove them from it. I never say that they will be punished later.

I believe it is important to be specific when I praise or punish my children. ("I love you and it makes me so happy when you get dressed without having to be reminded." "I love you and it makes me very angry when I must always tell you to dress yourself several times.")

I don't believe in hitting or spanking. There is never a need for that. Problems with behavior can always be dealt with by talking to and moving the child to a time-out place. To me the most important part is to always bring the punishment to a close by letting them know that you love them and you like other things that they do.

After Benjamin was born Sosia went through a terrible two phase—and terrible it was. She acted out all kinds of weird schemes. And then suddenly it ended.

Benjamin gave me more of a run for my money during his twos because he really did throw temper tantrums, anywhere, anytime. I knew what to expect, having seen tantrums in other children, so before they occurred I had decided what to do. I decided to give him pretty much full rein, to calmly tell him that I felt he had every right to be angry and that he could have a temper tantrum if he wanted to, but that I didn't want to be a part of it, and I would just wait for him somewhere else.

The first time you try this in a public place, you may feel really embarrassed. Older ladies will of course cluck their tongues at you and may even make comments like "Such a terrible child, you are obviously spoiling him." Now, I assure you that those comments made me much more angry than my child's tantrum, but I would pay no attention. I'd let the child work it out and ignore him (or her). He would soon tire of his rage because it was of no effect whatsoever. If he really worked into a steamy number where he was flailing around and kicking, I would grab him in a full body hug (so I wouldn't get scratched or kicked) and remove him to the car. Then I would let him work it out in the privacy of the car, with me standing outside of course. The most important thing I would do is sit with the little one afterward and share my honest response. Sometimes the children would be so upset that they really just needed to be hugged and reassured that they were still loved. Other times I would tell them how embarrassed I was because all the people were looking at us.

The big tantrums fortunately almost always occurred at home.

Here I would remove the screaming child to his or her room and close the door, telling him to come out when he was finished. The giant tantrums almost always required a wonderful close time for the child and myself afterward. Tantrums are tough experiences, and as devastated and upset as I would sometimes get, they must have been much more frightening to the child.

Rule No. 1: I always tried to remember who was having the temper tantrum. Although I was usually furious, I tried to remain as level-headed as possible.

Rule No. 2: I tried to disregard what was happening around us and focus on what was happening within the relationship of our family. It really doesn't matter what anyone else thinks about any of it.

Rule No. 3: If I felt confused about any of this, I would consult with a friend about what caused the tantrums and how she would have handled them. Another mother's perspectives can be wonderfully enlightening. One mother I know would pick up the child and wrap her arms around him and turn in circles. Another would take her child to a mirrored area and let him see himself. But my favorite was the father who had tantrums with his son, getting right down on the floor and flailing himself around the room. His son's reaction was just about the same embarrassment and intrigue that we feel, and they both ended up laughing at themselves.

It is true that when we are the most tired or upset ourselves the children seem to zero in on our instability. Then it is best to have a little time out for everyone. I find that it helps to anticipate the certain times in the day that are strictly one foot in front of the other. When I found that the "arsenic hour" was occurring at precisely 4:00 every day and lasting almost to 6:00 P.M., I scheduled a wonderful walk for that period. Dinner would be a crock-pot concoction or a long-cooking something or an already prepared quick cook-up. Believe me, it was a wonderful solution— and the amazing thing was that there were many, many families that also chose that exact time to walk. If your husband has a dinner engagement that evening, or is out of town on business, that's the perfect time to explore the fast-food restaurants, or schedule a long walk through the airport corridors, or even walk to the nearest shopping mall.

Jan 🦢

The corners of the rooms in our house have sheltered Jaclyn more than once. "Stand in the corner!" has slipped across my tongue many times.

When Jaclyn was born my husband and I agreed that we wouldn't use any physical punishment such as spanking. I had been secretly wishing that my child would be such an angel that we would never have to discipline. Ha!

We believe that the child should first be warned—and sometimes warned again—before being sent to her room or to the corner. We also agreed that if one parent disciplines, the other will not interfere. We came to this agreement only after a heated argument. It's so hard for me to see my husband discipline Jaclyn. My heart goes out to my baby.

Between John and myself, I am the more lenient. I spend more time with the kids and know their "games." John tends to discipline Jaclyn when he's tired after a long day of work and she's doing something that annoys him. We both seem to have less patience during the evenings, yet this is the time we spend with our kids. (Doesn't seem fair, sometimes.) Often I know Jaclyn is doing something only to get our attention. She doesn't realize that what she is doing only serves to irritate and annoy us. But who can really blame a child for wanting attention from two working parents?

I had heard of the terrible twos. Then I went through the terrible twos with Jaclyn, and now I'm on the brink of it again with Jenna. In all honesty, it really wasn't bad. We had our share of tantrums, but nothing in public that is particularly memorable, thank goodness. However, my husband did say more than once that he was awfully glad children start out so small and innocent, because if you got them ready-made at age two, you would probably send them back!

216

Each child responds to discipline so differently. Jaclyn will almost push you to the edge. She can really test. Jenna responds so quickly. A simple "No, Jenna . . . this will hurt you" often is enough to stop her.

It's so tough to discipline, yet I know it's necessary. We can't be raising delinquents. Children have to know what is acceptable behavior and what is not. Why can't babies be born with the rules already memorized?

In our home hitting is unacceptable behavior. I always give a warning—most times two—and then it's "Stand in the corner!" After what seems like endless minutes in the corner, Jaclyn *must* apologize to the person she hit, otherwise it's back to the corner.

There are times I think we will never pass this hitting stage. My pediatrician explains that when a child at this age hits, it is usually out of frustration. When a child is able to verbalize and articulate emotions, desires, frustration, the hitting will subside. Great explanation, right? Right! Try to remember that the next time your child hits. I can't recall the last time I did!

On the flip side of discipline, I try to teach my children manners. Although they are only three and one, "please" and "thank you" are magic words in our home. You do begin to think of yourself as a broken record though, always saying to your child "How do you ask?" ("Please") and "What do you say?" ("thank you.") I'm trying to be consistent, and I'm hoping the record will never wear out.

Katherine ❧

In our family the term "discipline" means setting realistic limits, being fair, and following through on the family rules. Of course this is easier said than done when you have two miniature geniuses disguised as children trying to outreason you—and if that fails, resorting to unfair temper tantrums, threats, and slammed doors.

217

With our firstborn, Deren, I observed that he was becoming contrary at about eighteen months. "This is six months too early for the terrible twos," I told Jack. Deren's terrible phase lasted about three months, off and on, and would return every six months for a brief rerun.

At home I was really at a loss over how to respond to Deren's unreasonable demands and belligerent behavior. I would stand there dumbfounded when he'd throw his toys, hit me, and purposefully turn over his lunch dish. I wasn't expecting this because I had been rational, loving, and nice to him. Why would he want to be mean to me and hurt me? He'd throw his bottle at me, then beg me to get it. Nicely, I would—again and again. I became exhausted and dismayed with him. I'd tell myself, "I can't hit him, or reason with him, or put him in his room, or abandon him!" I felt stuck.

Since I was stumped, I appealed to Jack, who said he wasn't having any problems with Deren. I felt worse until I realized that Jack really *didn't* seem to be having the same kinds of problems with Deren. Jack would have a calmer way with him and was not around as much as me. Gradually Jack and I would hash over the types of problems and potential solutions from a parenting perspective. In these early days I naively thought if I handled Deren's needs, gave him lots of love and was fair, then everything would work out. Wrong! Deren had a pattern and a demand system all his own, and I wasn't understanding it or handling it effectively!

I had heard somewhere that children get thousands of no's throughout their lives, starting almost at day one. I decided that I would not actively say no to Deren except in harmful situations where he could get physically hurt. I thought I would try this out for his first year. This system worked fine. It took a lot of creativity on my part not to jump into an automatic "No."

However, when he started going through the contrary stages of the terrible twos, I needed every tool and creative thought I could muster in dealing with his behavior. Almost every other word of mine was "No!" I felt sad to have to be the "heavy person," continually curtailing his fun as he would explore electrical cords and switches, put things in his mouth, hit me, scream, or whatever. I was glad, however, that I hadn't lessened the impact of no by overusing it in Deren's first year.

218

The cue for his tantrum would be a two-letter word said twice: "No! No!" With this he would begin to wail, jump, and scream and put on a performance for anyone who was near. His favorite place was in the grocery stores near the candy and gum section.

My usual reaction to a tantrum (Deren had them 20 to 1 over Alexandra, and I'm not sure why) would be to leave the grocery store, deli, movie, laundry, store, or whatever. I'd take the child to the car or away from people. I would continue to hold the child tightly and remain calm while talking to him or her in a firm voice. I would say things like "That doesn't work with me" or "That's not okay with me" or "You're having a tantrum and I don't like it." I would tell the child that if he or she would calm down, we would go back to the place we were, otherwise we would have to go right home. The merchants with whom I do business knew I'd be back for my groceries, laundry, or shopping. Fortunately, they understood.

Both my children seemed allergic to the word "no." After I caught on to that I would make deals with them about what was possible and what was not *before* we went to the store or movie or whatever. I would let them get a small treat or a package of sugarless gum and that would be it—no ands, ifs or buts. If they balked, acted out, or had a tantrum, I would do the same thing—pick them up tightly and carry them out.

While you can't avoid stressful situations all the time, I do find that it makes sense not to get into impossible predicaments with a young child. We would go to cafes and family restaurants where I could pay in advance. That way we could leave anytime since the food was paid for. Neither Deren nor Alexandra could "blackmail" me with a tantrum because I could leave a full table of food. (In some establishments a nice busboy would pack it up for me so I could return later to pick it up privately.)

To me making sure you can always leave immediately is a big trick with tantrums. Usually rushing out of a place while tightly holding a kicking, screaming child will quiet him or her right down. Children also seem to sleep deeply after a tantrum—perhaps this is related.

I tune in to my children's up times and down times. Naps have been exceedingly important for both of them each day. Deren finished his naps at age four and Alexandra will probably do likewise. I think preventing a child from becoming overtired is very helpful in heading off unpleasant situations.

When Deren became old enough to play with a friend and the standard "He hurt me" from either of them began, I finally came up with what I think is a brilliant solution. I decided to banish both of them to separate bedrooms for five minutes where they would have to remain isolated on their beds. They couldn't play with toys or read books. At the end of five minutes I'd ask them if they were ready to apologize to one another and play again. (This became the prototype for the time-out behavior to cool down.) After the five minutes of isolation (which I termed the "penalty box" after hockey game punishments), life became extraordinarily smooth. Whenever Deren and any friend, or his sister, would fuss and start to fight, I'd yell out, "Is it penalty-box time?" The two of them would immediately look innocent, with big tears in their eyes, and say, "Oh no! We're fine. We're just playing. There's no problem."

Before this solution I had struggled through several years wondering how to handle who did what to whom, and it was never clear who hit whom and why. Nothing could be solved. Everyone would be miserable waiting for me to judge behaviors that were impossible to ascertain.

Alexandra, now over three, is finally old enough to clearly understand the penalty-box concept. I have hardly ever "banished" her to her room alone because she is far more sensitive than Deren and catches on more quickly about how to be nice and respectful of others.

The main problem I have now is that Deren is older and more "streetwise." It's not much of a problem for him to be confined to his room for five minutes. In fact, sometimes when he's in a bad mood he'll ask me if he can go to his room for five minutes or orchestrate a situation so I'll send him there. Alexandra literally falls apart at just the mention of going to her room. So when either of them comes to me in tears reporting what the other did, I feel I don't quite have the adequate tools to deal with both of them together on this yet. It's unfair to confine just Deren, and yet Alexandra is still not old enough to spend five minutes by herself. Maybe I'll limit it to two minutes so she won't go into deep sobs.

In the past I would threaten to turn off a favorite television program, not take them to the movie or park, not take them for a treat that had been previously promised. If those things didn't work, I would threaten to leave them to themselves while I went to a different part of the house to do something more enjoyable for me. Neither of them liked that very much, and they usually became more contrite and cooperative.

Deren and Alexandra stage their biggest and noisiest battles when I am on the phone or when I have a friend over. Their racket gets so loud that I can't hear and have to stop what I'm doing and direct them to "knock it off." In these cases I know clearly that they are both competing for my attention. If I don't give it, they escalate their antics until one of them or both of them wind up getting "hurt." Of course I must pay attention to that—right? These kids are so smart! I try to set up my phone calls or visits with friends after I've given them lots of hugs and kisses and they are feeling cuddled and complete.

Discipline is one of the most difficult parts of being a parent. It is also a very necessary part, since the child must learn to show courtesy and compatibility. It was a difficult day for Deren in the Dusay household when he learned that the whole world does not revolve exclusively around him and that he is not the person to give the family orders.

Overall, Deren has calmed down and become much more cooperative. His free spirit still wants to negotiate and change things, and when it's possible to accommodate him we do. He knows that we're fair, and he is trying much harder to be fair himself, which means making an effort to see our position too. (We'll know when the fairness issue is no longer a major one when he accepts a piece of cake without looking to see if Alexandra or someone else got a bigger one.)

Our family is neither authoritarian nor democratic. We are somewhere in between. We view each family member as an important part of the team. Jack and I are available to listen to the children's wants and we make every effort to accommodate them. The children's feelings are every bit as important as ours. Each child feels energized to solve family problems and knows that he or she will be treated with dignity and respect. We set up family meetings at dinner to discuss the daily events and problems. We ask our children how they would solve the problems that they have or we have. There is an air of sharing and positive energy. Neither Jack nor I believe in shaming children, insulting them, or berating them so that they feel bad when they are naughty. Instead we set up an automatic time-out so we can all cool off and then rationally listen to what the other person is saying, thinking, or feeling. Our goals are win-win so that no one is wrong.

We are all free to apologize. I frequently behave in a manner I am not proud of and apologize to the children. They apologize, too, and we accept that and don't make each other suffer.

Occasionally Deren will confide that he knows it sometimes must be hard being a parent. I smile and wink and say that it is, and that sometimes it must be hard being a kid. He and Alexandra laugh.

Mary ❧

Frank and I did not discuss discipline until Natalie was at least six months old. Before that, how could we? She was so sweet and she could not even go anywhere. But at six months she was able to crawl all over the place, and we had to say "no" for the first time.

Some of my friends don't believe in using "no" before a certain age, but I believe it is just another word. How you say no—your facial expression and what other words it is accompanied by—make a whole lot of difference. Of course just to say "no" is very unfair to anyone, baby or adult, without further explanation. We are all entitled to know "why."

Consistency is very important as we help develop Natalie's personality. As she grew she needed more consistency and discipline. Children even in the toddler age are so smart, they recognize every single mistake we make. I am definitely more into discipline than Frank.

When Natalie was a little over a year old she got into a very bad habit of slapping people's faces. We told her many times that

222

was not polite, but she still did it anyway. Finally at one point I was very angry at her; she was crying and mad, rolling on the floor. I ignored her and left. I thought it would be good to let her know I meant it and to let her cry for five minutes or so. Frank could not stand it; he was mad at me instead, in front of Natalie. Discipline will work only when all parties involved in the household cooperate, especially the parents. Unfortunately a part of it is having a strong stomach for listening to crying for several minutes at a time. Frank has a problem with that. He is a very sensitive man and hates to let his little girl cry.

Both of us have the problem of tending to spoil our daughter. I think a big part of it is because we see her so little during the day that we all bend over backward to ease the losses. Basically we feel guilty. However, now that Natalie is over three years old, discipline comes much more easily and naturally to me.

Understanding the child's behavior at every stage of his or her age makes a lot of difference in how we will have to discipline the child. However, we as adults should have much more control over our feelings and emotions, regardless of how exhausted we feel.

One method of discipline I've used over and over again since Natalie was little over a year old, and which seems to be the best for us so far, has been "looking at the wall." I've created this method on my own, since it is hard to find an empty corner in our house for her to sit in. Many times we end up laughing instead when Natalie asks for help from another person in the house or tries to peep with her eyes or play with her fingers.

We have always taught Natalie to say "sorry" when she is naughty. I do not know how much she means it, but she manages to come and give me a hug to say "sorry." Then everything is fine again, as if nothing had happened.

Natalie never had tantrums until she became two. That year was not a terrible one for Natalie. However, I could not say it was terrific, either. Two-year-olds require lots of patience and understanding. They start to recognize their new abilities, but they don't have all the requirements met yet. It can be a frustrating year for both child and parents.

Once when we were shopping at our local supermarket, Natalie insisted on getting bubble gum. Usually I was able to turn her attention to something else, but not that time. She was so upset that she went flat on the floor screaming, creating quite a scene. It was so embarrassing, since it seemed as if I could not control my own daughter. From that time on we just avoided going to certain places with her.

Soon I learned, too, that staying calm and firm was the best approach to Natalie's tantrums. If I catered to her tantrums they only became worse. First I always pretend that it is not too serious. If that doesn't work, I use some firm words and leave. Usually Natalie will scream even more at first, then follow me and hug me and say, "Sorry, Mommy, sorry."

Two-year-olds might have their little idiosyncrasies, but for us it is another introduction to a new challenge to be a parent. We have to come up with a new trick all the time to keep the household running smoothly.

Susan ❧

I have given a great deal of thought to the subject of discipline, but I have come up with very little by way of a method that I feel is worth passing on. There have been various techniques that have worked for me in certain situations, but nothing works all of the time or for all children. Much of what I do is done by instinct, although my reactions are tempered by ideas I have heard other people discussing, material I have read, techniques I have tried, conversations I have had with Dick, etc. I am also guided by my personality, the child's personality, the phase of the moon, how tired I am, and countless other factors. Unfortunately, too much of what I do is out of the frustrations of the moment and is without adequate thought.

I think that disciplining very young children is harder than disciplining older children who have begun to have some control over their actions, emotions, and reason. For the later stages there are many fine books written and lots of helpful techniques. Two that I found particularly interesting and helpful were *Children, the Challenge* by Rudolf Dreikurs, M.C. (1964) Hawthorn/ Dutton, and *Your Child's Self-Esteem* by Dorothy Corjukke Briggs (1970) Doubleday & Company, Inc. But I found very little helpful information regarding disciplining during the first three or four years.

I would like to read more on the subject of discipline, not because I think that there is a perfect method somewhere out there, but because I am always looking for new ideas, new techniques, and, more important, greater understanding of child development. It helps to know about normal behavior patterns, levels of understanding the child is capable of, and at what point it is reasonable to expect what type of compliance. I think that greater understanding helps avoid some of the frustration that comes from expecting too much too soon.

I do believe in two very basic tenets. For discipline to be effective, Natasha and Ariana must know that they are loved, and they must know that it is possible for them to please us—that is, they must also get praise. It seems fairly apparent to me that it is the fear of losing our love that really causes Natasha to want to conform to our wishes. If she does not think that she can please us, she will have no reason to try. When she has pushed me too far and I have gotten unusually stern with her, Natasha sometimes hovers closely, behaving angelically, as if she is trying to win back my love and affection. She has even asked whether or not I still love her.

After I have disciplined Natasha and the message has gotten through—or at least I think it has—I always talk to her about why she was punished and I tell her that I still love her. I often tell her that I will always love her even when she misbehaves and even when I get so angry with her that I don't want to be with her at that moment. Depending on the situation, I sometimes also tell her that I know it is sometimes hard to do what she should, but that I know she can if she tries. Then I ask her to try. She always says that she will—and she usually does!

How I discipline depends a great deal upon why I am disciplining. It seems to me that I discipline Natasha for three very different reasons. The first, and most important, is for her safety, the second is to socialize her, and the third is for my convenience.

225

Natasha must learn (and therefore we must teach) that some things she may not do or must do in a certain way because to do otherwise will cause her great bodily harm. I do not forbid her to do things that cause her less than great bodily harm. I may warn, but often I just hold my breath. I think that growing up involves a certain amount of physical injury and children must learn their own limits by trial and error. If I try to prevent all injury, not only will I fail, but I also will stifle my child's development and may create an overly cautious or overly daring child.

When it comes to safety, discipline is easy. I use whatever force is necessary in the particular situation to keep Natasha from injuring herself and to teach her that such behavior is totally unacceptable and will cause her harm. Natasha learned the meaning of the word "dangerous" very early in her life. In this category, if in no other, I am entirely consistent. I am vigilant. I think ahead, I warn, I watch carefully, and I constantly reinforce my warnings. I yell, I shout, I slap hands, I spank, I do whatever is necessary to get her attention and impress upon her the importance of my message. The urgency that I feel obviously comes across because there is never a problem with this area of discipline.

Disciplining Natasha in order to teach her how to get along in society is particularly difficult because I have competing goals. On the one hand I want a child who is well behaved, who is not spoiled, and who behaves in a socially acceptable manner. But on the other hand I want a child who questions everything, who can and does think for herself, and who doesn't act in a certain way just because that is "the way it is done." I want a child whose creativity and enthusiasm for life is left intact. I also want a child who understands the reason for the rules and who does what is right in a given situation because it is right, not just because she's been threatened or cajoled into certain behavior. There are times when the "correct" thing to do is not what the rule book would prescribe. It is a delicate balance between functioning in society and maintaining individual strength. I often feel that I am working at cross purposes when I try to decide what discipline is appropriate. When I am feeling ambivalent, Natasha senses it immediately and intensifies her level of resistance or insistence, as the case may be, and the battle rages. She is also exposed to this kind of discipline at play group or in school, but in these situations there is usually little debate about what should be done.

On occasion I discipline Natasha for my convenience. There are times when I need peace and quiet, for example. I am not trying to teach her any important lesson in life, I just want her to shut up and leave me alone. There is probably some overlap here with the second area because she must learn that she is not the center of the universe and that other people's feelings and needs must be considered. This area of discipline is difficult because of the guilt I often feel when I push her away. How effective I am here depends upon how desperate I am and how guilty I feel.

The amount and type of discipline Natasha receives has changed greatly as Natasha has changed. For the first six months I didn't do anything that I would put into the classification of discipline. If she cried, I went to her and gave her whatever she needed. That's all there was to it. I didn't worry about spoiling her. I held her whenever she wanted for as long as she wanted. I nursed her whenever she wanted for as long as she wanted. I smothered her with hugs and kisses. I smiled at her and I talked to her. Looking back, it seems blissfully easy.

By the time Natasha was six months old she was quite mobile and had begun to get into things that were potentially dangerous. Although I put as many things as I could out of her reach, discipline began at this point. Until about sixteen months about the only reason for discipline was her safety, although occasionally it was for my convenience (especially if a mess was imminent). For the most part the method I used was to tell her no and remove her from the situation. Her resistance, if any, was short-lived, and this method worked quite well. She learned rather quickly which things were worth her effort and which things were going to be taken away from her. She began to respond to the word "no," and life wasn't all that difficult.

At sixteen months the "fun" began with her first (and by no means her last) tantrum. Until then Natasha had been an absolute delight to be around—always happy, full of joy, and eager to please. She would do just about anything that you asked her to do, and do it with a giggle or a screech of delight. I think the fact that she was such a wonderful baby made her new behavior seem even more terrible.

227

It seemed to happen overnight. One day she was her usual delightful self, and the next day she went into a rage over something so insignificant that I don't even remember what it was. But I will never forget that first tantrum. I had always thought of a tantrum as something that, although it involved some kicking and screaming, was purposeful. I was not prepared for the full-blown tantrum Natasha had. It was anything but calculated or intentional. It appeared to be a totally involuntary response. She went completely out of control.

Somewhere I had learned that one must not give in to a tantrum—that to do so would reward the behavior and thus encourage it. I had always assumed that it would be easy to ignore tantrums because I dislike manipulative behavior and am not usually one to give in to manipulation. But I was not prepared for what occurred. I just watched in horror as Natasha kicked and screamed and cowered in the corner. The best way that I can describe her behavior is to tell you that it looked similar to a seizure. There didn't appear to be any voluntary movement on her part at all. It was as if she were possessed. Rather than feeling angry or firm with her, my instinct was to try to protect her, to hold her and hug her and tell her that everything would be all right. With some difficulty I restrained myself for a while and just watched. When it seemed as though her fury was subsiding a bit, I couldn't resist any longer and I made a motion as though to pick her up. This only caused her to go back into a rage. This time I waited and watched until it had stopped completely and her energy was completely spent. She was exhausted and now wanted comfort and nurturing. I gave it to her, although I did wonder if this would somehow encourage the tantrums.

I don't remember how long it was until the next tantrum, but I remember that in the interim I decided I would walk away from her next time, thinking that even watching might somehow encourage the behavior. When it started I walked away. She got up and ran over to me, throwing herself down in front of me, screaming and kicking and carrying on all the while. The more I tried to get away from her, the more she clung to me. But if I tried to calm her or comfort her, she only raged more. It was unbelievably frustrating.

From then on she vacillated between being angelic and responding with tantrums. She didn't like to be told no, and she didn't like being told what to do. Her level of resistance was beyond belief. I tried ignoring the tantrums, but that didn't work. Finally, at the suggestion of her pediatrician, I found that the best way to respond to her was to put her in her room, close the door, and leave her there until the tantrum was over. At first they lasted a long time—fifteen or twenty minutes wasn't uncommon. When your baby is kicking and screaming uncontrollably for fifteen minutes, it seems like an eternity! And doing nothing but waiting for it to end is difficult. There were many times when I just could not stand there doing nothing while she screamed and I would try to reason with her from outside the door. Of course it was to no avail and probably counterproductive, but I just couldn't help myself! When she learned how to open the door I put one of the childproof doorknob covers on the inside of her door so that she could not open it. In time it wasn't necessary to close the door, and the threat of closing the door became a useful tool in later attempts to control her behavior.

Fortunately, with one or two memorable exceptions, Natasha's worst tantrums occurred at home. When she did have a tantrum in public, I picked her up and carried her away from the situation as she continued to kick and scream. I tried to ignore the stares and hoped that no one would report me for child abuse, because to listen to her scream, you would be sure that she was being severely abused!

Natasha's most outrageous tantrums occurred intermittently over several months. Then they became increasingly more controlled. The worst part didn't last more then six to nine months. After that she would lose control occasionally and we would have to put her in her room until she regained control. Gradually she learned to throw what I call "controlled tantrums." This is what I had expected from the start, and these are much easier to deal with. She doesn't lose her ability to reason, and thus more traditional forms of punishment become effective.

When I first commented to Dr. Smith that Natasha had started the terrible twos early, he told me that they were no longer referred to as the terrible twos—now they are the terrific twos. Well, I have nothing against focusing on the positive, and it is true that during the same period of time that Natasha was having the most outrageous tantrums she was also capable of being the most delightful she had ever been, but the tantrums and the trauma they caused us were definitely the more significant behavior for that time period.

Natasha has always responded well to the admonition that something was dangerous, but with great resistance to the admonition that something is socially inappropriate or that she must behave in a certain way. I respond to her resistance in various ways. Often the process goes something like this: I tell her (or remind her) what I expect. Occasionally I am surprised by compliance at this level. If not, I change my tone and increase the volume of my voice. If that doesn't work, I try the old universal method of counting to three. If I get to three with no compliance from Natasha, she gets punished. Usually she is sent to her room (as a time-out). Sometimes when I start to count she will say "Mommy, you don't have to count, (sigh). I'm going." Recently I have begun to use other punishments occasionally, such as taking away a privilege. Until now I didn't think that she would remember what she was being punished for by the time the privilege was actually withheld, and mere threats aren't very effective. Now her memory is good enough to make this type of punishment effective when I can think of the appropriate thing to withhold. In general I try to make any punishment follow quickly after the infraction (preferably instantaneously) because the connection is better and thus the message clearer.

I'm not sure why the twos get the top rating when it comes to obnoxious behavior. Natasha has just gone through another difficult stage, in many ways more obnoxious than the terrible part of the twos. She would do exactly what she knew would annoy me. I would say "Natasha, don't do that." She would look right at me with a look that said "Up yours, Mom," and proceed, in an even more exaggerated way, to do exactly what I had told her not to do. Her defiance was beyond belief and since she obviously knew what she was doing, I had no problem being firm with her. Once again the stage was relatively short and we all lived through it. What can possibly be in store for us next? Never mind, don't tell me!

I don't always discipline with any logic at all, but I try. A friend has told me about a method that advocates the use of "logical consequences." I think it's a great idea. Punishment is designed to teach, and letting a child suffer the logical consequences of his or her behavior is a terrific idea. But I have difficulty thinking of logical consequences that will punish Natasha without totally destroying me! I'm working on it—and I know that I'm going to have lots of opportunities to practice.

Everyone talks about how important it is to be consistent. Wonderful advice. Just try it! I've tried and I've failed. I've tried again and I've failed again. I'm going to keep on trying, but I don't think that it is possible. I've lowered my expectations with regard to consistency. My opinions concerning what is appropriate depend on so many variables that consistency is just not possible. I do try especially hard not to condone unacceptable behavior, but I sometimes just ignore it, usually because I'm too tired to deal with the situation. I'm not sure that it isn't sometimes better to ignore some bad behavior and avoid constant controversy. I don't think that ignoring it is the same as condoning it.

Because she appears so mature, I have often expected more of Natasha than she has been able to give. I expected self-control before she possessed it; I expected her to remember the rules before she was able. These unrealistic expectations caused us both no end of frustration. I don't suppose it has caused any real damage, and she eventually learns, but if I had waited until she was better able to comply with my wishes I wouldn't have had to repeat my message so many times and perhaps her resistance would not have been as great.

Natasha is often a very difficult child. Dick doesn't like it when I say this. For him it conjures up images of problem children. Natasha certainly is not a problem child, but she can be difficult. She is very manipulative and very creative in her attempts at manipulation; she is very persistent in her unwillingness to take no for an answer; and she has a very strong need to be in control. I have learned that the best way to deal with her strong personality is to give her an opportunity to save face. If we find a compromise position she will always comply, but if I maintain a hard stand, so will she. We spend a lot of time negotiating.

I have also noticed that much of Natasha's difficult behavior occurs when I am not treating her as an individual. I'm too busy trying to fit her into my busy schedule without really taking the time to consider what her needs are. Often with very little extra effort I can accommodate both of our needs; then there is no need to discipline because she is no longer resisting. It takes a little extra thought and a constant reminder to myself that she is a person and needs to be treated as one.

Natasha saves her difficult behavior for me. Baby-sitters *almost* never have as much trouble as I do in getting her to do things, and my friends couldn't believe it when I told them that Natasha threw tantrums and was difficult to control at times. Whenever they were present she was an angel. On one noteworthy day Natasha was in a particularly bad mood. She had been fussing about anything and everything and she was driving me crazy. At about four in the afternoon my friend Elaine stopped over for a visit. Natasha ran to the door to greet her and couldn't have been more charming during her entire visit.

In disciplining Natasha I have learned a great deal about myself. First, I discovered that I don't like disciplining and I don't like being tough. I want people to just do what they should do—I don't want to have to force them to! I'm sure that this dislike of toughness has caused me to ignore more than I should and to allow some bad habits to develop. But I'm learning. I've also learned that I have quite a volatile temper. Prior to having children, it really took something of enormous magnitude to get me to raise my voice or to express anger of any sort. I was controlled. Well, not anymore. Children just seem to know how to get to the most sensitive spots. They keep you up all night and then they push, push, push, until you just explode! Can it be unintentional on their part? It seems so calculated and it is sooooo effective!

Before I had children I thought that it was possible to raise them without the use of corporal punishment. I still think that it is desirable to avoid force, and I'll even grant that it might be possible for someone else, but I don't think that it is at all practical. Sometimes a slap on the hand or a swat on the butt is the most efficient way to get Natasha's attention. I don't use corporal punishment much and I think that it is seldom the best method, but at times it just seems appropriate.

I also used to have no understanding of how child abuse was possible. Although I have never come close to hurting Natasha when I spank her (her pride, not her body, is injured), I have had the urge to hit her much harder than I ever have. Children know how to push you beyond your limit. Child abuse is

232

unconscionable, but I can now understand how parents who have no way of getting any relief from the stress of caring for their children could totally lose control and punish a child with greater force than they intended. I feel very fortunate that I have been able to find ways to get away from my children from time to time and find some relief from the stress they create.

It is a little early to know for sure, but I suspect that Ariana will be more compliant, more anxious to please, and less manipulative than Natasha. Will this be better for her in the long run? Perhaps not. I have often said that Natasha's personality will serve her well in life, if I don't destroy her in the interim!

I started disciplining Ariana later than I did Natasha because it wasn't necessary as early. She wasn't as mobile as early. Currently we are still at the first level. Soon, though, we will begin to expect her to learn the rules of socially acceptable behavior and the honeymoon will be over.

As hard as it is for me to discipline and be tough with Natasha and Ariana, it is much more difficult for me to watch Dick mete out any punishment. When I put Natasha into her room kicking and screaming, I know that there is a good reason, but when Dick puts her into her room kicking and screaming, I am sure that he is torturing the poor child and I yearn to rush to her aid. I know that I cannot, so I bite my lip, clench my fists, and sit telling myself that I must not interfere. I think that I have been remarkably good about not interfering (Dick may have another perception), but it has been very difficult. I don't like being a passive observer. We all make mistakes with discipline and it is much easier to make them than to sit silently by while someone else makes them.

Dick has probably made fewer mistakes with discipline than I have, if for no other reason than he doesn't discipline the children as often. Although I think that Dick is overly stern at times, he is more consistent and thus probably more effective.

Dick and I are very fortunate in that we see eye to eye when it comes to discipline. I'm a little softer, he's a little firmer, but our goals are the same and our immense love for our children is the same. It's going to be a difficult journey for both of us, but we have each other's support and I have every confidence that we are going to make it.

I don't think that it is essential for Dick and me to use the same techniques as long as one of us doesn't sabotage a particular plan of the other. We spend a great deal of time talking about what we are doing by way of discipline so that we can, in our own way, reinforce the message that the other is giving.

Disciplining a child is the most difficult task a parent has. I worry about it a lot. I just hope that with enough love, they will recover from all our mistakes—and if anyone has enough love, Natasha and Ariana do. Other parents may love their children as much, but it would be impossible to love them more!

Chapter 16

DEPENDENCE/ INDEPENDENCE

- Our views on encouraging our children's independence
- Hating to let go
- "I do it!"
- Getting dressed, walking alone, and other milestones
- Stranger anxiety—and overfriendliness
- Regressive behavior

Diana ᴥ

From the moment both of my children were born they were actively working their way to independence. As an infant Sosia almost seemed angry to be so helplessly immobile and dependent. She worked hard to become independent. I tried to give her plenty of opportunities by making things in the house her size or accessible to her.

I wanted my children to be independent—most of the time. (They grow up so fast! Sometimes I want to freeze them right where they are.) I try to foster their independence by assuring them that I am there all the time. If they venture further than they have ventured before, I am there when they come back for assurance and/or security. I have always felt that if I am reliable, the children will feel they can be independent without fearing that they could somehow go too far and lose the tie between us.

In many ways I try to overdo the warmth. To hug and kiss and snuggle as much as I can fit in. If they needed to sleep right next to Yogi and me, we would let them. If they needed to be carried around in a backpack all day, then they were. If they couldn't face the first day of nursery school without me sitting next to them, then I would be there. I found that pretty soon they didn't want me at nursery school and they learned to trust my return to the room. The more assurance and warmth Yogi and I gave them, the safer they seemed in pursuing their own independence.

I have noticed a pattern in my children's seeking independence. The greatest test of independence is followed by the biggest regression. Toilet training is followed by diapers, and the diapers are followed by real independence. Going to nursery school and being unable to say good-bye is followed by complete independence at school. If I try to deny the closeness or love that they seem to crave and try to force them to grow up faster or act differently, they don't seem able to overcome the regression as quickly.

Yogi and I followed our children's leads when they were regressing. When Benjamin was born and Sosia was almost three, she "forgot" how to feed herself, forgot that she didn't nurse, even forgot that she didn't wear diapers. We played along with her completely. We held her when we fed her. We had her sleep with us in our big bed and we kissed her simultaneously on both cheeks. We diapered her like she had never been diapered before, complete with baby powder and baby games. I even went so far as to "nurse" her in earnest one day, until even she had to laugh at herself and admit to us (and to herself) that she was no longer a baby. And when she "forgot" again, as she seemed to do frequently for a while, we "forgot" along with her. She was able to explore Benjamin's world frequently according to her own needs without any ridicule or resistance from us. Our pediatrician assured us that Sosia's regressions would pass, and of course they did. We stressed the wonderful "grown-up" things she did and helped her to see her independence as a wonderful thing, even when the baby seemed to get all the attention.

Even now, at six, Sosia sometimes seems to "forget" how to dress herself. When I run upstairs to help her she often wants to use this time together to share something that is on her mind about growing up.

I have been told the regression itself may be caused by the child's fear of going beyond his level of skill, or the realization that he is both gaining and losing something at each milestone.

One of the things that continues to save my sanity during the regressive periods is the realization that the behavior that is bothering me can usually be attributed to the child's developmental stage. A baby with colic is not giving a parenting ability review, a six-year-old doesn't really hate his parents when he yells it from his room. All the regressive stages are just a way for children to come to grips with their separateness from their parents. Their realization that they are human, that they really are not connected physically anymore, even that they will die someday—it's all part of the events that motivate them to grow. They are, after all, just looking for some sort of guidelines in this immense world of possibilities that they have found themselves in.

It makes me sad when I hear people say that they must "train" their babies to sleep through the night by letting them cry it out, or that they don't want to give in to their cries all the time and spoil them. A little baby is helpless and utterly dependent. By responding to his need for security, I feel you can actually free him to be more independent. There were many nights that I felt like crying myself, and days that I could barely stay awake, but now my children are remarkably self-assured and confident. And fortunately for me, and for them, they trust Yogi and me. They know that they can bring problems of every variety to us and that we will always respond.

We live in an environment that is tragically and alarmingly treacherous. Children need to be independent, but they also need to be protected. Coming from a small town, it took me a while to realize that ALL kinds of people are very interested in babies. I became extremely cautious of strangers. I never let anyone hold or touch my babies. Kind strangers were treated pleasantly but firmly. I have found it easiest to simply discourage any communications between my children and strangers. I don't want my children to feel comfortable in any way with any strangers. It is an unfortunate commentary on our society, but any newspaper will give a number of reasons why I keep my decision firm.

Jan 🍂

I want both my daughters to grow up to be independent, thoughtful, and strong individuals . . . but does it have to begin at such a young age? I guess it does.

When Jaclyn makes her own egg-salad sandwich it is a messy experience for Mom, but such an accomplishment for her. It's an ordeal for me to watch her cutting her own fingernails, but she's got to learn somehow and learning is growing. (Mom, however, grows more gray hairs.) My motto is "Learning with Supervision." I've never wanted to put a damper on my children's curiosity, but I've never been foolish enough to sacrifice their safety, either.

I instill in our baby-sitters the importance of caution when they are out with the children. On shopping trips they are never to let the children out of their sight, never to take their hands off the stroller if they stop to turn around. With Jaclyn getting older now, I talk to her about staying close by. Holding her hand is important to me, because I love her so much. There are so many people about in a shopping center, I don't want to risk losing track of her.

I regard the terrible twos as a time when our cute and cherubic critters are growing up and want to be independent. They want to try everything from drive the car to cook a nine-course meal. "I do it!" was a line we heard many times. In truth, they really can't do many of the things they want to—yet. But they have to learn. It's so much easier and faster to just do things for a toddler. I had to constantly remind myself that we all had to learn sometime. Compromise was my salvation. You can carry the keys to the car, but Mommy has to drive. You can drive when you're sixteen (maybe)!

Giving Jaclyn an age reference seems to make sense to her. You can wear Mommy's makeup when you're sixteen; you can pierce your ears when you're sixteen; and you can wear tampons (they see all!) when you're sixteen. Sixteen is going to be a big year in our house. Try twenty-one at yours.

Although many times I find myself saying "No, don't do that," I really don't think it enhances growth and creativity. But by giving an age reference you're not really saying no, you're just postponing the activity. And although we know sixteen is a long way from three . . . Jaclyn seems to think sixteen is next month!

Katherine &

With both children since birth I have observed their quests toward independence. It seems that they have indefatigable wills to grow, learn, and master biological, social, psychological, and intellectual endeavors.

In the beginning their little heads would bob with a powerful will to reach the breast and nurse. They would strain and keep trying to raise their heads, or hold on to our fingers with an iron grasp to be pulled up, or try and try to flip over, sit up, crawl, and take those early steps. And they are as overjoyed by each milestone as they were determined to attain it.

For Jack and me the hardest part is letting go. Before the child masters a new skill, there are many failed attempts. It's frustrating for us to either hold them back or patiently go through a learning phase, or stand by as they learn to cut an orange with a knife (while we nervously think of cut fingers and sloppy orange juice all over), or try to get out of a car by themselves (while we fearfully watch their feet reaching for the curb). Of course any assistance on different tasks from us is loudly and strongly rebuffed. Each new step becomes exciting and frustrating for them and us.

When children become tired they regress quickly to babyhood. This usually means that they go limp and want to be carried, or they scream because they are so tired, or have to eat immediately, or have to go to the bathroom, or go home, or whatever. It is fascinating how they go from an independent powerful human beings back to helpful infants in two seconds flat!

I have had many conversations with the children through the years about strangers and strange animals. I want them to begin to recognize the "good guys" from the "bad guys" in real life. They're aware that "strangers" are people you haven't met yet and that they are strangers themselves to people who don't know them. They are clear that they won't accept rides or go for walks with people *without* prior permission from Jack and me. We chuckled with surprise the other day when a friend asked Alexandra what she wanted to be when she grew up.

"A stranger!" she answered, with a sly smile on her face as she gives Daddy and me a pseudo wink.

Mary ਏ▲

To grow from a dependent little infant into an independent human being is a big change, maybe the biggest adjustment we have to make in our entire life. No wonder kids are so confusing during the toddler years. However, we are not perfect either, and it's easier to get mad at them now than when they were still totally dependent on us.

To us "two" was not all that bad. In fact, two-year-olds are so interesting. They are making a big stride in their independence, and yet they still want to be babies too. At two Natalie was also feeling somewhat insecure. She did not even like it if I touched my friends' babies; she got jealous immediately. Wherever we went she would cling to my dress, and she was also afraid of clowns. At home she became a little bossy, telling us all what to do and how to do it. She wanted to do everything herself, and it is very hard to reason with or teach a two-year-old. They don't seem to listen, because they feel they know it already, even if they have never seen it yet. This was the time when Natalie first learned how to say "sorry" and give a hug and a kiss. She soon learned that by saying "sorry" she made everyone feel better.

Natalie can be so funny at times. Sometimes she insists on flushing the toilet herself, another time she will teach me how to flush the toilet properly, and sometimes she doesn't even want to flush the toilet at all.

I feel it is up to us parents to help shape our toddlers into happy and confident little children who will need more and more of our support and understanding throughout the first twenty years of their lives. This means to recognize and respond when they need us as well as to let them know if they do something wrong. It is hard at times for me, especially when I come home from work very tired and Natalie needs extra attention and keeps on nagging me. In our family we use the term "sorry" followed with hugs and kisses. After all, we are all human.

Susan ❧

Natasha has always been an extremely independent child. That term can mean a variety of things and applies to both desirable and undesirable behavior. In general, I think that having an independent child is wonderful but difficult. I have often been very frustrated by Natasha's strong independence. When I look for sympathy from people I am always told that it will serve her well when she gets older. In theory, of course, this is correct, but there have often been times when her independent behavior has created such conflict between us that I wonder if I will allow her to live long enough for those traits to benefit her!

Natasha's independence manifests itself in her ability and desire to do things for herself; the fact that she isn't always running to Mom or Dad for defense and/or comfort; her knowing exactly what she wants and figuring out ways to get it; her lack of shyness and her ability to adjust easily to new situations; her stubborn resistance to others helping her; her resistance to others' suggestions about what should be done and how it should be accomplished, and her desire and ability to control most situations with her friends. Despite her independence, she does not play by herself much. Natasha likes a lot of attention and needs an audience if not an actual playmate. Because of this, Ariana, who loves being with Natasha, has been a great relief.

Natasha's independence was apparent at a very early age, although I don't now recall just how early. Sometime after eighteen months she decided that she could dress herself. She could manage some things herself, and when I had plenty of time I just watched as she struggled until she either accomplished her goal or became frustrated enough that she would ask for help. But if I was in a hurry and tried to help her before she was ready to be helped—watch out! All hell broke loose! I learned to try to get her moving well in advance of the time I needed to leave the house so that she would have plenty of time. On those occasions when I just couldn't wait, we fought. Believe me, it isn't easy dressing a rapidly moving target who is trying to put you out of commission as you work!

Then, just as Natasha began to get proficient at dressing herself and could do it in relatively short order, she decided that she didn't want to. Suddenly she needed help with everything. At first I didn't mind because it sped up the process of getting her dressed, but then she used it for game playing, both in the selection and application of her clothes. The battles we had over getting her dressed were unbelievable! By a process of trial and error I gradually found ways to defuse the situation but it was ages before I discovered the obvious. No breakfast until she was dressed and hair combed. It was amazing how this turned a battleground into a cooperative effort. She still likes to have help getting dressed but the times she does it herself are increasing.

The same switch from total independence to dependence came in the area of feeding herself. The first time I gave her any food on a spoon, she would turn her head and refuse to take it. If I put food in front of her, she would pick it up and eat it. The messes were awesome. Then, just as she started getting fairly neat about feeding herself, she began asking for help. This was less problematic because I'm not usually in as much of a rush during meals, and her hunger would eventually bring her around to my way of thinking.

One sign of Natasha's independence that has caused me some concern is that she has never been the least bit afraid of strangers. She never minded being held by a stranger, and once she began walking she would walk right up to perfect strangers and take their hands as if they were her friends. Once she began talking she developed a love of talking with strangers and will carry on a conversation with anyone who will talk to her—not that she gives *them* much chance to talk! She is not the least bit guarded in her conversations and is willing to tell anyone anything. Although I am concerned about her safety, I also love this warm, independent part of her personality. When we travel we meet lots of interesting people because Natasha starts conversations with them. I have started to tell her that she must be cautious about strangers in certain situations, but how do I go about teaching her that it is okay to talk to some strangers but not others? And that sometimes it is okay to talk to certain strangers but it is not okay to take anything from them or go anywhere with them? And how do I teach her that even some people whom she knows well and thinks of as her friends should be considered strangers for some reasons? It is very difficult, yet I don't want to stifle her wonderfully friendly personality. We live in a very impersonal world and it has become necessary to be very cautious about many things, but I don't want to teach my children fear, only appropriate caution.

I have begun to try to teach Natasha these subtleties, and we talk about various situations and what she would do in them. I try to use people she knows or has met briefly, place them in lots of different situations, and ask her "What if?" questions. She has been amazingly perceptive in her ability to answer my questions appropriately, and I am hopeful that I will be able to get my message across without making her paranoid.

The hardest stage so far in this regard was when she loved running away from me and hated to be held. Grocery stores and department stores were the most difficult. She would struggle to get out of my arms, then run away from me. Chasing after her made shopping difficult and I began to leave her at home rather than struggle with it. But I also began teaching her that it wasn't safe for her to be out of my sight even for an instant, and that if she wanted to be allowed to run around she must watch me and not get out of my sight. It wasn't long before she learned this rule and now we almost never have any problems.

We also have a very strict rule. Any time we are in a street, parking lot, or other place where cars might be, Natasha must hold on to my hand. If she is standing beside the car and I am not holding her hand, she must be touching the car.

There are no exceptions to these rules. Very quickly she learned them and could be trusted to get ahead of me while we were walking and stop well back from the street to wait for me to hold her hand. When she is with another adult who isn't quite as strict as I am, she tells them the rules and waits for him or her to take her hand so she can go across the street.

Ariana is beginning to show signs of independence, too, but she is too young for us to predict how she will compare with Natasha. For a while I thought that she would be less independent, but she is beginning to make me wonder. One thing is for sure: Ariana will find new ways to exert her independence so that even all of our experience with Natasha will not prepare us completely for what she has in store for us!

Part Four

ORGANIZING YOUR LIFE

Introduction 🐦

Organizing your life is not easy when there is a baby. Babies just seem to find ways to create disorganization. However, all of us have tried in our own way to organize our lives and Part IV lets you know how we have gone about this difficult task.

Chapter 17 is about working after having children. The five of us cover a broad spectrum when it comes to working. Among us we've gone back to work early and waited a long time; we've worked part-time and we've had very busy professional lives; some of us feel torn between two worlds and some of us feel perfectly satisfied with our decisions. There's the decision, the execution, and the reaction to the reality of living with the decision. We cover it all.

One way of getting your work life going again after the arrival of children is through the use of child care. There are lots of options available, some better than others. Among us we have tried most of them. We tell you in Chapter 18 what we've tried and how we liked the various options. How did we go about making the choice? Once we had someone, how did we take advantage of their services? We also talk about our children's reaction to child care, and how they handled changes in care-givers. Also, what about letting sitters drive? Discipline? Did our sitters just take care of the children or did they do other tasks, allowing us more time to be with our children?

We all eventually found that we needed some time away from our babies. How soon this happened varied widely. In Chapter 19 we tell you about our need to be away, how we accomplished this, and how we felt about it afterward.

Chapter 20 is on eating out with baby. Some of us did this more often than others. We all tried it from time to time with varying degrees of stress and success. From our experiences you may pick up some ideas about when it works best and how to go about doing it. You'll also learn that even those of us who just loved taking our children along had some difficulty. So if you are struggling here, you are not alone!

We have all traveled with our children. Some of us love it while others have decided to stay close to home for a while. In Chapter 21 we tell you what we have learned about traveling with our children on both short and long trips, on airplanes and by car, staying in hotels and camping. We've got some ideas about what to pack and how to keep the children entertained while en route.

Chapter **17**

WORK

- Deciding to stay home
- Deciding to work full-time
- Deciding to work part-time
- How we felt and how we reached our decisions
- How our husbands feel
- The trade-offs

Diana ‍

I decided not to work full-time after Sosia was born. It was a difficult decision. Going to work would have given me a feeling of accomplishment every day and a sense of self-worth and personal growth. But it also would have added tremendously to the pressures of my family, my husband, and myself. I decided to spend the majority of my time and energies with my children. Staying home gives me an opportunity to see them and to supervise them regularly, and it keeps everyone happy. Although I decided not to go in to an office every day and work full-time, I still wanted something to keep me feeling active and productive once the children started nursery school. I wanted to have some sense of accomplishment outside the home when my mornings became free. I began helping Yogi in his office by filling in during vacations or helping with his printing and banking needs. Now I manage his office on a part-time basis. It gives Yogi some extra time to spend with our family and gives me a sense of purpose without tying me down to a long workday schedule. I also do free-lance writing and volunteer for the annual fund-raisers at Benjamin's and Sosia's schools.

My schedule is perfect for me and my family. When someone is sick, in a school production, or just wanting to share a story over a glass of milk, I am able to be there with them. Yogi and I feel fortunate to be able to have me stay at home.

Not having daily career goals can be frustrating. Some days I feel like nothing is happening. For that reason I have put a list of goals on the refrigerator, including: happy children, children that are read to regularly, children who go to the park daily, a mother with a positive attitude, etc. This helps me feel that I am accomplishing long-term goals and helps me keep a handle on the fact that *I am* accomplishing the raising of my children in my own way.

Not working is difficult at times because it brings a totally different persona along with it. I was no longer Diana Bert; suddenly I became Mel Bert's wife. Now, I don't want you to think that it was anything other than what I wanted, because I most certainly did want to stay home with our baby and I love being Mrs. Melvyn Bert. However, it was a big surprise to find out how much of your identity is tied to the kind of work you do. If you are at home with children, people seem to find you pretty boring and confine their conversations with you to simple topics they feel you can understand ("And how do you feel about *Sesame Street*?") This can be frustrating because you will feel like talking about topics of some importance to adults. It is aggravating that people forget you once did something other than raise children. And it is infuriating that in general people have such little regard for the job of rearing children.

In order to be a better conversationalist with gentlemen I met at parties, I would indicate that I was "in advertising." That would at least get an intelligent conversation started. But with the women I discussed the *real* issues. Is the baby sleeping through the night? Teething? Walking? Found any good baby-sitters?

Some of my friends got around the issue of "adult stimulation" by starting a book study group. They met on Sunday nights and put the dads in charge of the little ones. Over coffee, wine, and cheese they discussed books that they had read, and when stumped for different titles to study they called the local university and asked for some good titles. The university even offered to have graduate students come and lead discussions.

I guess one of the problems of not working (and of working) is wondering whether the grass is greener on the other side. I was happy being able to be at home. And I was frustrated that I was never regarded as a woman who was just as capable and intelligent as one who held down a job. I find that many women place such a high value on the power they have attained in the workplace that they feel a little strange around someone who has chosen to walk away from her "seniority" and stay home with her little ones.

My children brought along a moral commitment. Fortunately, Yogi makes a good living for us. I could hardly justify having two little children at home with baby-sitters just so I could attain a promotion at a job. My most important job was to be at home raising my children. Not that I know everything; I don't. And not that I don't use baby-sitters; I do. But I'm Mom. I'm the one who calls the shots. I decide where the children play and when they take their naps. I referee the squabbles and kiss the boo-boos. I feel that someone must be at home to supervise the overall picture. My being there makes our quantity of life so much better. I feel that I am in control of the life that I have chosen for our family and myself. I would be very unhappy to have only a few hours at home each day with my family. And after a day of job pressures, I would have a hard time slowing down enough to enjoy my family and be able to nurture them.

Some of the most important conversations I have with my children seem to pop up unexpectedly while I am brushing their hair or putting on their socks. Life just doesn't seem to yield its deepest, darkest secrets at specified times. We try to have "quality time" at the table during our meals and invariably the children squirm, complain about certain foods touching other foods, and describe how much they hate chicken. Sosia usually helps us all lose our appetites by asking what happened to the rest of the chicken if we are eating the legs. From there it is hard to move into a meaningful conversation about what they learned that day or what happened to them at school—especially when they are still speaking English at a halting pace. Now I am in definite favor of trying to arrange quality time, and we spend a lot of energy in that pursuit. But I have found that the children break down at precisely the same time that everyone gathers in the evening. There is bathing and dinner and before you blink it is time for them to go to bed. I opt for "quantity time" mixed with quality time—reading stories, playing games, and watching performances of my children's favorite fairy tales on TV. Quality time comes by just being available a lot. Being around to explain "how it works" or having the time to play checkers.

No one ever said that it was fair for someone to stay at home and someone else to go out and "win the bread," so to speak, but children certainly do not ask to be born, and they do require a certain value placed on their well-being and future development. I do not feel that "a woman's place is in the home," but I do feel that one parent should be there for the little everyday occurrences.

Yogi fully supported and encouraged my staying home. He also supported my desire to work occasionally so that I felt I was still in touch with the working world. But he also believes, as I do, that one person should assume the responsibility for the home running pleasantly and smoothly.

When I did the publicity for *Having a Baby*, it was my first experience away from my children. They functioned very nicely in my absence because of the extensive organization that went into the trip. Yogi and I cooked and froze dinners for each day I was going to be away. We set up different activities for specified times each day. The children were in the park and doing something outside during the daytime, and then having their regular quiet time in the afternoon. I think that traveling with them along would have been a tremendous burden on me and on them. It was much easier on all of us to let them be at home with their regular schedules and their regular friends. We set up a daily schedule and made daily telephone calls that kept us well informed of each other. The experience showed me that the family could function beautifully without me. However, while going away is something I would enjoy doing occasionally, I'm definitely happy not to be working full-time.

Jan ₰

I absolutely love my babies. I absolutely love my work. My life is my babies. My work is so very much a part of my life. I think about my babies while I'm at work. I often think about my work while I'm at home with my babies.

It's a constant challenge trying to balance both. At times I think I'm close to reaching that delicate balance . . . then, boom! For some reason, it's thrown off.

I have learned that I thrive on the stimulation and challenge that working can give me. I *need* to work outside of my home. Hats off to the women and men who choose to work at home to take care of their children. It certainly is the most personally rewarding experience.

You have to be honest with yourself regarding what you'd like to do. How will you be fulfilled, satisfied, challenged? Being a working mom is never easy. I often say that I need a wife! I don't have any secrets or any special elves helping me (how I wish, sometimes), and I do have my moments (lots) when it all gets to be too much and I'd like to throw in the diaper.

Diana once told me that she is the best mom her children have. I so agree with her. But I also feel I can't be the best mom for my children if I'm not happy, fulfilled in myself. I've heard it so many times before—from my own mother, who worked—that quality time, rather than quantity, is the key. There are no easy answers and no guarantees, but you've got to grab hold of one concept and keep going. What I try to do is squeeze in my work week (some fifty to sixty hours) in five days, leaving two days strictly for my kids.

My kids have been waving bye-bye to me ever since they were a month old. For them it's part of their lives. I try to put "going to work" in a positive light. At three Jaclyn is asking "Why is Mommy going to work?" I tell her it's because I love what I do,

I'm learning all the time, I meet some very interesting people, and I'm constantly challenged. And then I tell her that when she grows up, she might want to work too. And then of course I ask her what she might like to be when she grows up. Why not start them thinking now? And why not think big!

Do I feel guilty about going to work and leaving them for ten, twelve, or fourteen hours at a stretch? You bet! Am I tired when I see them at night? Do I have less patience with them then? You bet! But staying home with them—for me—is not the answer. You try to do the best you can to please everyone.

I do get to travel with my job—some pretty plum assignments. Two weeks in Shanghai. Ten days on the Mexican Riviera. Two weeks in London. But en route home I can't push the plane fast enough. I miss my children terribly when I'm gone. I call as often as I can. I think I miss them more than they miss me. Before going on a trip I tell both girls (even though Jenna may be too young to understand) that I'm going to be gone for two weeks, but that I'm going to come back. I really think instilling in them that you *are* going to come back is important. I never wanted my children to miss activities important to their development just because I work. As you read in Chapter 12, my girls participate in play group, swimming lessons, gymnastics, and music lessons. I worked it all out with our care-giver, who was able to take them to their activities. And I try to make special appearances at the activities whenever I can.

The only thing that seems to be lacking for a working mom in any given day is *time*. I find my duties stretching into the wee hours of the morning. That seems to be the only time available to get organized, write notes, pay bills, read the newspaper, shower, and sneak a snack. If there is any sacrifice to be made, it seems always to come out of *your* time. Of course it's not fair. Of course I get awfully jealous of my husband, who seems not to have the same kind of pressure from the kids as I have. But I'm not willing to give up anything. So I try to do it all as best I can. Sometimes "best" is seen through some very tired eyes. But luckily children do grow up . . . and maybe, just maybe, will give back some of the time.

Funny how one big hug, or one wet kiss, or one quick laugh from your child can erase any fatigue—at least for the moment.

Katherine 🦆

I love to work! It seems I've always worked. I started working in an ice-cream parlor during the summers in high school, then was a flight attendant for nearly ten years after college, then did my training for six years as a psychotherapist, and eventually I started my own private practice of psychotherapy.

Working is not the issue. How many hours I work a week is! Before having babies I would happily work as a flight attendant for ten hours a day flying my international schedules. I would book eight or nine patients into a day of therapy without a second thought. After having babies I wanted to dramatically curtail my work schedule—yet not stop working completely.

After carefully trying different options and experimenting with numbers of hours and times, I have found that part-time work (twenty hours a week) is perfect for me. Any more than that and I begin to feel out of balance.

I have the good fortune to be my own boss and create my own schedule. I schedule my work hours while the children are in school or napping. I also make sure that I schedule some private time for myself into each workday. It took me a few hours of trial and error to work out a routine. Right scheduling is what makes it work for me. I feel in good balance with my husband, children, myself, and my work. I also realize that any one of these delicate balances can change—and I'll have to go back to the drawing board when it does.

The children, Jack, and I are together from 7:00 to 8:30 or 9:00 every morning. I see them each afternoon when they're home from school. We have "family dinner" at 6:00 each night, which we use as another attempt to "socialize" them and teach them some rudimentary manners. The dining-room table frequently looks like a war zone. Of course the weekends and holidays are bonus times because we can all sleep in later and see each other off and on all day.

Mary ❧

I have my own business. It is a business serving others, which in turn has always given me lots of satisfaction. But my business depends on me to succeed. To be absent for a while is okay, but the company is not large or formal enough to go on by itself. I am a mother not just at home for Natalie but also for my company.

There was no big decision for me. I *had* to go to work, and all my anxiety and concern and missing my clients made me go back to work when Natalie was two months old.

It was not easy. I was torn, but I knew I had to do it. At home, because Natalie was still so young, she did not really know anything different. Life always gives us new challenges. We need to be flexible.

The most interesting part of all this to me is that before we had Natalie, Frank and I would come home from work and collapse. After we had our little girl I felt like I had a new shot of energy when I got home. When I got home I like to take over Natalie's care completely. Our house that used to be so quiet is full of life and laughter now because of Natalie.

Natalie understands that Mommy and Daddy go to the office every morning. She knows I will be home in late afternoon. From time to time I've taken her to the office; she thrives on all the attention she gets from the clients as well as the staff. She definitely needs more attention as she grows.

Sometimes Natalie gets difficult, just when I am tired or in a hurry to go somewhere. I have a schedule to meet, so this can be a problem. I've learned the best thing is to stay as calm as possible at such crucial moments. It only makes things worse otherwise, and she cannot help it at times. On the other hand, those hugs and kisses when I get home mean so much. Sometimes I do feel like collapsing and Natalie goes all over me, talks to me, anything to get my attention—and that is okay too.

256

As she gets older I have to make more plans for Natalie. Since I have to go to work and therefore don't have all day to attend to her, organization and consistency are crucial.

Susan &

For many women, whether or not to work while their children are young is not open to debate. They must work to support or help support their families. For these women the problem is not whether but how to do it.

Others of us have the option of working or not working, and the financial impact of our decision varies from great to not much. If our basic needs are being met on some level by our husbands' incomes, the question becomes which way we think our children will be better off. The debate rages, and there may never be any definitive answer. I continue to debate with myself about this issue constantly.

A real problem that I have observed is that once we have made the decision about whether or not to work, we feel that we must defend this decision to the death. As a result everyone who has made a different decision is somehow wrong, bad, neglectful, or worse. Still, we feel the impact of other women's opinions. I have tried not to fall into this judgmental trap, although I have noticed a tendency to do so. I hope that one day women will stop criticizing each other and begin to work together toward increasing our options and helping each other feel good about our choices. I think that if we recognize the value of caring for children we can work at improving child care for those women who work and also recognize the important job of those who choose to stay at home with their children. Our interests are not so different. Don't we both want quality care for our children and a strong, positive feeling of self-worth?

I work part-time, and I continue to be torn between the two

worlds. I feel a strong need to be at home with my children. I think that they are better off not having me work full-time. And I know that I am better off experiencing firsthand the joy of observing my children grow and develop. Whether or not they would suffer long-term effects if I were working full-time I don't know, but I don't want to find out.

On the other hand, I feel a strong need to be in the work force. It has been very difficult for me to give up the financial independence that I have had for much of my adult life. Moreover, during the years before I had children I developed a deep-seated prejudice against housewifery. Before I had any experience on the subject I became convinced that being a stay-at-home mom was boring and demeaning. In fact, I find being Natasha's and Ariana's mom to be one of the most challenging, exciting, enjoyable things that I have ever done. But still I can't seem to overcome the panic I feel when I think about not working. So I attempt to be involved just enough to be able to say that I am working and to stay abreast of what is happening in my field so that I can return in the future.

When I am in my office I find that I am quite happy to be there. I fantasize about the day I will begin to spend more hours at work, and I can't imagine not working. But when I am away from the office I can't imagine why I'm working at all. I don't have the hours to spare! Then I'm not sure that I will ever want to return full-time. I am truly having fun being a mom.

I don't know when I will be ready to work more hours. Sure the girls will be in school all day before I know it, but all day for school does not mean all day for work! And what about summers and school holidays? I don't know the answer. I don't even know all of the questions. I've even thought about going back to nursing, where it would be much easier to work part-time and only part of the year. But it seems a shame to waste all that law school education. I haven't even paid back my student loans. Besides, I like being a lawyer.

I think that I will always feel torn between my many lives—the life of mother, of wife, of worker. Now that Ariana is here I am increasingly comfortable with my current situation—more than I was after the birth of Natasha.

When Dick and I decided to have children I thought that I would want to go right back to work on a full-time basis. I had no way of knowing the feelings I would have and the difficulty I would experience when I was away from my children for long periods of time (for me, a long period is anything over four hours). Nor did I know how happy I would be staying home with Natasha and, later, with Ariana. Dick wanted me to stay at home with Natasha for at least two years, and I agreed to try. Much to my amazement I made it through the first year with almost no difficulty at all.

Around the time that Natasha was one year old, I began to feel that it was time to consider going back to work. I didn't really want to be away from Natasha, I just felt that I should be working, at least part-time. Fortunately, my boss wanted me back and was willing to take me on my limited schedule. Perhaps because she has faith that one of these days I will return to the full-time work force, she has been extremely accepting of my very slow reentry. I don't think that she suspected the process would be quite this slow, but so far she has continued to be extremely patient and accepting. When I told her that I wanted to work part-time, we agreed that I would begin to develop a mediation practice. Our firm specializes in family law (divorce), and divorce mediation as a subspecialty is relatively new. Mediation is an alternative to divorce litigation, where the mediator meets with both husband and wife to assist them in working out their own settlement agreement. Because I work with the husband and wife rather than their lawyers or the court, I am able to control my schedule, making part-time work feasible.

Just about the time I got the mediation practice going, Ariana arrived and the tug of war between home and work began pulling me back home. I worked very little during Ariana's first year. I hope to gradually increase my hours of work as Ariana gets older, and perhaps the day will come when I will no longer feel so torn between work and home.

Chapter 18

CHILD CARE

- What our options were
- Selecting a care-giver or day-care center
- How to live with a live-in
- When care-givers discipline the children
- Letting baby-sitters drive the children
- Giving care-givers other tasks
- How our children felt about child care
- Compromises

Diana 🐾

Although much of my time is spent at home with the children, Yogi and I did and do frequently require the help of a baby-sitter or care-giver. So I tried a lot of different types of child care. Most of them were too expensive, too inconvenient, or hopelessly unreliable. Because San Francisco is in deficit when it comes to teenagers who are available for baby-sitting, we had little luck there. We don't have any grandmothers who live close by to call upon in an emergency or on the spur of the moment. Sometimes we would arrange for a sitter and then be too tired to go anywhere. Other times we would be in the mood to go somewhere and be frustrated because we were unable to get a baby-sitter. When a new baby-sitter came to the house all the time for instructions would often make us late for our engagement; even then we would worry that we had forgotten to tell her something. We finally opted to try a live-in baby-sitter with the hope that our baby-sitting problems would be over.

When we decided to explore live-in baby-sitters we realized that our house was perfectly suited for it with private quarters that were useless for any other purpose. We thought we would try having a student live with us in exchange for baby-sitting. This would allow us the flexibility to go out on the spur of the moment or on baby-sitter-competitive weekends, at the minimal cost of one extra mouth to feed.

It was nice to be able to teach the routines and schedules once and know that whenever we decided to go somewhere our sitter would be well versed. A live-in also provided a whole person who became a part of our family and was a consistently special person to the baby. She also was available to help when I was home. That gave Yogi and me the opportunity to have dinner at home without baby interruptions. Our live-in baby-sitters were able to assume a variety of tasks besides child care. I was able to read to or bathe the children while the dishes were being done. Errands could be run while I took Sosia or Benjamin to Child Observation class. Our various live-ins were happy because they were able to attend school or pursue hobbies without having to pay rent or worry about meals. Having a live-in has been the next best thing to having myself cloned. And the best part is that it was an expense equal to calling a baby-sitter only when we were going out.

Yogi was very happy with my choice to have live-in help with the children because it meant he could come home and whisk me off to impromptu dinners and have me all to himself after a tough day. It also allowed me to run the house more effectively. It saved a lot of wear and tear on all of us.

When Sosia was a newborn we found our first live-in. She was a student who was attending language school. Having a young adult move in on top of a new baby proved to be extremely stressful. We established a few guidelines that have proven to be helpful for all our live-ins since.

> We allow female visitors *only* and limit two per visit.
> Phone calls are okay during regular daylight hours.
> Friends may not ring doorbell after bedtime.
> Dates should be met outside the door only.
> Privacy on both sides strictly enforced.
> Public area is kitchen—available to everyone all the time.
> No going upstairs (to bedrooms) after Yogi came home.

We usually find the live-ins through previous live-ins or their friends. We check their references very carefully. There have been a few failures along the way when the sitter wanted more time off or fewer responsibilities or simply didn't like caring for children. On those occasions we have changed the baby-sitter as soon as possible. Firm, established guidelines and a respect for each side has proven to be a successful formula for our live-ins.

When the children were tiny the live-in was sometimes helpful simply to provide an extra lap or set of arms for one of the children. We established a schedule that was good for both of us during the day. The sitter could attend school or pursue her interests when she was free. Then I would arrange a few hours when she was expected to be working. Her working hours always included a few hours around dinnertime. She always had a Sunday and Monday off. Sunday was set aside for family activities without a baby-sitter. If a baby-sitter was needed during our sitter's time off, she could either work for more pay or I would get another sitter. I kept a list of people who were available to baby-sit for those moments. I also had a nearby home day-care facility that I used occasionally. The children loved to go there too.

Since my live-in baby-sitters were consistent, they were sometimes put in the position of providing discipline. We established several guidelines for them to adhere to. Time-outs were used by all of us. When one child was acting up they would be asked to leave the room for a specified amount of time (two minutes maximum) and to return when they felt that they could behave in a more acceptable manner. Fights were never to be refereed.

(Taking sides was too complicated and usually the younger one gets the benefit of the doubt—not always correctly.) We took the stand that no one was right or wrong in a fight and both fighters would have a time-out. (Surprisingly, being separated was real punishment for them and they would both try to shape up quickly so that they could play together again.)

Since my children were born there has always been a time during the day that is more stressful than the rest of the day. When they were babies it was right at dinner. When they were older it was late afternoon. Now it is right after they come home from school. I try always to be there at those times, and if possible have the live-in there also. It seems that the children will test limits at those times and I like to be the one who establishes the ground rules. Also, the baby-sitter has limited resources to draw on; she can get involved only to a certain degree. The baby-sitter is not allowed to use any harsh disciplinary styles. Doing so is grounds for immediate dismissal.

If the children are on a roll of bad behavior, we hold a meeting. This includes the child, the baby-sitter, and me. We discuss it from the child's point of view: why it is happening and what the child recommends should be done about it. The solutions that my kids have come up with are better than anything I could possibly have thought of. For instance, Sosia once suggested that a good punishment for her and Benjamin giving the baby-sitter too much trouble would be to stop them from watching the *Disney Sunday Movie* for two weeks (unless *Davy Crockett* was on, and then to let them watch that week in exchange for the next week). They felt good about that and they also shaped up. For them it was extremely strict punishment, and they had done it on their own. We are especially careful that the baby-sitters and the children show respect for each other. The baby-sitters may not be called names or treated poorly by the children. They are also not there to do the children's chores or to be the children's "servant." The baby-sitters may not treat the children with any disrespect, either. The live-ins often become so much like a younger sister to me and an older sister to the children that one reason we established the rules is so that they do not begin to act like brothers and sisters.

I found that it was too much of a bother to have my baby-sitters drive. I was afraid of their skill, afraid of them under the pressures of having children in the car, and I didn't want to give up my car to them. We found that since we live in the heart of San Francisco, public transportation was completely adequate for their needs. The children considered taking the bus one of life's great parties, the baby-sitter had a pleasant, safe way to travel, and the children loved it! When necessary I made myself available for transportation and always left taxicab numbers in case they were needed.

Although I originally began with the idea that the baby-sitter would do stimulating activities with the children, I found that often our expectations were vastly different. I felt that my children should be offered a variety of different activities. I provide different entertainment even when I am doing things around the house. Whenever possible I include my children in the different tasks, but I found the baby-sitter often just couldn't be bothered with letting them help her sweep the floor or do the dishes. Some baby-sitters just wanted to plant them in front of the television. (That was never allowed.) Some care-givers just don't have the motivation to encourage the child's interests. Sometimes they simply don't know how, and sometimes they just don't seem to think it is important. I found that if I wanted the children to be stimulated, it was up to me to arrange it. I would tell the baby-sitter to take down the children's toys, take the kids on outings, and play with them when they were in the park.

When I was instructing them I found it easiest to communicate with the baby-sitter through notes. My Household Information Book (see pages 266 and 267) contains all the emergency information, so my notes were for day-to-day occurrences and schedules. I also encouraged care-givers to write me notes about pertinent things (when the baby ate, eliminated, slept). That can be important information when two people are caring for the same children.

You can see that this is a lot more than you would usually tell a baby-sitter coming into the house for an evening. But I thought rather than write it all down every time we hired someone new, or when we had someone new taking charge for the evening, I'd do it once and do it completely. It gives me tremendous comfort to know that almost any type of emergency that could come up is covered. I expand and change it as our needs change. Now that my children are in school, for example, the book includes the names and addresses of their teachers and schools. When I see an article in a magazine that I feel is pertinent information on first aid, for example, I tuck it in the booklet. I also leave blank pages and pencils for phone messages and an envelope with emergency money in case the baby-sitter must take a taxi or buy supplies. I leave the house knowing that any information that my care-giver may need is at her fingertips and that unforeseen emergencies are covered even when I am not available.

Jan 🙢

I never dreamed that my children would come to mean so much to my life, my entire being. They *are* my life. But my life is also my career. If I couldn't be with my children all day, then I wanted them to at least be in their own home and with the best possible, most loving, kind, considerate, intelligent, resourceful "Mary Poppins" on the face of this earth.

Because my career necessitates travel, I have opted for live-in help. I have been lucky to have some wonderful care-givers. If you're looking, friends are your greatest resource, otherwise there are several nanny colleges around the country and agencies that deal strictly in child-care person placement.

It's not easy having someone live in your home and care for your children. My husband had a terrible time adjusting. After three years I think he's finally getting the hang of it. You do lose some of your privacy. You have to share your home, towels, dishes, food, car, and of course your children. But for my family, for now, this is the best answer.

The first care-giver I hired stayed a year, the second stayed three months, the third was with us for a year and a half, and we now have hired a fourth. Every time a care-giver opts to leave, I panic. I can't tell you how vulnerable I feel every time I need to look for a new care-giver. Will I find someone good? Can I find anyone at all? The answer is yes.

Diana's Household Information Book

The first section is a title page that lists who we are, where we are located, and our phone number. (Ever wonder if the baby-sitter remembers your phone number and address? Could she remember in case of an emergency?)

Our name: _____

Our address: _____

Our phone number: _____

The second section is for emergencies. I try to give it in the order of importance. It is clearly printed and highlighted in red.

IN CASE OF A PHYSICAL EMERGENCY CALL 911.

Fire: _____

Police: _____

Poison Control Hotline: _____

Children's doctor: _____

Ambulance: _____

Drugstore that delivers: _____

Drugstore that delivers at night: _____

First-aid kit located: _____

Earthquake box located: _____

Fire extinguisher located: _____

Father's office: _____ (Secretary's name) _____

Mother's office: _____

Other possible locations where I may be reached:

Closest neighbors: _____

Closest relatives: _____

Relatives living out of town: _____

_____

(This might include parents, brothers, and sisters.)

Other good friends: _____

_____

(This may consist of the names and addresses of friends who would respond to the needs of my children in case of something unforeseen.)

Other emergency phone numbers:

   Lawyer: _____ (include name and address and phone)

Insurance Companies:

   Household: _____ (name of agent and phone)
   Liability: _____ (name of agent and phone)

Veterinarian: _____ (include the name of the pet)

Other Emergency Information:

   Extra keys located: _____
   Security systems: _____
   Garage door opener: _____
     Garage door repair: _____
   Water shut-off valves located: _____
   Gas shut-off valve located: _____
   Circuit breaker (or fuse box) located: _____

Repair Service:

   Plumber: _____
   Appliances: _____

The third section contains day-to-day information about running the household.

Typical meals for the children: Any food allergies or food dislikes. Favorite recipes. Foods that are not allowed and marketing lists.

Activities: Those that are permitted and those that aren't. Children who may be visited without prior approval and children who may come over. (Include the names and phone numbers of the mothers and children.)

Special rules: Guidelines for television, games, or books; snacks for children; and what is off limits.

House rules: No food allowed outside the kitchen, etc.

Care-giver rules: No smoking, phone time limits, visitors, etc.

Our live-ins have needed to drive, cook, nurture, shop, and even wake in the wee hours for a cranky crying baby. It's not an easy job. But having the right person in your home, caring for your children, is crucial. It means relief. It means you can get on with your career. It means that life in general can move on. I tell each and every one of my care-givers how very important they are to me and how much I appreciate what they're doing. It can be a thankless job; you really don't get a lot of strokes from young children, let alone from tiny babies.

When it comes time to part I tell my children that so-and-so is going to another job but that she loves them and will definitely come back to visit. On the great advice from Diana, I had my children's pictures taken with their care-givers. We put the photographs in their rooms. You don't want your children to think that the person is leaving because of something they might have said or done.

I screen all applicants by phone first and give them a very realistic picture of what I expect. If I haven't scared them off and they are definitely interested, I invite them to my home for an interview. I tell all the applicants to look at other child-care situations, because I want to know that they choose to come to my home as much as I choose to invite them. I check references and I always conduct a second interview.

I always interview prospective care-givers with the children present. (This on the advice of Katherine.) You can see immediately how she relates to your children. Our first care-giver just loved babies. When she took Jaclyn in her arms you knew this woman could nurture and love. This was important for me when Jaclyn was a baby, but now that the children are three and one our needs have changed, although I still look for someone who can nurture. Our present care-giver brought to our interview an alphabet game she had made in nanny school, plus a book full of games and projects she had done with children. Jaclyn, who was acting up during the interview, was immediately taken with an activity at hand. So was I. We hired her.

Here's what I expect from a care-giver: First, her workweek begins at eight in the morning on Monday and ends at eight in the morning on Saturday (two days off). She is in charge of my children from the time they wake up to the time they go to sleep. (I didn't do this with the first several care-givers, who assumed they were through working the minute I came home from work. I let this go for two years and then got smarter. I realized I just couldn't do everything. I was pooped when I got home, worse later in the evening. These days I can *choose* to put the children to bed and read them stories; it works a lot better.)

In the past I told our care-giver that she was in charge of keeping the children's clothes washed and pressed. I did not say when. Often I found dirty clothes in hampers when I thought they should have been washed. I have learned to specify that the children's clothes are to be washed Monday, Wednesday, and Friday. This works. I have learned to be specific right from the start, at the time of hiring. Beds are to be made every day, toys put away before bedtime, and children must have their hair washed daily and teeth brushed twice daily. I have learned that care-givers are not mind readers—they don't know what you do or don't want until you tell them. I did feel somewhat shy at first about being so precise, but I have learned this works best.

I have also learned that as my children grow, the type of person I need changes. Our present care-giver *teaches* the children: Jenna her colors, Jaclyn the alphabet. She does all sorts of crafts—they make birthday cards, they make gifts (paper flowers), they make welcome-home signs when I'm gone. She takes them on nature walks around the neighborhood, picking leaves and flowers that are presented to me when I get home. They also pick wild blueberries and put them on their ice-cream for dessert. The children love her. I hope she never leaves me, except of course to get married and perhaps have a family of her own. Which I hope is a long way off.

As for age, I have had care-givers whose ages ranged from sixty to twenty-one. The woman who was sixty just didn't have the stamina to keep up with my toddlers (please, I'm not saying this for all people who are sixty, just the care-giver I hired). Our present care-giver is twenty-one, and initially I thought she was too young. After all, I was looking for someone to run my home and take care of my children when I would be on another continent for two weeks straight. But after checking references and talking to her about my concern as to her youth, I decided to hire her anyway. She is a wonder, with great energy and maturity beyond twenty-one years.

On the subject of discipline: Again, at the very beginning, I

269

explain our preference (warnings, no physical punishment, definitely use the corners of the house) and really have had no problems on discipline.

Some friends ask their care-givers to sign a contract (usually stating they will remain for at least a year), and although I don't think this is a bad idea, I just don't believe in doing it. I believe that if someone wants to leave, they will leave, contract or no contract. And I certainly wouldn't want anyone watching my children knowing they preferred to be elsewhere.

I also believe in making the care-giver part of the family. She is not the "hired help"—she is to be respected, praised, and definitely thanked for all that she does.

Katherine &

I was very reluctant to give the responsibility of caring for Deren, my first baby, to anyone other than my husband. I really needed some free time to go off by myself (to aerobics, lunch, or a movie), but I couldn't bring myself to leave him. I figured that nobody would be good enough to care for my precious baby. I had myself convinced and felt stuck.

Finally, after almost six months, our faithful housekeeper convinced me to leave him with her for a few hours. With her help, I gained confidence about being separated from Deren, although Jack and I would still plan outings and even dinners out that would include Deren accompanying us in his little portable traveling basket. I could really enjoy myself on these family adventures because I wouldn't become distracted worrying about Deren and phoning the housekeeper every half hour to check on him.

After Alexandra was born I was confident I could get good child-care helpers and I became much more clear about the personality qualities to look for in these people. I felt the helper

270

must have common sense, must authentically love to cuddle and play with children, and must have a sense of humor.

Jack and I decided to investigate live-in helpers who could also help with the housecleaning and meal preparation, since I was resuming my work on a part-time schedule and didn't want to send both children off to day care. We found that in the long run, a live-in helper would save both time and money. Jack and I were used to a lack of privacy anyway with two active children, so we decided one more person living in would make only a positive difference for us.

The first person I hired was overweight and quite young. I rationalized that she would be like a plump, good-natured older sister for the children. Wrong! She just sat around, miserable, and ate us out of a week's groceries in two days. I had a little better luck with the second girl we tried. Her problem was that she loved to dance until 2 A.M. and sleep until noon each day.

I began to feel discouraged, and asked my women friends for help. They told me about au pair girls, who usually come from Europe or South America to live in with American families in order to understand their language and customs. They function as members of the family and help with all facets of child-care duties. Success! We found a wonderful twenty-year-old from Sweden who enhanced our lives in many ways. When she left after a year we were sorry to lose her. Our next three au pairs were from France, and we had a marvelous time with them as well. We found out that au pairs usually stay for a one-year commitment and will frequently find a replacement for themselves when they are ready to leave.

When desperate, I have put an ad in our local newspaper under "Domestic Help Wanted." The ad simply states, "Energetic young woman needed for child-care and light housecleaning in exchange for small salary, room, and board." Usually I get ten to twenty responses to this ad and I set up personal interviews with the children present—so that I can see how they will relate to one another.

Another way to find good baby-sitters (live-in or -out) is to post notices on bulletin boards at the local colleges and universities in your area. Nursing and dental schools can also be good resources because many of these students are unable to find affordable housing and would be willing to trade some domestic

271

services for a convenient room and board situation with flexible hours so they can go to school.

The clearer I am with my helpers about their job assignments and my expectations, the more pleased I usually am with my helpers.

It's an enormous step to imagine inviting a stranger to move into your home and work for you. However, remember that you already brought a stranger (in the form of a baby) to come and share your life for the next fifty or so years. After you meet and get to know someone, he/she is no longer a stranger—that goes for child-care people as well. Some of the warmest, nicest people I have ever known have come to work for us!

Mary ❧

I work long hours, sometimes six days a week, so I could not think of anything other than live-in child care. In addition to allowing me to work flexible hours, this arrangement also lets Natalie stay in the same surroundings. I wanted Natalie to develop a recognition of the house we all live in and a feeling that it is also her house.

In the beginning my mother was with us, and she took care of Natalie for a month with so much love. My mom is a wonderful mother. I often wish I could be as good a mother as she is, but I also know my way will have to be a little different. Unfortunately my mom could not stay forever with us. When she had to go home we had a new challenge: to find a reliable au pair. I was a little panicked.

I find that an infant is the easiest to take care of as long as he or she is healthy. Little babies need only to be fed and changed regularly, otherwise they are cuddly and cute. It is not difficult for someone who loves babies to care for them well.

I talked to everyone, both friends and clients, for ideas about how they solved their child-care problems. We decided to get a European au pair. Since we all used to live in Holland, it would be nice to also expose Natalie to the Dutch language.

We asked my mother, who lived in Holland, to find a girl who was interested in learning what the American life-style is like and willing to exchange child care for a stay with us, being a part of the family plus a little compensation. Apparently there is much interest among the European girls in this type of opportunity. We have always been very lucky to find nice, honest girls. However, I have also heard some horror stories from friends and clients.

Unfortunately we live in a somewhat remote area, with no easy public transportation, and no evening entertainment except television. I had to make sure our live-ins met other young people so they could have some fun on the weekends. One of my Dutch girls used to take day tours every weekend to see Yosemite, Carmel, etc. She was very independent and had a ball while she was in the States. Unfortunately she could stay only six months.

We never allowed anyone to drive until Natalie was two years old and she needed to be driven to different classes. Driving a child around is a tremendous responsibility.

There was no guarantee that every time we got a new care-giver she would be perfect, no matter how many times we had interviewed her. Instinct was my best judgment. The qualities I needed in a care-giver when Natalie was an infant were different from those I looked for when she became over a year old. The most important qualification was that we needed someone who was happy and full of life. When Natalie became a toddler we learned that she was very active and always wanted to work on a project. Naturally we needed someone who had lots of patience to do that with her and have fun doing it.

When Natalie turned one year old we had a more mature lady live in. She was the mother of a little girl herself, whom she left behind in Indonesia. She was wonderful to her. She gave Natalie much affection and love and care. She was a mother to Natalie during the day and a friend of ours in the evening. She also took care of our house and cooked delicious meals for us. Giok Lie was a Chinese lady originally from Indonesia, just like me, and we had lots of unspoken understandings. Unfortunately she was able to stay with us for only about a year. We missed her terribly. We did not know how we could ever replace her.

We went through a couple of months of trial and error. We were desperate. We would take almost anyone, and some lasted only a week. Natalie was a little over two years old then and in the midst of being toilet trained. Well, so much for that. With no consistency and so many different people taking care of her, it was devastating. Then we settled on Carol, who is an American lady from Pennsylvania. Carol is able to drive, which is a big convenience for us, since she can take Natalie to school. Unfortunately she could stay for only seven months.

Child care is a topic that most of us working parents wish we didn't have to cope with. I wish my parents lived in the neighborhood so I could drop Natalie off at her grandparents' house while I am at work.

To have a live-in also means a lack of privacy. I always feel obligated to entertain them. I have to be able to trust her, and I have to be flexible enough to have another person in the house. It is important that she be happy with me, because she takes care of my most important possession, my little girl.

Fortunately, I don't have many problems with Natalie. Every time I had a new care-giver she started on the weekend while I was home. I introduced Natalie to her new baby-sitter, and I would show the care-giver all our daily routines in detail. Natalie does not have to adjust to a new routine; the new baby-sitter has to adjust to mine. Again consistency is my main rule. The people may change, but the surroundings and daily routine are the same.

Since I am hardly home during the day, I have to rely on my baby-sitter to discipline Natalie. However, when it comes to giving her a little punishment, I am strongly against it. Both Frank and I believe only we should do that, and no one else.

Susan 🙡

My child-care story is long and, as with those of most moms, one of considerable frustration. I've tried just about every type of child care I can think of—part-time, full-time with housekeeping, full-time without housekeeping, live-in, live-out, even day-care centers.

I'll start with the success story. Finding sitters for those evenings when Dick and I wanted to go out without our wonderful progeny has been a relatively easy task—not cheap, but what is these days? At first I didn't know where to begin. I wanted someone mature, so that I would feel comfortable, yet someone young at heart, so that Natasha would have fun. I also wanted someone with a car, not only for the convenience, but also in case of an emergency. I tried getting referrals from our friends who have children, but they either had live-in child care or relied on high school students who couldn't drive. With some reluctance, I called an agency, and it turned out to be perfect. The sitters they have provided have been superior. The agency's fee was high but justifiable: You pay for a one-time match, and thereafter it is acceptable to call the sitter directly. By using the agency periodically we have developed a list of reliable sitters and now rarely have to call the agency.

If Natasha didn't like a sitter, I wouldn't call her again. I want to know that the children are having a good time while I am away. There is enough guilt associated with being a mom; I don't need to feel guilty every time I walk out the door! At first I judged Natasha's opinions from her responses to the sitters when they arrived and when I left. Later she began to tell me her preferences. Now I usually ask who she would like me to call. Sometimes her opinions change overnight for no apparent reason. Jutta, for example, had been sitting for us off and on since

Natasha was about one year old and was a great favorite when suddenly one evening Natasha went absolutely crazy at the sight of her. I thought it was just because Natasha had been tired that day, so I tried again. She said she hated Jutta and ran from the room. Needless to say, I didn't call Jutta for a while. I never discovered what the problem was. Several months later we ran into Jutta on the street and Natasha greeted her like a long-lost friend. She is again one of Natasha's favorite baby-sitters and Natasha almost always gets excited when she hears Jutta is coming.

Finding good sitters to come during the day has been, with a few periods of reprieve, nothing but frustration. I've tried everything as my needs have changed, as the amount of money available to spend on child care has changed, and as I became totally frustrated. At first my choice was to have someone in our home part-time so that I could work for a while and have some freedom to do things such as exercise. I wanted someone in our home because I wanted Natasha to have one-on-one care in familiar surroundings. Also so I could be with Natasha every spare moment I had. This arrangement causes some problems for sitters (and thus problems finding sitters). When Mom leaves the children adjust and then relate with the sitter out of necessity. When Mom is at home, however, she is just too tempting for the kids. Why should they go to the sitter when Mom is in the other room? I don't mind if they come and check on me occasionally. That is one of the joys of working at home. But it takes a very good sitter to be able to judge when to allow this to happen and when to intervene and keep the kids away without their being terribly unhappy. The sitters that I've had accomplished this with varying degrees of success.

With a lot of reservations, I put an ad in the local newspaper looking for someone to work about fifteen to twenty hours per week. I got an amazingly good response. I automatically rejected those who admitted they would be short-term and women who wanted to bring their own children with them. I interviewed several applicants and hired Debbi, a young high school graduate who was undecided about college. She met my needs quite well and her hours were flexible. Unfortunately she decided rather quickly what she was going to do about college, and within two months she left for Oregon. Such a short stay was not to be the exception. During the first year of hiring regular sitters

I averaged one every two months. I stopped rejecting applicants who said it was to be a temporary job for them, since it became obvious that it was a temporary job whether the applicant and I admitted it or not.

Except for the obvious problems of the time involved in having to advertise, interview, and train new sitters, having sitters change regularly wasn't as bad as I thought. Fortunately, Natasha took to new people almost immediately and each new person brought something new and exciting to her life. She actually seemed to enjoy the variety. Some sitters were full of energy, some liked silliness, some were quiet but liked music or reading, and one in particular liked to dance. Natasha loved dancing and still does.

By this time I had gotten used to having a sitter available and liked the luxury. I thought that I might be able to find someone who would stay longer if I offered a full-time position. I did, and she did. We had a full-time sitter, Big Tasha (as opposed to little Natasha), for almost a year and a half. It was nice to be completely spontaneous again about my life. I could run or go to exercise class whenever the spirit moved me. I could go out shopping or have lunch with a friend on a moment's notice. I could get work done around the house whenever I was in the mood to do it. No more concerns about when the sitter would be there and whether or not her schedule fit with mine.

Big Tasha was there all day, five days a week. Since I spent a lot of time with Natasha, Big Tasha also helped with the laundry and keeping the house tidy. I even learned to let her do the errands so that I could have more time with Natasha. Tasha had a very quiet manner, which was very effective; she could get Natasha to do things that I could not (nap, for example). The first year that she was with us was wonderful. It was a pleasure to have her around. The only drawbacks—besides the expense— was having her there whether I needed her or not and finding things to keep her busy.

Then something happened. I don't know if Tasha got bored with the job or if she began to have problems in her personal life, but things changed. I refused to notice until things got so bad that they were intolerable. I had become dependent upon her and I didn't want to have to interrupt my comfort to find a new sitter. I wasn't sure that I could find someone as good as

Tasha had been in the past, and I was almost certain that I couldn't find someone as good for the same price. Still, she was obviously lying to us about a variety of things and I could no longer trust her. To make matters worse, she lied with such apparent ease that I began to wonder if I had misjudged her personality from the start. Could she have changed so much or did I just not see? I still wonder about my ability to judge people.

Next we tried an au pair. Although having someone live in is usually the least expensive way of getting full-time help, neither Dick nor I had wanted someone else living in our home—we value our privacy too much. But I knew of an au pair who was available and I was unexpectedly without help at a time when I had planned on having lots of help and when Ariana was only three months old. So we decided to give it a try. Diana seemed very nice and was willing to do the housekeeping as well as take care of the children. It sounded ideal to me. The problem was that she was young and beautiful and stayed out until the wee hours of the morning playing so that I felt guilty getting her out of bed in the morning to help. She didn't stay long enough for me to find out just how inconvenient her habits would be. After one week she left, giving us one day's notice. I was extremely disappointed, even though the situation had not been perfect. This convinced Dick more than ever that he didn't want live-in help. I still wish for it at times, although I'm not convinced that it is "the" answer.

When Diana left I tried using the agency to find sitters when I needed to be away during the day. The agency was great for evening sitters but very iffy during the day. They always found someone, but not always someone with whom I was comfortable.

When I could no longer stand the inconvenience of not having a regular baby-sitter I decided to forgive myself for whatever errors of judgment I had made with Big Tasha and began the search for another sitter. This time the response to my advertisement was not so good, so I hired a sitter with a fourteen-month-old daughter. For Ariana, it actually worked out well, since the babies got along great. As I'd suspected, however, there weren't enough hands to go around and Natasha was often left to fend for herself. She was old enough at the time that it wouldn't have been terrible except that she always came to me when she needed something. When the sitter was tending to her own child, Ariana would find her way into the room where I was working and try to help me with my typing. Needless to say, I didn't get a lot of work done at home. Still, there was someone there when I needed to go out, and I could get to my office on a regular basis. I was getting enough work done that I was willing to stay with it, but the job became too much for the sitter. So once again I was without a care-giver.

The ad went in the paper again. I was convinced I would never find another sitter when Natali answered the ad. She seemed to be everything I had ever hoped for and didn't blink when I quoted her the salary. She worked for one week and the following Monday called to tell us that she didn't want to work for us anymore. That was the end of that. This brings us almost to the present.

I had begun to go it alone again when Dick saw an advertisement for a new family day-care center in our neighborhood. When Natasha was a baby I had rejected the idea of a day-care center because I had wanted one-on-one care for her. Natasha is now in school three mornings each week and she can stay after school as late as 5:30 P.M., so child care for her isn't a problem anymore. When Ariana was about six months old I had looked into day care because I was desperate, but the only day-care centers I had found wouldn't take drop-ins. It was with little hope that I called this new center. Eureka! They take drop-ins and I like the two women who operate the center. I have left Ariana there a few times and it seems to be working out fairly well. I still would prefer someone coming into our home if I could find the right person, but Ariana seems to like the center. She never cries when I leave her there and she likes playing with the other children. So, until the next crisis, I have adequate child care.

Chapter **19**

TIME AWAY FROM BABY

- When we left our babies for the first time
- Learning to separate—both mother and child!
- The importance of private time
- Vacations—without the kids
- How we found time to be with our husbands
- Whether or not our husbands pressured us to take time away from the children
- How our children felt

Diana 🦢

I feel that I am a better mother and a more relaxed person if I allow a little time to meet the needs that I have. When I have been away from home for several days or when I have been writing at home, I need a day or two to rejuvenate myself.

I have also found that my life at home runs more smoothly if I set aside a day for errands and activities outside the house. If they are impossible to do with children, I use child care. During these days I plan to do my own activities as well, such as getting a haircut or having lunch with a friend. By blocking out one day a week I feel that I have established the time as mine. It helps me to plan my life with a little more control. I know what I will accomplish on which days. I know that the other days are set aside specifically for the children and their needs and activities. I can anticipate the whole week. There are days that I can stay in my Levi's all day, and others when I must dress up, but my life feels more controlled and I avoid the yo-yo sensation.

How much I go out socially depends on how much time I have spent away from the children. It also depends on how much I like and trust my baby-sitter and how much time she has already spent with the children during the day or week. What makes me choose to stay home and cancel social obligations depends on how the children are doing. If they are starved to spend time with Yogi and me, we stay home and spend time with them. If they are occupied with the baby-sitter on some project or some new interest, they really don't care if we go out.

Leaving the children too frequently can be a big struggle. Somewhere along the line you just have to strike a happy medium between social obligations and family obligations. It helps to eliminate unnecessary commitments.

I find I must set aside a little quiet time for just Yogi and me. Dinner after the little ones have gone to bed helps us have a conversation without interruptions.

Separation can be tougher on Mom than on the baby. At different points in a child's development he either waits by the door for the baby-sitter or cries as if his heart will break when she comes. At any age talking about it beforehand helps immensely, even if you feel that you are only talking to yourself, for it will help ease some of the stress. When your children get a little older dramatic play can help them get over their fears of being separated. My favorite tactic was to give Benjamin something precious to keep for me while I was away. Sometimes I would take off my watch and let Benjamin keep it for me when I was gone. In the morning he would bring it to me. This was very effective.

Leaving our children with a care-giver is just a natural part of parenting. Ninety percent of the time Sosia and Benjamin were happy five minutes after we walked out the door. No one can be there every minute, and baby-sitters are a normal part of life.

Even though I was often sad or felt guilty leaving them, I usually benefited tremendously from a little time away from them and the responsibility of parenting.

At one point Benjamin suddenly developed a terror of a particular baby-sitter. Every day he asked if Yogi and I were going out to dinner and begged us not to. Since it was not his typical behavior (I'm sure there *are* children who respond with fear when "Mary Poppins" baby-sits), I sat down and asked him about the problem. Since he was two years old the explanation took some time. He was finally able to communicate that the baby-sitter had told him that unless he was a good boy, Yogi and I would not come home. He was terrified. The baby-sitter got a job doing something else, and we found a fabulous care-giver to take her place. It took him a long time and an immense amount of reassurance from us to get over that fear.

We still go out frequently, sometimes just to take a walk around the neighborhood. Parenting is an important job, but we need a break now and then. We both benefit from some time away from parenting and sharing the responsibility with a kind caretaker is a happy solution for us.

Jan ≈

John and I went out to a small dinner party when Jaclyn was ten days old. I must admit, I felt good getting all dressed up, putting on some makeup, and going out just like a "big person." Of course I worried about the baby, but luckily my mother was taking care of her and I knew Jaclyn was in very confident and special hands. As it happened, she slept through it all, never missed us, and woke up way after we were home.

I really think time away from baby, if only a few hours, is necessary. You miss them when you're away, so you can love them extra hard when you return. The world does go on even though we new moms think it should stop awhile while we tend to baby.

People always ask me if I take my children on my work-related trips, and the answer is almost never. The travel schedule of a "road trip" is rough: 6 A.M. crew calls; flying at night, arriving in the morning; three hotels in ten days are tough enough on me—I wouldn't wish it on my children. In the ten years I have been working on my television show, my husband has traveled with me twice—once to Las Vegas and once to Japan. After the trip to Japan he said it would be a long while before he wanted to come along again.

I did say "almost" never because there is that chance that someday the opportunity would be right—and I'd love to take my kiddies with me. I miss them terribly when I'm on a trip. And always, the evening before a road trip, I never accept any social engagement. I need to spend the time explaining where I'm going, how long I'm going to be gone, and that Daddy and their care-giver will be here. Recently I bought Jaclyn a globe so she and Jenna can see the countries I visit and how far away they are. Of course Jaclyn thought San Francisco was awfully close to Mexico City on the map and felt I could walk!

And I must admit we are being more selective about accepting social engagements, mainly because I really much prefer being at home with my children. Perhaps because I work long hours, perhaps because I do have to travel, but I think it's simply because I enjoy spending time with them.

Katherine ❧

When Deren was born I wanted to be with him every minute. I was struck with wonder and awe at seeing such a tiny, well-formed creature. I didn't want to share him with anyone. Only a few special people, with the exception of Jack and my parents, were freely allowed to hold him. I was possessive and insisted that I wanted to be the primary person in his life. Perhaps I wanted to prove myself a good and competent mother. Perhaps I wanted to observe the positive influences my parenting would have on him. All I know is that Deren slept in his bassinet by our bed and accompanied us everywhere—to restaurants, movies, parties.

We left Deren for the first time when he was six months old. I remember we were attending a fancy dinner party and I felt a bit miserable missing him. I called home several times and he was sleeping.

After this first outing it became easier and easier for me to leave and take some much-needed time for myself. The biggest problem I faced was Deren's distress every time I left the room. Sometimes I would think, "I've created a 'monster'—he's too dependent on me and doesn't know anyone else!" I had very mixed feelings leaving him and it became more difficult when I went back to work part-time. He would fuss and cry nearly every time I told him I had to leave for work. I would sneak back and listen; fortunately the tears were for my benefit *only* and he would cheer up quickly.

I learned in the first year with Deren that although I was afraid he would change, grow, or reach a milestone while I was gone, a day or two either way didn't make any difference. I was there for each of his developmental performances (new teeth, sipping from a cup), and I cherished the experiences and the memories.

When Alexandra was born I was still supersensitive to Deren's emotional needs and how he would feel about having a new sister. I would spend as much time with him as possible because I felt he really needed my closeness and reassurance.

Jack would hold Alexandra a lot while I was with Deren. I would try to hold her privately, out of Deren's sight, so he wouldn't get so jealous. I let other people hold and cuddle Alexandra.

I discovered that Alexandra was extremely content as long as she was being held, and I didn't necessarily have to be the holder. What a revelation this was. She became used to the many people and helpers we had in the house. Of course I felt that she would save her biggest smile for her mother. I was enormously pleased.

Possibly because Alexandra has been exposed to many loving people, she is comfortable when I leave the room or tell her I'm off to work. She runs to me and says "A kiss! A kiss! A hug! A hug!" When we complete our ritual she goes happily back to playing. Deren really never got through his tears and "Don't go, Mommy" until he was nearly three.

My children have had very different personalities and attitudes since they were born—from the first minute, hours, days, and weeks! I don't think Deren or Alexandra would have been much more different if I had let Deren be with more people during his early years and if I had been the primary person around Alexandra.

I use my own intuition about how much or how little time to be with the children. I find it's very important to create time for myself to read a book, go for a walk, go to my favorite coffee house, shop, or go to the health club. This valuable time is precious because it can help reaffirm who you are—a separate identity from your baby.

Today the children are eight and four and life is wonderful! Last year Jack and I decided to accept an invitation to lead a seminar in Switzerland and take a minivacation in France and Italy with the trip. We planned this entire adventure for months. I was in heaven, dreaming of restaurants, shops, and sightseeing. It was to be our very first trip without the children. We were leaving them in excellent hands at my parents' home with our beloved live-in student helper.

The whole week before our trip I became sicker and sicker, sadder and sadder. I would cry and tell Jack that I was really questioning the trip. I thought about canceling it. Each day that passed brought me closer to doom. I felt that a death sentence was imposed on me, and each day brought me closer to the ominous end. I would brood every day, and when I tucked the children into bed at night I would look at their gorgeous angelic features and say to myself, "Why do I want to leave them? How could I?" Jack and my parents would reassure me that this would be a great trip and that the kids would be in excellent hands, but I resisted. I knew I didn't want to take them with us because five days of the trip was business and five days were pleasure. It would be a big schlepp putting them on a twelve-hour polar plane flight and driving for five to six hours at a stretch through Europe. I could barely stand driving for fifteen minutes with them in the backseat fighting.

I decided we would go through with this trip and that we'd come home early if we couldn't stand it. I cried and cried the entire night before we left. I kissed them and sobbed secretly inside. I could hardly bear to leave. We had made my brother Jamie the executor of our will, and my brother Mike and his wife, Jan, the guardians of the children if anything happened to us. Our life insurance was in order.

With a heavy heart I boarded our flight to Paris by way of New York. When the plane was somewhere over Chicago I began to lighten up quickly. Pretty soon I was elated. No responsibilities! Only pure joy and a magnificent well-earned vacation with my darling husband!

We squeezed hands and I cuddled into Jack's shoulder. He patted me on the head and smiled. We stayed the full ten days on our trip and I wanted to stay ten days more.

We phoned home every two days, and sometimes the children were too busy playing and having fun to even come to the phone for more than thirty seconds—if at all!

This vacation was wonderful and I can hardly wait to do it again!

Mary ᐓ

The first time I ever left Natalie was when I went back to work two months after she was born. Despite the feeling of guilt, it was very important for me to go back to work again. I made it up to Natalie by spending most of my time with her after work and on the weekends. I became a believer in "quality time." We hardly ever went out anymore, but we did not feel we needed to.

It was wonderful just to be home and play with our little girl.

When Natalie was almost one year old, we took her to visit my parents in Holland. Since it was actually a business trip for us, we left Natalie with her grandparents for two solid weeks. This was the first time we did not see each other daily. It was terrible, we missed her so much. Every time we saw a little girl, she reminded us of Natalie. We ended up buying too many presents for her, while Natalie was actually having a super time with her grandparents. She got so much attention—almost twenty-four hours a day! When we came back we were surprised that Natalie was able to take several steps on her own and looked so happy. But at first she did not want to turn to me. This brought tears to my eyes. It had been just two weeks, but it felt as if we had not seen each other for two years.

Since then I've left Natalie once a year for two to three weeks while going on business trips to Europe. There have also been several short trips where I had to leave her at home with a care-giver. All my trips have been mostly for business purposes. Otherwise, I spend my time with Natalie.

Frank was most supportive about all this. We were working together, so he understood that I couldn't be in two places at the same time.

Susan ❧

Today I find it is so important to have time away from my children that it is hard for me to remember when this wasn't so. But in fact, when Natasha was born and for about six months after, I didn't have any desire to be separated from her. Actually, I felt some reluctance every time I let other people hold her. I wanted her with me every moment of the day. I was quite surprised by this strong feeling of attachment. I was in absolute

287

awe of the whole miracle of life. I knew that the day would come when I would want to have some time away from her, but it was hard to imagine. Fortunately, she was an incredibly easy baby to take places, and that is exactly what I did. I took her everywhere with me. Even when Dick and I went out in the evening, we took Natasha with us. There were a few exceptions where we felt that it would really be inappropriate or just wouldn't work for one reason or another, and on those occasions we hired a sitter and left Natasha at home. She did fine, of course, and I managed reasonably well.

Dick felt much the same as I did. We both gradually wanted time away with increasing frequency. I think that Dick progressed a little more rapidly along this line, but not so much more quickly that it created problems.

When Natasha was about six months old it became increasingly difficult to cart her along. She slept less and was more mobile. It was then that I began the never-ending process of finding baby-sitters.

When I first began leaving Natasha with sitters during the day, it was because I wanted to go somewhere where it was difficult to take her along. I still didn't really experience a desire to be away from her. I don't remember when it was that I first felt that desire, but I must admit that I feel it fairly often now. There are times when I long for peace and quiet—just a weekend away by myself with nothing to do but sleep (oh, for some uninterrupted sleep) and read. I want to be *alone*! But I settle for a few hours away because I know that I would miss my girls soon after I left the house and missing them would spoil my fantasy weekend.

My need to be away from Natasha increased as she got older because as she got older she became more demanding of my time, noisier, and more difficult to deal with. Now she goes in and out of stages where she is particularly difficult. During these stages I feel the greatest need to have time away. Since I don't have family close enough to drop her off on short notice, I resort to hiring baby-sitters—thank goodness we can afford them!

When Ariana arrived I had already become accustomed to having sitters take care of my child, so it was not as hard letting go. Still, it was a gradual process. Also, the addition of a second child increased my need to get away. I find that being a mom is more than a full-time job; there is no time during the day or night that you are off duty. And with two children, the occasions when I can find a little time to myself without a baby-sitter are few.

It's difficult to find time at home to do things like pay bills, talk on the telephone, read, or do anything that requires undivided attention. Cleaning house or cooking are easier because they are physical activities and don't demand undivided attention; it's easy to find ways of including the children that they find exciting and fun. I try to do my quiet activities when they are asleep. The problem with this, of course, is that by the time they are asleep I am so exhausted that I have a hard time finding the energy to do anything. Also, this is the only time that Dick and I have together without the girls putting constant demands on us for our attention.

Dick and I are beginning to feel a need to be away from the girls for a weekend. I know that other parents leave their children for weekends and longer periods when they are very young. Sometimes I wish that I could do this, but I can't. I prefer to wait until a night or two away from us will be looked upon by Natasha and Ariana as an adventure rather than a problem. I think that Natasha was three years old, or nearly so, before I felt that leaving her overnight was a possibility. I suspect that Ariana will be ready sooner because she will have her big sister to keep her company. I don't know yet when Dick and I will have our weekend away, lounging in bed in the morning with the newspaper instead of two little munchkins, but I suspect that when it does happen we will both miss the girls very much.

20

EATING OUT WITH BABY

- Where to go
- What to bring
- How to ensure a happy restaurant experience
- Picnics
- Difficult experiences we have had
- What to order for baby

Diana ⚬⃕

There are times in a child's life when you can go out to eat, and there are times in a child's life when you definitely should not. I suppose that there are children who are wonderful additions to a dinner out at any point in their development, and I am sure that the reverse is true also.

Yogi and I loved to go out to dinner. One of our favorite activities was catching a nice coffee while watching the sunset— before our babies, that is. Like many of our solitary pursuits before children, this one, too, became a totally different matter after children. We became the fastest eaters in the world even as we constantly asked each other when Sosia was going to start crying, or whether she was wet, or had been fed. We soon discovered that eating out with a child is not relaxing. Since we really enjoyed a fine meal in a restaurant, we decided that we would hire a sitter and go out every Wednesday night.

On other occasions we would pack up baby and off we would go. "Packing up baby" may be a bit of an underestimation of what we actually did. We are talking here about Cheerios in little Tupperware containers, teething cookies with a little ribbon tied around them, little toys and little distractions galore. We became masters at inventing a thousand things to do with spoons and ice cubes. There were times when the meals were a joy and having the baby with us was a plus. Those times were few and far between, but they did happen. Success depended a lot on whether the baby was tired or needed some physical activity. It also depended on the restaurant. There are wonderful restaurants that cater to children; however, there are also restaurants that are not suitable for children, and we began to steer clear of them. Careful planning can save the day when eating out with the baby.

Jan ❧

Let me be honest. It is no picnic eating out with the kids. They *think* they are on a picnic, and the place *looks* like a picnic after they've eaten, but for Mom it was a meal she hardly remembers eating.

Eating out with baby is best when baby is very new and wants to sleep. We took Jaclyn to one of the nicer restaurants in San Francisco when she was two months old. My husband had an old friend visiting and wanted to entertain him with a view of the city. I called and checked to see if this particular restaurant allowed infants. They did. I asked for a corner table (just in case the little tyke wanted to exercise her lungs a bit), and Jaclyn sat in her own chair in her infant seat. I had nursed her before we left, and throughout the three-hour meal she never woke up! Hooray! We assured the waiter that she'd had a great time and had really enjoyed herself.

Since then Jaclyn has done whatever she can to impress the restaurant—throwing food, spilling the water, dropping the silverware, and generally letting us know that home looks awfully good. Every time I take the kids and have one of *those* experiences, I say never again. But of course "never" lasts only a few weeks. My mother always says, "How can you teach them how to behave at a restaurant if you don't teach them at a restaurant?" Does eighteen sound like a good age to start?

We do frequent the fast-food restaurants in our neighborhood. Somehow, because these places cater to kids, they seem to be more forgiving of these messy six-napkin-apiece diners.

There is a book called *Eating Out with the Kids in San Francisco and the Bay Area* written by Carole Terwilliger Meyers. It gives you everything from hints to picnic sites to the establishments that welcome toddlers. Perhaps if there isn't such a guide or book in your area, you could write one?

Katherine &

Since I really don't like to cook and my husband, Jack, calls me the world's worst cook, I needed to figure ways to take my baby out with me. I have a repertoire of three delightful luncheon spots where I can get delicious soups and sandwiches for less than four dollars. These cafes are very charming—the opposite of stuffy! The owners and staff truly love children and go out of their way to be helpful and sweet. Since these places are in the immediate neighborhood, I could stroll Deren and/or Alexandra there from their youngest ages, and I would plan their outings around lunches. This was a fine arrangement because there was a positive payoff for each child and me. Deren and Alexandra would have a nice walk outdoors with their mommy and were able to see lots of shops, people, cars, dogs, and activity along with way. I would have a terrific lunch that someone else had made for me and feel confident and content that I was doing some positive things for each child.

I especially appreciate my neighborhood after having babies because the joys and excitement of walking places with my children keep all of us in shape. I learned to keep my errands close by so that my life is more streamlined.

I found that when both children were babies a lunch outing would be the major occurrence of the day. It was exhausting to get each of them ready, me ready, and the stroller loaded up.

I would time my lunches to avoid the mad rushes of the usual diners at noontime. Because my babies are separated by three and a half years, there was only a short time during which I took them both. I would usually be taking only one of them, because after Deren turned three he was in a morning nursery school program. Taking one was infinitely easier than taking them both out.

Usually each child would get impatient and want to leave. I would order my cappuccino in a "to-go" cup so that I could leave on a moment's notice. One can feel so precarious when dining out with a small child. One minute everything is calm and peaceful; the next moment everything is falling apart.

I greatly appreciated the waitresses and busboys who were so understanding and pleasant to my children. I am also extra attentive to other mothers and small children when I see them on outings because I remember how vulnerable I would feel if other patrons gave me or the kids a critical look.

When we had only Deren, dining out was less complicated. Jack and I would frequent the ethnic restaurants that abound in San Francisco. We found that babies were welcome in Italian, Chinese, and Greek restaurants and that nice fusses would be made over them. Because we would take an infant travel basket, we could place Deren next to my chair without a problem. It seemed that the noisier the establishment, the more soundly

Deren would sleep. I loved these occasions of going out because I would get dressed, put on makeup, and fix my hair. I would feel like we were "stepping out" and Jack and I could have some good old-fashioned adult conversation, yet we didn't have to leave Deren home with a sitter.

After Alexandra came we didn't take the kids out for dinner anymore, only lunches. It's far easier to take both of them now that Deren has turned six. His manners have improved considerably and I can gently coax Alexandra through her lunch.

The little baby seat that hooks to the tabletop and collapses flat when not in use is quite portable and a good investment. Many high chairs in restaurants are dirty and unpleasant and the child doesn't feel like a part of the gathering. With this seat the baby is at table level and it's quite easy to keep his or her interest.

I love to take babies and children for picnics at the park. This is probably the most relaxing of all for me, especially if I pick up the food "to go" so I don't have to prepare it. Here we can all stretch out on a big blanket and the children are free to go running back and forth. They can check in and have a sip of juice and then be off again.

I have learned how to eat left-handed (I am right-handed), nursing one child, eating with my fingers, and bouncing another child on a knee—all with a big smile.

Mary 🐦

Having only one child, we did not feel constrained to stay home. If we went out, we always took Natalie along with us, unless it was for business purposes. We did stay away from fancy restaurants. Chinese restaurants and McDonalds are perfect. They are more family oriented and are flexible about almost anything, including messes or screams. Going to a fancy restaurant with a one-year-old or two-year-old can be disastrous if the toddler is not in a good mood, which you will never know.

We had one very embarrassing experience in Squaw Valley, which was not even our fault. We stayed at an inn that was supposed to have a wonderful restaurant that was not fancy. The owners were a young couple with young children. We had read about them in a magazine and thought it might be nice to go there. Well, the place was lovely, we got a very nice room, and we had a reservation in the dining room for 7 P.M. The innkeeper was aware we had Natalie with us. She was then a year and a half old. In fact, the innkeeper told us she would put us in a corner table just in case. When 7 P.M. arrived we were there promptly, but the table wasn't ready. Apparently the staff was using the table, so we waited for fifteen minutes. Natalie started to become fussy. Our waiter, once we got one, seemed to have never been exposed to children or babies. It took a long time for us to order dinner. Then he told us that if Natalie could not be controlled soon, we would have to leave, since she was disturbing everybody else. I certainly did not see any sign of it. Everyone looked at us with compassion rather than anger. We were still having only bread and butter when we decided to leave. I couldn't stand it anymore. I ran to our room and cried. To me it was a new humiliation, not just that Natalie did not behave well, but also that the waiter dared to treat us like that.

Since there is a baby boom again, it might not be a bad idea for some restaurants to reserve space for families with children. We as mothers feel guilty already when our babies cry—we don't need to go to a restaurant and be reminded of that over and over again.

Susan 🙚

For the first six months of Natasha's life she was the easiest baby in the world to take to a restaurant, and take her we did—often, and to every sort of restaurant. She had her first restaurant experience when she was seven days old. I had not been out of the house since her birth, and Dick, knowing that I needed to get out, took us to brunch. We weren't sure exactly how it would work with Natasha, but we were more than willing to try. This was our first experiment with carrying out our pact not to let a child interfere with our life-style—one that included lots of travel and lots of dining out.

It was amazingly simple. Natasha was awake when we entered the restaurant and looked around a bit, getting lots of oohs and ahs from the waitresses and patrons. Then she nursed a little and fell asleep. We put her down in her basket and she slept while Dick and I enjoyed a leisurely brunch. This scenario was repeated countless times during her first few months of life, not only at brunch but at many dinners too. We soon discovered a convenient portable bed that folded up to the size of a diaper bag for easy carrying. There are several of these on the market. The one I bought was relatively inexpensive, made by Gerber, and at that time it was available from the Penney's catalog. Occasionally, if we were eating breakfast or lunch out (which we did when we were traveling), Natasha would stay awake during the meal, but she never created a fuss and never caused Dick or me to enjoy our meal any less.

When making our reservations we let the maître d' know that we would be bringing an infant with us and asked for a table against the wall, preferably a corner table, so that we could put Natasha's bed down someplace out of the way. We felt it was only fair to warn the restaurant in case they objected. We never got even a note of reluctance—even from the formal restaurants, except from one extremely formal restaurant in New York. When Dick called for a reservation he made the usual request and warning. The maître d' hesitated and called for the owner who indicated that she had never had a baby in her restaurant. I probably would have taken the hint and gone somewhere else, but Dick assured her that Natasha would be no trouble and that no one would even know that she was there. They took our reservation. Naturally it was on that night that Natasha decided to fuss a bit before eating and going to sleep. She really wasn't making much noise, and the other patrons didn't seem to notice—and believe me, I was watching carefully. We got a few stern looks from the owner and one strong hint from the waiter that we should leave, but then Natasha conveniently fell asleep and never woke again until we were walking out of the door.

Not only was taking Natasha *not* a problem, but on several occasions it was a decided advantage. By giving the restaurant advance notice, they had time to arrange our seating away from the main crowd. On several occasions we were given lovely private rooms that otherwise would not have been available to us.

Occasionally, as we entered a fancy restaurant with Natasha in our arms, there were some skeptical looks from the other diners, but invariably as we left we were told how wonderful our child was and how she had not created any problems at all. Often people who had not seen us come in never knew that she was there until we were walking out. Then we got looks of amazement— they couldn't believe that a baby had been in the restaurant!

When dining out with Natasha I was very conscious of any noise she made. On those rare occasions when she cried I would always take her out of the restaurant until she was quiet. I felt that it was my responsibility to make sure that she did not disturb anyone else in the restaurant. I also felt that people should be tolerant of our bringing our child as long as she was not disturbing them.

After Natasha was six months old it gradually became more difficult to take her to restaurants. She liked to see what was going on around her and thus we weren't always able to get her right to sleep. We began leaving her more often with baby-sitters. When we were traveling we still often took her to the dining room with us, with varying degrees of success. When we

297

couldn't get her to sleep we took turns entertaining her so that she would be quiet. This definitely detracted from our dining experience, but it wasn't impossible and she still slept often enough that we felt it was worth risking.

By the time Natasha was nine months old, taking her out to dinner was almost always a problem. When we wanted to enjoy a quiet meal together or with friends, we hired a baby-sitter. In fact, from that point until she was about two I didn't want to be in a restaurant with Natasha. She was a terror. A happy, delightful terror, but a terror nonetheless. She babbled and chirped and squealed with delight. For me they were wonderful noises, but I was very concerned that other people eating their meals wouldn't feel the same. She also complained a lot if we didn't let her wander around the restaurant, and if we did let her down she would wander off and we would have to chase her. This, of course, turned into a game, and didn't leave much time for our meal. If Natasha ate anything, she did so extremely messily, leaving more food around her than in her. She absolutely refused to let anyone feed her, so we either had a mess or she didn't eat. When we were traveling during this phase of her life, we made sure that we ate in very informal restaurants or left her with sitters in the room. When we were forced to take her to restaurants during this period, I had to become a little less concerned about some of her noise and activity. I still took her out if she was fussing, but the other disturbances were minor and I learned to deal with them.

Sometime after Natasha was eighteen months old it again became easier to take her to restaurants. She wasn't quite so demanding and could sit quietly for short periods of time. I had gotten used to some noise and she was remarkably well behaved most of the time. Natasha has a charismatic air about her; people seem to enjoy her, and when we have taken her with us out to eat, we have received more positive comments than negative looks. It will never be as easy as it was those first six months—at least not for many years—but we have once again arrived at a time when she is fairly easy to take to a restaurant. In fact, Natasha is so much fun to be around that I would usually rather take her than leave her. She can eat without destroying the table and floor around her and she can sit still through almost an entire meal. She is absolutely no problem when we are someplace informal enough to allow her to wander around, which we let her do after she has eaten, or in between courses if it is to be a long meal. She enjoys going from table to table talking with other people, and for the most part the people she talks to seem to get a kick out of this very forward, jovial little girl coming to their table to entertain them.

We often meet Dick's parents for dinner and have found that Chinese restaurants are some of the best for this. The food is good and the people love children and are tolerant of their noise and mess.

We have never had a problem obtaining food in restaurants for Natasha. Before she could eat much solid food I would order cottage cheese and fruit for her, or cut up tiny bits of whatever we were eating and let her gum them. There was always something that she could eat, and if she was still hungry, she nursed. Now that she's three and a half, we seldom order anything special for her, we just give her a little bit of what we order. At dinner we may order an extra soup, and at breakfast perhaps an order of French toast or pancakes and fruit.

Ariana was more difficult during her first six months. She didn't nurse in public as easily and thus it was harder to get her to calm down and sleep in a restaurant. Now Ariana likes to eat so much that if you keep food in front of her she is happy and will, relatively quietly, stuff food in her mouth—and I mean stuff! She can't seem to get it in fast enough. Fancy restaurants are still out of the question, however, because for every bite that goes in, one goes on the table and another goes on the floor.

If you try, you will find a way to eat out with your child— unless you would rather not bother, which is okay too.

Chapter **21**

TRAVELING WITH BABY

- Shopping trips
- Short expeditions and day trips
- When you're going to be out late with baby
- Staying in hotels
- Plane travel
- Car travel
- What to pack when you leave the house
- Entertaining children while en route

Diana 🦆

The shock of having a baby wake me up in the middle of the night as though I simply did not need an ounce of sleep was nothing compared to the shock I experienced when I realized how long it routinely took to get out of the house with Sosia in tow. No more quick errands. No more traveling light. We're talking diapers, wipes, one change of clothes, a sweater in case it gets cold, a blanket in case the baby needs to sleep, sunscreen in case of sun, a pad in case the baby needs changing, a teething cookie in case the baby starts to teethe, a pacifier, Vaseline, socks, a burp cloth, a favorite toy, a bottle of sterile water in case the baby gets thirsty, a thing to hang in the car window in case the sun shines in the baby's eyes, and half of everything that the baby owns. That takes about five hours to pack. Then you get yourself dressed, and just as you are walking out the door you remember you should change and feed the baby. That takes approximately forty-five minutes. Then you are ready to go. Oops, Daddy will be coming home in five minutes—better put these errands off until tomorrow. No wonder new mothers get depressed. The whole day is spent just getting ready for the whole day!

After a few weeks of this grueling schedule I hit upon the bright idea of packing the bag for the baby the night before. I started leaving it packed all the time. That way, if I had to go somewhere, it was all there. Of course the baby's necessities change as the baby matures, and as the outings vary, so my little bag reflects those changes. The bag can be stored in the trunk of your car or by your front door. Now you are fairly mobile for short expeditions. Remember to change your perishables and you are all set.

I followed a simple guideline when I considered how long it would take to do something with the baby. What used to take an hour would now take two; what used to take two hours would now take four. Simple logic followed that I could accomplish roughly half of what I used to accomplish without a baby. To cut down on frustration, remember to allow for all sorts of surprises! Dirty diapers, baby's spitting up, and naps at unexpected (inconvenient) times. Almost anything is possible.

We changed our mode of long-distance travel when we had children. We felt committed to traveling with them rather than leaving them at home, which meant we did more trips with an emphasis on "family" activities. We camped out for the first time and loved it! It was complicated to pack for, but it was a wonderful way to enjoy our children without worrying about disturbing people in restaurants.

Taking babies along on long-distance trips requires a few preparations. Since diapers require a lot of space, I usually took along enough for one day and planned to buy the rest as needed at my destination. (I would check to be sure they were available if I was going to travel out of the country.)

We arranged for baby beds in hotel rooms. When we visited relatives we usually put the babies on folded blankets on the floor. They were very happy, and protected from falling. They could be in our room with us, we could watch over them when they woke up. (A good idea since babyproofing someone else's house is impossible.)

High chairs were usually available in restaurants. But eating while camping out proved to be a challenge! We purchased a simple little chair that folds up compactly and connects to the end of a table like a sling. The baby would sit at the table in it. I found it so convenient that I started carrying it in the trunk all the time, just in case. Now that the children are older, they are much easier to travel with. I gave them both a small bag for playing in the car and let them pack it with anything they can fit in. I supervise enough to be sure it includes water-soluble coloring pens (crayons melt in a hot car), plain paper pads, scissors, tape (leave the glue home), favorite tapes, books, and a deck of cards. We are able to draw, write, cut, play tic-tac-toe, and listen to music for hours with these simple supplies. Car travel does require a few tricks. We have found that rotating the people in the car on a regular basis is a lifesaver. Separating the children after lunch is a priority. Planning a midmorning breakfast helps break up the day and saves time on unnecessary pit stops. An early morning departure and an early evening arrival make driving pleasant. It gives everyone time to unwind after dinner. When we followed a few simple guidelines we were able to enjoy including the children on long happy journeys by car. They have been great times for our family to share.

We took a baby-sitter traveling with us once, but it felt as though we had ten children, not two. She insisted that her schedules and needs came first. We found that traveling with the children by ourselves was a lot more pleasant. We took suites when we stayed in hotels and were able to feed the children simple foods, then call for room service later for ourselves.

I have never used hotel-supplied sitters, but our trips were pleasant and enjoyable without them. Best of all, we got to enjoy our children.

Jan &

'Tis always better to overpack than fall short of diapers! For my first child I packed everything: two dozen diapers, extra clothes, bibs, socks, shoes, and lots of bottles. Somehow with the second child you relax more—diapers for sure, extra clothes only if you remember. Wherever I went, even on short trips to the market, hardware store, or shopping center, I always packed diapers. I fear the day I run short of diapers and one of my children decides to do you-know-what!

Besides diapers, I always packed bottles of juice. To shop in peace I provided lots of juice to pacify any potential crying child. Small hint: apple juice doesn't stain like grape juice, which is important if you want to continue shopping and the bottle has leaked onto your clothes.

Airplane travel can be a challenge. As a former flight attendant, I really thought I knew how to handle my kids on a flight. I took their own food, books, toys, and of course lots of diapers. Jaclyn still got bored on one of our trips to Hawaii. She was two and a half at the time and started to wander around the plane, but always came back. One time she didn't. She got lost. They announced during the movie that there was a lost child in the galley, would her parents please come forward? Most embarrassing.

Do take your own child's food if he or she is eating only baby food or drinking formula. I can't tell you how many disappointed parents I had on my flights when I was a flight attendant, not to mention hungry babies, when the parents found out the airlines did not supply baby food or formula. On two occasions I've given away extra formula while traveling because a parent forgot it or didn't bring enough. If you're on a five-hour flight, it will be even longer before you get to a market, and believe me, baby will be *very* hungry.

To heat up formula on a flight, have the attendant fill up the air-sickness bag (one third full is fine) with hot water. Put the bottle or jar of baby food in the bag, seal it up, and in a few minutes it's warm . . . even hot. I don't remember being taught this in flight school, it was something another flight attendant taught me, so you may have to suggest this to one of the attendants on the plane.

Take lots of diapers. Airlines don't supply these, either. Actually, at one time they did, but with cost-cutting measures, diapers got dumped.

If you are planning to make a major trip, let the airlines and airport agent know. They can give you seats on the plane that afford the most room for baby (or babies). Some planes have wonderful bassinets that you can put an infant in. On takeoff and landing, if you're holding an infant, be sure to strap *yourself* in and hold your infant. You do not strap yourself and baby together with the same seat belt. In an emergency your forward weight would surely put too much pressure on your tiny baby.

One last tip: The slim-line collapsible stroller can save your back . . . and arms and energy. I've strolled my baby up to the gate, into the plane, and practically onto the seat. The stroller can be stowed in one of the closets of the plane. Other times I've sent the stroller as luggage.

Up, up, and away . . . and good luck.

Katherine 🐦

Both of our babies have traveled in arms, baskets, strollers, car seats, taxis, buses, gondola cars at ski resorts, and airplanes. I believe that strollers are the easiest on the children, followed by short car trips in car seats where they can fall asleep. I don't know that traveling with children is ever very easy on parents.

For me, I feel continually on duty, trying to make sure the child is safe, comfortable, and not disturbing others too greatly. It's hard to relax when traveling with a child because a child by nature can be completely spontaneous and unpredictable. I'm not really clear when the child will laugh or cry. I put a lot of energy into amusing the baby so his or her mood will be mellow. It is extremely difficult to be in a car or airplane with a fussy baby.

Jack and I usually try to plan any travel trips around the baby's sleep time. This is great on all of us because no one's serenity is disturbed (including ours) and we have some special time to talk together while baby naps.

When we had just one child (Deren) we could travel places with relative ease because there was only one child's personality to work on. With two children it's been quite difficult. When one sleeps the other doesn't, and that one wakes up the sleeping one, and on and on.

Traveling with children also means taking lots of paraphernalia such as bottles, diapers, wipes, food, toys, clothes, strollers, and car seats. Jack and I've decided to curtail trips of any great distance until both children are older. We truly enjoy being home with them and doing activities close to home.

Recently we have been exploring more of the countryside with the children. If we are taking day trips, I pack snacks, books, crayons, and activity books and little pillows. We play road games such as Who Sees a Little Horse First? and How Many License Plates from Other States? The rewards from these trips are arriving in the mountains or at a fishing stream, swimming pool or a ski lodge. We'll drive to the ocean or to an abandoned gold-mining town. Jack and I love to introduce the children to new places.

Mary ❧

Frank is someone who will take the whole household along for just a weekend trip. Naturally he insists that the same be done for Natalie. Her little traveling bag is ready at all times. Whether it is for a trip to the supermarket or spending a day with grandparents, the same supply is ready.

At the beginning the bag was mostly filled with diapers, a squeeze bottle filled with water, tissue paper, wipes, and one extra set of clothes and pajamas. A friend of mine suggested a lunch-box-sized Igloo for taking food and bottles on day trips. It is very handy to carry other essentials too.

Our first travel experience was a trip to Los Angeles by car when Natalie was ten months old. Since it was a business trip, we left Natalie and our au pair at my cousin's house. We took everything from formula to rice cereal to jars of baby food along, plus plenty of clothes in the suitcase. We had more than enough for three days. It went very well; we all enjoyed the trip. Whenever we went out of town we took our au pair along, since she was like a part of the family. I have never had to use a baby-sitter service in a hotel. If that should be necessary, I'd prefer to leave Natalie and our live-in baby-sitter at home.

When Natalie was approaching one year old we took her to Holland for the first time to visit her grandparents. We had no idea what to expect. We took our usual bag with us, including several bottles of milk and jars of food. The plane left in the evening, but all seats were filled. Natalie traveled for free, but we did not have a seat for her. As she was sleeping on the seats, Frank and I were practically on the edge. Natalie slept almost all the way, but we were all stiff when we arrived.

On the way back the plane was empty and there were extra flight attendants, so Natalie got all kinds of attention. They were very nice to us and our little girl had a ball! We were lucky.

When Natalie was able to walk and participate in different activities, the contents of our bag changed. We now have more changes of clothes and underwear and socks and some toys. She manages to get herself dirty easier and I hate to see children in dirty clothes. Our laundry bill went up!

We've loved traveling with our daughter. However, on business trips we'd take her only if we could leave her with my parents or someone close to me who would not mind. Otherwise, she is better off staying at home.

Generally I think babies travel much better than we think. We, the adults, are mostly the ones who worry too much and are not flexible enough with the little inconveniences.

Try it. You'll be surprised how they can make your little trip an enjoyable one.

Susan 🐛

Getting out of the house can be a problem at times—at all times. It took me years to remember to plan extra time for all the problems that occur just as I'm about to leave the house. I keep a diaper bag packed, ready to go, at all times. Since I nursed both babies and didn't use baby food, keeping it packed was easy. I didn't need much. Just diapers, wipes, burp cloth, a change of clothes, plastic bag for dirty diapers, Vaseline, and the front pack. I kept the stroller in the car. When Natasha was an infant there was one more essential item that I wouldn't be caught dead without: the pacifier. It was so important, so easy to forget, and so easy to lose that I kept a large supply on hand at all times. I kept one in the car pinned to the car seat (not where she could reach it, but as a spare), one or two in the diaper bag, one pinned to the pack, and usually one in my pocket. Since they have gotten a little older I also take along pajamas and a toothbrush if we are going to be out past bedtime so they can go right from the car seat into bed. Just having the diaper bag packed does not solve all of the problems of course. It is still necessary to remember to take the diaper bag. With Natasha I almost never forgot. With Ariana I almost never remember. Being more relaxed with the second child is not necessarily good.

Inevitably, just as I am ready to walk out the door, something critical is needed. When Natasha was a baby she would need to nurse; later she needed to go to the bathroom. (It wouldn't matter that I had just asked her to go within the last fifteen minutes.) There is no way to predict how long it will take to get out of the house. The only sure thing is that no matter how much time you plan, you will need more.

Once out of the house, taking Natasha along wasn't much trouble at all until she was older and started causing a nuisance no matter where she was—at home or away from home. But even then she was usually somewhat better when we were out grocery shopping or running errands than she was at home. In terms of nap time, it didn't matter how long I was planning to be out (except that I had to pack extra diapers) because whenever and wherever Natasha was sleepy, she slept. With Ariana I tried to be home or at least in the car sometime near her nap time because she didn't sleep well except in her crib or in her car seat. Otherwise, she has been easy to take along.

With two children it is much more difficult to accomplish much while I am out. I spend more time trying to keep them from making too much noise, running away from me in a crowded store, taking things off of the shelves, asking for everything in sight, and less time accomplishing my goals.

Dick and I have traveled a great deal with both Natasha and Ariana. When we first traveled with Natasha she was four weeks old. We went to Florida for a week. It was easy. Natasha slept on the flight and never cried except once to let me know that she was hungry. We always made sure that she either nursed or sucked on a pacifier during takeoff and landing to avoid ear pain. It worked—she never complained.

When Natasha was three months old we decided to try a longer trip. We spent four weeks in Europe. Since we were going to be in a very small resort town much of the time, I was concerned that we would not be able to buy diapers, so I packed as many disposable diapers as I could without taking extra luggage. We had diapers everywhere. Then I packed enough cloth diapers to use in an emergency. All of this proved unnecessary. Even in the tiniest of towns in the most out-of-the-way places, disposable diapers were available. Now when we travel we take enough diapers for several days and buy more as we need them.

Many people think we are crazy to take our very young children with us on vacation. "How can you relax and enjoy yourself?" they ask in amazement. Well, *we* wonder about people who travel without their children. "How can you stand to be away from them so long?" we ask in amazement. I can't yet imagine the day when I will want to leave them for a long (more than three days) vacation. The amusing thing is that when some people first consider their children old enough to go along, we will probably consider ours old enough to leave.

We have found that traveling with children increases the problems a little, but increases the joy so much that the problems are overshadowed to the point of being almost forgotten. We travel a little differently now than we did B.C. (before children). For one thing, packing is much more difficult. I am packing for myself and two children. I have minimized the difficulty by keeping a list of the essentials so that I don't have to waste time trying to remember what I am forgetting. I adapt the list according to our plans. Here is my list. I hope it will be of some use to you.

table seat
portable crib
pack
blanket (*especially if there is a favorite*)
favorite toy
sugar-free desserts (*or other special dietary needs*)
diapers
wipes
bibs
special cup (*or bottles if you use them*)
breast pump (*and bottles and detergent to wash everything with*)
clothes
shoes and socks
jacket and/or sweater
pajamas
robe

slippers
books
travel kit (*I keep this packed and ready to go at all times—it makes overnights a breeze*)
    toothbrush
    toothpaste
    shampoo
    barrettes
    rubber bands
    night-light
    brush and comb
    fingernail clippers
medicine kit (*this is also kept packed and ready to throw into the suitcase*)
    thermometer
    Tylenol (*with dosage chart*)
    decongestant
    Band-Aids
    calamine lotion
    ipecac
sunscreen

By means of careful planning, we still take fewer suitcases for the four of us than most people take for two. We have a rule that if Dick and I can't carry it, it doesn't go.

To avoid missing flights due to the inevitable delays that children cause, we no longer rush to the airport at the last minute but plan to arrive well in advance of flight time. Rather than relaxing and reading during the flight, we spend our time keeping the children entertained so that they don't disturb the other passengers. Occasionally they both sleep at the same time and we can read a little, but I never plan to finish a novel during the flight. Keeping children entertained on an airplane where they are confined in such a small space can be difficult at best, but we have gotten quite good at it. During the young-toddler stage a cup of ice can keep them entertained for an unbelievably long time. You may end up slightly damp, but it's only water! As Natasha got a little older and was no longer fascinated with ice, I started bringing books and a little bag of toys (small animal figures, tiny cars, cards, and pencil and paper). It takes some creativity and lots of energy, but children can be kept entertained and thus relatively quiet and still. Now, especially on long flights, Natasha walks around the aircraft. She invariably attracts the attention of a flight attendant who misses her children (or just loves kids).

The most difficult part is keeping a toddler in your lap during takeoff and landing. Then after a child gets his own seat, it's difficult keeping him seated. Natasha is a pro. She buckles up on her own and watches for the "Fasten Seat Belt" sign to go out so that she can get up.

The flight itself is such a minor part of the trip that we don't consider the task of keeping our children entertained a major problem. In my opinion it is much less of a problem than dealing with bored children when traveling by car. Once you take off the kids can move around some in an airplane, but in the car they are confined to their car seats for the entire trip. When traveling by car it is difficult for us to travel long distances (more than three hours for us) once they get to the restless stage (about the time they started walking). When they are at their most restless, we found that the only way to drive even three hours was to plan the trip around nap time. We're still at that stage.

Once at your destination there are some things that cannot be done with children—unless, of course, you are lucky enough to be traveling with a baby-sitter (which has its own problems). Still, we have found that the things that cannot be done are few. It just takes a little more planning. You may need to plan some time in the room for naps, but isn't the idea of a vacation to relax?

Yes, we have made some changes in the way we travel, but we definitely do not enjoy it less. We enjoy it more. Watching children play, grow, and develop is some of the best entertainment in town, and when we are on vacation we have time to really watch the process. Plus, the process is enhanced by the children being in new environments, experiencing new things, and meeting new and different people. We see the places we visit through the eyes of our children. They see and ask questions about things that would otherwise escape us completely.

On seeing us traveling with Natasha and Ariana, people have commented from time to time "It's a shame they won't remember any of this." It's as if they are saying that the children don't

311

benefit if they won't remember the specific places and things we are seeing. I think this attitude couldn't be more incorrect. First of all, the children are learning from their experience, even if they aren't learning what an older child might learn. Every experience is a building block for the next. Even more important, they are enjoying themselves and we are enjoying ourselves watching them.

There is another decided advantage to traveling with children. They attract people. Almost everyone is attracted to children. It provides an easy opening for friendly conversation. And one of the most interesting aspects of travel is the people we meet.

Part Five

FAMILY CHANGES

Introduction ❧

And now you're a family. What does that mean? Personalities, changing relationships, finding time for sex, and some comments by dads are the subjects that comprise Part V.

In Chapter 22 we tell you about the different personalities of our children. You probably know them pretty well by now, but do you know how early they were who they are? We talk about how soon we saw certain personality traits and how much input we think we had on framing their personalities. What about the differences between boys and girls, first children and second?

In Chapter 23 we talk about relationships, about both the relationships our children have with family and friends and about how our relationships with others have changed as a result of the existence of our children. Has it been positive or has it created problems? Relationships do change—Mary has had the unfortunate experience of divorce. In this chapter she gives you some of her thoughts on the subject. How did having a young child affect her decision to divorce? What was it like for the child? For Mary?

In Chapter 24 we tell all about siblings. What did we do to prepare our children for their siblings? What types of problems did we experience with rivalry between the siblings and how soon did it manifest itself? Were we prepared by what we had read or were there surprises in store for us?

Chapter 25 is written by Averil, one of the authors of *Having a Baby* who was unable to contribute to the rest of this book. In this chapter she gives us some insight into what it is like to have twins—almost triplets. Zoe, her first child, is only thirteen months older than the twins.

If you're wondering whether or not there is sex after childbirth, read Chapter 26. How soon were we ready? Was it the same as before we had our kids? How did we find time for this once spontaneous activity?

Finally, in Chapter 27 the dads get their chance to add their comments. In their own words they tell you from their perspective what it is like to have children.

And then it is time to say farewell again. We hope that you have enjoyed sharing in our experiences and that perhaps we have given you some helpful hints. If nothing else, we hope that this book has given you some comfort knowing that you aren't alone. In Chapter 28 we tell you some of our best and worst moments, and then each of us says her own farewell.

Chapter 22

YOUR CHILD'S PERSONALITY

- Like Mom, like Dad—or neither?

- Recognizing your child's personality type

- Nature or nurture?

- Learning to live together

- Adjusting discipline to personality

- How we encourage "good" traits and build our children's strengths

- Dealing with bad tempers or thoughtlessness

- Boys versus girls

- The influence of school and other children on personality development

Diana ❦

My children showed their personalities distinctly in the first few days of their lives. However, since the physical limitations of a little baby almost eliminate his self-expression, the full impact of my children's personalities was felt during the first years. As they gained more physical abilities, the little ones were able to show more clearly who they were and I felt that I knew them better and better. But I never looked back and felt that somehow they had changed. It was almost like watching an artist at work: As time passed, the picture became clearer and more detailed. The children's personalities have intensified, and they will probably continue to get more distinct.

Sosia demanded my attention from the first day of her life. She resented her physical limitations and demanded that she be shown things. Benjamin seemed more adaptable. His demands were simple. Possibly second children get so much vicarious stimulation and unrequested attention that they don't need to be as demanding.

When I see Sosia or Benjamin get into trouble because of a personality trait, I try to show them how they can make things easier for themselves. For instance, when Benjamin launches into a problem without looking at it and then loses his temper because he can't control things, I try to show him ways to deal with the anger and hopefully avoid the frustration. When Sosia becomes fixed on accomplishing impossible goals, I try to help her ease up and become more varied. But the personality traits are there before we even recognize them. We just begin to see them more clearly as time passes.

As the children get older we are surprised (sometimes positively and sometimes negatively) at how some of our own personality traits come through in our children. Benjamin is sometimes so much like Yogi that it amazes us. Sosia is a little bit like me (she loves art) and a little bit like Yogi (she loves math). It is hard

318

to say whether these traits come from living together and mimicking us or whether they are inherited, but we definitely see them.

When disciplining I always take into consideration which child did something wrong. Sosia is strong and independent and takes strong words with a grain of salt. Benjamin can be shattered by a look or can sometimes simply ignore me. Most of the time he turns everything into a big joke.

Working all the personalities into one household feels like I am conducting a symphony! The differences and the similarities can be beautiful! Sometimes they're fun when we all act silly or playful. Other times the strong wills or different interests can clash. I suppose part of being a family is learning to deal with all the similarities and differences effectively. It will probably be a life-long pursuit for all of us. If I ever get it just right, I'll let you know!

Jan ॐ

Having a baby can shatter all your private theories of development. I had been pretty convinced that a child's personality is shaped by her or his environment. My husband and I were both surprised to see *personality* when Jaclyn was less than a day old. She was active, alert, and of course cried and fussed through the first night. Never having had a baby before, I thought this was normal. Jenna, my second daughter, was noticeably calmer and slept through the first night.

As a baby Jaclyn never wanted anyone to hold her hand, nor would she grab hold of anyone's finger. My husband tried to get Jaclyn to hold his finger when she was only a few hours old, and she refused. He tried when she was a day old, two days old, a week . . . and then gave up. He was a bit disappointed. Jenna immediately latched on to her daddy's finger.

Jaclyn is so much like her father in temperament that even he can see it clearly. She's got a quick temper that flares up quickly,

319

then calms down easily. She loves to be constantly busy and is easily bored. She's very independent and we like to think bright. In front of strangers she's reserved and observant; at home, full of the devil, with lots of energy. My mother-in-law says she is exactly like her daddy was. We have nicknamed her "Pumpkin."

We call Jenna "Sweet Pea" and her nickname couldn't be more apt. She smiles and laughs and loves to flirt with friends and relatives. She fusses only when she's tired or hungry. She seems to have a calmer disposition and long attention span and, again, we like to think she is very bright.

It is incredible to imagine such distinct personalities (at such a young age—from Day One, we like to say) from the same parents in the same environment. After some discussion and some thought, I've come to believe that the blueprint for each child's personality is imprinted before he or she is born. How we react to the children and their personality traits can be the deciding factors. I personally try to encourage Jaclyn's positive qualities and channel the positive use of her energies. I try to ignore her quick anger or speak softly to her when she screams. Her temper is not a trait I want to encourage.

I don't know how much influence we really have on the personalities of our children. I do believe we have direct influence in *shaping* their personalities. Wish me luck. I need it.

Katherine 🐛

The number one priority that I have in rearing my two children is infusing lots of hugs, touching, and authentic praise for them so they get a clear sense that they are loved and appreciated. Self-esteem is the foundation of a happy life, and I go to great lengths so each of my children realizes how important he or she is.

Our firstborn, Deren, is strong, independent, and fairly unaware of the many "trivial" things going on around him. He can easily forget to eat or go to the bathroom. Some days he'll button his shirt crookedly and become so engrossed in his Legos, the TV, a video game, a sport, a transformer toy, or a book that he won't hear people talking to him. Since he concentrates so deeply and intensely at times, he often does not hear my praise, feel my warm hugs, or respond to my jokes. He also doesn't hear me reprimand him unless I shout. However, once he realizes he is being criticized he turns on his tears easily, and then my concern is that I'm being too hard on him. Sometimes I fear that he will incorporate only the negative responses and not the positive. I have learned to make an extra effort so that he will hear me praising him and will feel my hugs and kisses.

When Deren was going through early babyhood, people would remark about how focused and intense he was. He would look so serious as he memorized our faces and expressions and listened to our conversations. He has had this same intense interest in action activities, outer space, and construction sets. He loves to analyze objects, take them apart, and try to put them back together. He has a delightful sense of humor and enjoys using expressions with double meanings.

Because his will is so strong (and mine is too!), he and I lock horns on many occasions with angry statements and bursts of tears on his part—and sometimes my part. I never knew I could get so angry at another human being! Sometimes I wouldn't believe how loud I was yelling or how much I would shake. I wondered whether I would have been able to handle these episodes at all if I hadn't had those long years of training as a psychotherapist. The main technique I would draw upon when I was at my explosion point was to create time-out! I clearly needed time away from this two-foot giant who was practically controlling my life. How did he know all my vulnerable "buttons" and how to push them? I would be incredulous with myself that I would let myself get worked up so quickly and passionately.

Deren and I continue to find ways to work out our differences. The bottom line is that we love each other deeply and want to work things out. We are both "natural" leaders with opposite ideas. When we are unable to compromise or work things out to our satisfaction, we will play "Ro Sham Bo." Deren told me the name. The game consists of making hand signs that represent a rock, scissors, and a piece of paper. We count to three and then show each other the signs. There's a clear winner because a rock can break scissors, scissors can cut paper, and a paper can wrap around a rock. Since we've come up with time-out, negotiations and "Ro Sham Bo," our lives have been more harmonious and we can enjoy each other more.

What I have found out is that children cultivate a reasoning ability from very early times and they also develop their own distinct personalities. I don't want to squash Deren's creativity and independence so we continually "make deals," which preserves both of our autonomous spirits. Our confrontations are invariably about who is in control.

Recently, Deren has gotten excited about earning money because money buys toys. I have been trying to teach him to budget and save his money so he can get a better toy at the store. He earns fifty cents a week by doing regular jobs around the house. I create extra jobs for him to earn more. Every little bit he makes he wants to spend immediately. He will also pull the "You said before . . ." or "You forgot to pay me before . . ." or some version of this so I will end up owing him more. We finally work it out accurately. I may end up still feeling some frustration and Deren will sometimes, without a word, run up to me with all sorts of hugs and kisses and tell me how much he loves me. My anger melts on the spot! He is so darling—a wonderful body, dimples, and blond hair. He smells so good, and when he directs his love toward me I feel like one of the most special, loved women in the world.

At night when we cuddle he'll ask me to scratch his back. In order to help him develop consideration for others, I will then ask him to scratch my back. In the beginning he was reluctant and gave me a five-second scratch and said, "My turn!" Now he is more aware that it gives me pleasure. He volunteers his back rubs at night, and since he recently started reading, he asks to read a good-night story to Alexandra and me.

Deren is very close to his father, Jack, and eagerly awaits his evening arrival from work. They laugh, play, roughhouse, and tickle. They play sports and ski together. His personality is unfolding gradually with each of us.

As parents we continue to set limits and establish what is fair. This is hard on Deren since some things are nonnegotiable and he wants to be the boss and run the show. I continue to tell him that someday when he grows up and leaves home, he can be his own boss and have as many toys as he wants to buy, eat ice cream and Oreo cookies every morning, and stay up all night if he wants. He smiles and lights up and says, "I'll watch the Playboy channel on TV too." I wink and smile and say, "Right!" My "someday when you grow up" speech is strangely reminiscent of what I heard from my parents.

Alexandra has a completely different personality from Deren's. If I give her a stern look and say "No Rice Krispies in bed," she will look scared and tiny. She'll immediately rush over to hug and cuddle in my lap, saying, "It's okay. It's okay." I start to question myself. "Did I look too firm? Was my voice too loud?" Alexandra is so sensitive, she practically reads my mind.

Alexandra is a calm, serene, affectionate child with a big smile and kind words for everyone. Compatibility is her trademark and her sensitivity seems never-ending. Because she is so busy relating to others and to her environment, she rarely becomes so fully absorbed in other activities (*Sesame Street* on TV is an exception) that she ignores her surroundings. She is an amazingly easy, happy child to talk to, play with, and negotiate with. The biggest problem in her personality is her lovingness. She'll crawl into Jack's or my lap frequently and give unlimited kisses and hugs. Deren, by contrast, will give his hugs and kisses while he's on the run. He's usually in a hurry to find his GI Joe, X-Wing Fighter, or a pen so he can draw a maze. Deren is "out there" and Alexandra is "present." Could this be an innate difference between boys and girls? I'm thrilled to have one of each sex. They teach me so much!

It's tremendously exciting for us to have these two children with such different personalities sharing our lives. We marvel at how wonderfully they relate to each other and to us. I am quite demonstrative and truly enjoy giving them hugs and kisses (even when Deren doesn't notice).

The major reason I had kids was to cuddle with them, tickle them, and love them. They have provided instant sources of intimacy in our busy, frenetic lives of hectic schedules and impending deadlines. They allow us to take breaks from ourselves and to stop being so caught up in the unimportant parts of life. With them we provide ourselves with refreshing opportunities to get out of our "hurry up" selves.

Mary 🍃

I believe that each child is born with a certain character and that we as parents play a very important role in helping our child's character develop into a distinctive personality.

I remember very clearly that Natalie's first two months were a getting-to-know-each-other time. Her needs were simple and routine, but Frank and I had to get used to that. Slowly she developed more alertness and we responded to her more. It was obvious how important it was to her how we responded about everything. We became her role model.

School has had a dramatic influence on Natalie's personality. As an only child she did not have enough interaction with other children. Basically she did not know what to do with other kids, even though she knew there were others in her age group. She has grown more confident and spontaneous. Since personally I've always been rather shy, I did not want her to be like me in that respect.

Natalie is a child who loves to receive and give affection, and she hates to be alone. This is the only insecurity of hers that I'll still need some help with in the next couple of years.

She is definitely a little girl. She has developed quite a vanity about her looks, what she wants to wear, and what type of hairdo to go with it. Now that she is three and a half years old, she has become like a little friend to me.

Since that Frank and I are going through a divorce, communicating with Natalie is very important. I tell her as much as her little mind can handle and also tell her it is okay for her to tell me what she thinks. She has matured quite a bit just in the last couple of months.

Fortunately, Natalie has always been a happy child who loves life. She has handled many changes in our family, such as baby-sitters changing and Daddy leaving, like temporary life disturbances. Life must go on.

As she grows older Natalie's life will become more complicated. I want her to learn now in a simple way that life is full of fun and games, but that we need some challenges at times, and that whatever the challenge may be, the reward is always worthwhile.

To respect what Natalie needs is a very important part of our communication. I believe that good communication will help her grow to be a happy person with a strong personality that will help her endure any life disturbances she may experience.

Susan ❧

My conclusions about a child's personality are simple. Each child has a very different, distinct personality; it is set from the moment of birth (probably conception); there isn't anything that a parent can do to change that personality; and if you try, rather than working with the particular personality, you're in for big trouble!

That all sounds pretty dogmatic, doesn't it? Well, before I had children I would have been much more equivocal. I once thought that behavior modification could be personality modification and that a parent had a large impact on what their child's ultimate personality was like. Natasha has changed all that. I still believe in behavior modification, but behavioral and emotional *tendencies* are apparent from birth.

When Natasha was born she had a delightfully mischievous look in her face that seemed to say, "Look out world, here I come!" She was so alert and ready to take everything in. It was as if she just couldn't begin to experience, and affect, the world around her soon enough. That eagerness in her eyes was just the beginning! So far, everything she has done has substantiated our belief that we have a ball of fire on our hands.

As an infant Natasha's bright eyes and big smile captivated the attention of almost everyone around her. It was as if she was showing off, even then. Now she still loves an audience. She still loves to show off, although now, at age three, she does sometimes exhibit a little shyness when someone asks her to perform. Left to her own devices, however, she will find a way to become the center of attention.

From a very early age, Natasha exhibited signs of being independent. She has a mind of her own, but it goes beyond that. Throughout her infancy and babyhood, she was never clingy. Anyone could hold her and she never minded if I left the room, just as long as someone was there to play with her. Natasha does not take no for an answer very easily. As I've mentioned, she started throwing tantrums at sixteen months, and still has difficulty accepting the fact that she cannot always have her own way. Fortunately, we are now often able to reason with her.

Natasha smiled and laughed early and has kept on smiling and laughing in the same infectious way. I can't imagine a more cheerful, fun-loving child. She has a delightful sense of humor and loves teasing people. When she was sixteen months old we were at the beach with her godparents. I was dozing while Dick and Natasha went for a walk. On their walk they found a doll's arm, which was slightly smaller and paler than Natasha's. They took Natasha's arm out of her shirt and put in the doll's arm, then came to me and woke me up. Naturally I panicked for an instant and Natasha and Dick laughed uproariously. Natasha had played along quite well, and now that she knew how it worked she put the arm back in her shirt and went off to play the joke on her godparents.

Her personality develops more as time goes on, but the basic tendencies were apparent remarkably early, and there is a remarkable consistency. Parents and others do have an impact on a child, but I believe that we either enhance and strengthen a personality the child has or do a great deal of damage by trying to change or disregard it.

When Natasha was about a year old I read a book called *Your Child Is a Person,* by Chess, Thomas, and Birch. It was wonderfully supportive of my beliefs. They gave examples to illustrate that working with a child's personality is the most effective method of dealing with a child. I don't agree with all of their opinions and conclusions, but I feel that their basic premise and many of their examples were very helpful.

Ariana arrived with an entirely different personality. She is much calmer and less manipulative. She has an adorable smile, but it doesn't have the devilishness that Natasha's smile had, and she doesn't have the fire under her that Natasha did. Ariana is sweet and affectionate. She plays well by herself.

In reading what I have written I feel as if something is missing. Labels are only generalizations. My children's personalities are so complex, so complete, so unique, so wonderful, yet oh so different. Thank goodness!

Chapter 23

CHANGING RELATIONSHIPS

- How we as parents relate to our children, and how those relationships change
- When children prefer one parent over another
- Fathers caring for babies
- Cultivating relationships with grandparents, cousins, and other relatives
- How our relationships with our own parents have changed
- Relationships outside the family that are important to our children
- Changes within the marriage
- Divorce

Diana 🙶

The relationships within our family have been changing constantly since the children were born. When they were tiny they were definitely all mine. When Yogi approached they would look at him with caution and sometimes even shun him. This made both Yogi and me feel terrible!

But as they grew all that changed! I often have to fight for some time with them. At one point or another both Sosia and Benjamin have been only Daddy's children. On one occasion after we had taken care of some basics—haircuts, cleaning up rooms, household chores, etc.—Sosia looked up at me pleadingly and asked, "When is Daddy coming home so we can have some fun?" On other occasions they both fight to sit next to me in restaurants. Perhaps when they were younger and more dependent on me, Dad played a lesser role in their needs. Time changes relationships dramatically.

Fathers can care for children as well as mothers can. Yogi loved to do the cooking. However, changing diapers or getting involved in "dirty work" was something that he felt I was better at. For the children there is a certain comfort that comes from the familiar and repetitive aspect of one parent handling everyday care, but a change in routine need not be disastrous. One ingenious father I know was caring for his new baby while his wife was working. He had been trying for several hours with no success to get the baby to sleep. It finally dawned on him that she was missing something about her mother, so he went to his wife's closet and got the robe that she wore when she nursed. He draped it over his shoulder and his baby fell sleep in moments. The baby had arms that loved her; she just missed Mom's smell.

My children came most frequently to me with their little bumps and bruises, but after they had seen Dad do the medical dressing on something more serious, the tiniest little bump became a big exchange between Sosia or Benjamin and Yogi.

At times the children have depended on me totally; other times they have depended on Yogi 100 percent. They may look to us at different times for different things. They seek us out for our experience in different areas. Dad handles blocks and trucks, Mom is a pro at water play and finger paints.

The biggest change we experienced in relationships around our house was between Yogi and me. We had only fully considered what parenting meant about the same time we became parents! After we had children we became much more team-oriented. Although Yogi may have shied from diapering, he certainly took a serious interest in being a good daddy. We found a bond building between us that had not been there before. A united front with a mutual goal. We began forming a unit of concern for our children. I saw Yogi in a new light. Now he was a man who shared all his talents with us. I never knew he loved to fly kites. He plays "Fish" like a pro! I gained a new respect for his desire to make our lives more comfortable, secure, and stable. We changed from a couple who really enjoyed fine dining and quiet evenings to a couple of parents who also enjoyed watching long performances of break dancing and serious attempts at juggling. We changed from a couple to a very happy family. Some of the changes were tougher than others, but growth always follows challenges, and I have certainly gained a new awe and a rich respect for the man I fell in love with. He is a great husband. And he is a fantastic daddy!

My friendships with other women have taken on new meaning. I realize now how important it is to have extended families. Our play group became our extended family. We check in on each other when there is sickness in the household. We visit each other as new mothers with a picnic basket lunch and we listen to every detail of the birth and the confusing feelings that follow. I have found that I have needed other women to share ideas and experiences with. The cooperation, concern, and understanding have made the friendships much deeper.

Grandparents are special. Their calm attitudes and wonderful surprises fill the children with comfort and joy. Sosia and Benjamin enjoy the stories they tell of their parents back then. They are ever curious about how all the people connect. "Who was your sister and your brother?" "Who was oldest?" "Which room did you sleep in?" We cultivate the relationships with the grandparents carefully and we see them as frequently as possible.

Having my own children has given me a new respect and love for my own parents. I know firsthand the kind of devotion they poured into my life. I often look to them for advice, comfort, and supplemental care. I often find myself stopping to ponder how much I appreciate a particular little thing my parents did for me. I find that something I have done with my own children will trigger a long-lost memory. Mom and Dad, thanks for giving me patience when I needed it most. Thanks for teaching me how to laugh at myself. Thanks for teaching me how to parent. Thanks for being my parents.

Jan &

A radio station in Hawaii once ran a contest asking where the safest place in the world was. The answer: a mother's lap. My husband is a wonderful, loving father who gives (as I've said before) the greatest horsey rides. But the nurturing, the terminal worrying, and, often, leniency come from me. Are these the reasons why, when the children are sick, or tired, or simply need to be comforted, they want me? I don't know. But there is something so wonderful about being able to comfort a hurt child. It is fulfillment like nothing I have felt. Of course there are times—say, at three in the morning—when I wish they preferred their dad more, and called out for *him* to get them a drink of water, or take them to the bathroom, or get the monsters out of the room.

One special thing has happened to me since I've had children. I so appreciate my parents. They are great baby-sitters when they come to town, but more important, can you imagine what they went through to raise us? I also find myself imparting the values my parents taught me. And, heaven forbid, I find myself sounding just like my mother! She certainly was wise and kind . . . and still is.

Recently I told my mother some of the things she told me while growing up that I'm now telling my own children. ("Try your best, that's all I ask." "Don't be upset, it was an *accident*, it was not done intentionally." "If you have nothing nice to say about someone, don't say it at all.") She told me she had heard them from her own mother.

I have often said that I have officially joined the boring parents club. I remember thinking B.K. (Before Kids) how boring it was to hear other parents talk about their son's soccer game or their daughter's skating lessons. And I remember thinking, "If I ever have children, I am *never* going to talk about the mundane things my kids ware doing." Well, if you're like me A.K. (After Kids), welcome to the club!

I love to talk about kids . . . mine especially! I don't want to bore anybody, or you, but it is *important* to me to find out about potty training techniques; about swimming lessons (and if the kids can swim across the pool); and yes, even about skating lessons, because Jaclyn loves to ice-skate!

I have also found that in the last few years we have become closer friends and even made new friends with people who are parents. I can especially relate to parents who happen to have children about the same age as mine. There's something very "clubby" and warm knowing that we are all having similar triumphs and trysts with our toddlers. I am not reluctant to talk to another parent at a cocktail party about taking a child off the bottle, but I'd have trouble chatting with someone who had no idea what a bottle looks like. I'm not saying I have totally given up on world hunger, peace, and the general state of the economy. I love to talk politics, travel, devaluation of the dollar, terrorist tactics, movies, cajun cuisine, job security or lack of it, and designer hosiery. But I absolutely relish talking about babies!

I had often heard that children do change your life. I now know how much they change it—but for the better. I am often accused of being on a personal campaign here at my office telling everyone they should have children. If the verdict came in guilty, I would never appeal it.

But I have noticed that having children does mean (at least with me) spending less time with my husband. Call it the exhaustion factor, call it more bodies in the house, call it what you will—but we both have had to make an extra effort in our relationship. It seems easier to talk about what the children have done during the day . . . what funny things they have said or done. Before we had talked about each other's day—the decisions, the difficulties, the plans.

Perhaps my not readily sensing the needs of my husband (and he not sensing mine) has led to our disagreements—some pretty big fights. And I know a lot of it stems from not communicating . . . and perhaps not feeding each other the proper "food": support, solace, and strokes.

We are trying. We have gone out on "dates." Out to dinner by *ourselves*, no friends or relatives ever on dates. I love our dates. We often are the last to leave the restaurant. We talk about our jobs, frustrations at work, goals, ideas, finances (ours), and bosses (mine). And yes, we even talk about our babies. We both agree we need to go out on more dates.

And we have taken two trips without the children. We went to London for eight days this past summer. And I must admit, I did wonder if we would bore each other to death, being constantly together. Instead, we were like two college kids, staying up late, eating whenever we wanted, and traveling the countryside by train. In other words, we had a great time! We also went on an "adult retreat" with another couple (also parents) to New Orleans for five days. It felt like we were four college seniors celebrating after finals! We stayed up late, slept in, shopped all day, and devoured raw oysters.

I missed my babies each time I was gone. I called home every day. I set up their pictures in the hotel room. But it was so nice just being with John. It reinforced for me the pair we were before children—and it just felt comfortable, familiar, and real good! We do plan to take more trips together. And the best part of these "retreats" is that I didn't feel any guilt. Not planning them, being on them, and returning home. The trips were too much fun.

I don't want to give you the impression that everything is coming up roses at my home. Because, as you know, roses have thorns. And I have felt them many times. Having children and taking on the obvious responsibilities of raising them adds to your financial and emotional burdens. My husband is not exactly thrilled that we pay almost two thousand dollars a year for preschool for Jaclyn. He looks at me with disbelief to see a bill for shoes costing $29 for each of the children. I, on the other hand, believe in the school (and I think he does, too, albeit with dollar signs) and not only liked the shoes for the children, but knew they needed them.

I know our priorities for our children are not always in agreement. (Aside from safety, well-being, and health.) I remember fantasizing once about how great it would be to move into a great big house with other mothers and children, raise the kids— and when they are eighteen invite our husbands in. But then whenever I have this fantasy (usually after some disagreement) I try to plan another "adult retreat" and work on picking those thorns off the rose stem.

Katherine 🐦

After I had Deren I felt an immediate bonding with him and Jack. I also experienced a deep closeness to my own parents, especially my mother, because I felt for the first time what she must have gone through when she gave birth to me. I loved her and respected her very much at that moment. I suddenly felt tremendous closeness, intimacy, and the sense of full responsibility that goes with being a parent.

I was so proud of my parents, and I become more so each day that I raise my children because as I expend tremendous time, energy, and love; I know they did the same for me. I can forgive them their shortcomings and the times they "blew it" for me and my brothers. I have taken on an enormous feeling that transcends the petty day-to-day concerns that go along with rearing children. I feel that I belong to an international organization of parents whose motto is "We're not perfect—we're only doing the best job we can, and often it isn't good enough." I had no idea how difficult it would be to raise children! They're independent from an early age and often don't want to cooperate, or feel empathy, or do what the parents want them to do. Knowing these things as a new parent has brought me much closer to my own parents in respect and love.

When Deren was born it seemed like he only wanted his mommy. He was fascinated by his daddy, who would make funny faces and throw him up in the air. He would go to the grandparents and Uncle Jamie for brief times. Yet he was most content in his mommy's arms and it seemed that for the first three months he wanted to nurse around the clock. We were rarely separated.

Both children went through daddy phases at about age three. They wanted their daddy to be home to play with them and roughhouse. Daddy became the focus of the family. Thank goodness this phase happened, because it's easy for daddies to feel left out when all the child wants is his or her mommy!

The children love visiting their grandparents, yet it is clear that their relationships with Jack and me are the most important. They continually seek us out no matter what they are doing.

Deren has formed a deep relationship with Minnie, the eighty-year-old nanny who was his first baby-sitter. She regularly visits us and spends the night. She calls him and he phones her every day. He loves her intensely.

I'm pleased that both children are sociable and enjoy being around people of all ages. I would rather that each child remain people-oriented and well liked by others than get straight A's in school. I make sure that they are aware of the needs and feelings of others. Frequently this has been a hard path for Deren, who concentrates on his wants and can easily forget about others. However, my efforts continue to bring him around and this has a beneficial effect on his relationships with his friends. He gets better and better at taking turns and giving praise.

I feel very fortunate to have married Jack and have him as the father of our children as well as my husband. He is not jealous or resentful about the extra time I give the children. He loves to watch me nurture and cuddle with them. Since we were married nine years before having kids, we had lots of time to firm up our relationship. We geared up for having children, and because Jack had already raised two children, he must have known how a parent's attention can easily become diverted from the spouse and focused on the child.

Jack and I make sure that we have special private times for ourselves during the week. We also get together for tennis and other activities, and this reminds us of our relationship and renews our marriage.

We don't socialize with many couples these days. Time is so short and precious—we want to be with each other, with the kids, and also have private times by ourselves. Jack will socialize by having a tennis "date" and I'll meet other mothers and their kids to go out for lunch. There is very little time to nurture old friendships and make new ones. Our lives are full, with each other and working. As the children grow up and want to spend more time with their friends, we will also have more time for our friends.

Mary 🐦

Even though Frank and I spend almost the same amount of time with Natalie and love her equally, I do believe a man and a woman have different ways of expressing their feelings.

Natalie has been able to charm her dad since she was an infant. While Natalie and I have lots of little fun projects together, she is definitely Daddy's little girl. A father offers strength and tenderness, a mother offers security and peace. These feelings were so strong with us, we never felt we had to compete with any of our baby-sitters, even though Natalie spent most of the day with them.

Natalie and I have developed a certain communication that no one, even her dad, could understand. A mother is more detail-oriented. She worries about everything—how the baby feels, how the baby looks, if she had enough food, where to go, with whom, school, projects, toys . . . everything including laundry. This is why children naturally turn to Mom for everything.

Frank took care of Natalie last summer when she was just three years old. She followed him wherever he went and he was there for her after school, but she looked like an orphan. She did not get changed from her school clothes and took her naps on the sofa rather than in her bed. Why? Because he is a man? But Natalie seemed happy.

There was a time when Natalie used to call everybody "Mommy." She used the word to get anything she wanted from everybody, male or female.

Having Natalie has made my relationship with my parents even closer. Natalie is their first grandchild. My parents and I have always been very close despite the fact that we live so far apart. They are always there when I need them. I hope I'll have the same relationship with Natalie as my mom and I have.

My cousins who live in the Bay Area are also very close to me.

They often visit. In fact, Uncle John was the first visitor Natalie had in the hospital.

Natalie is lucky to have grandparents and several uncles, aunts, and cousins too. I think a sense of family is very important for all of us. My parents always taught my brother and myself to have respect for the older members of the family. In my opinion family members can play a very important role in Natalie's development. They can set examples for her while she is growing up. Even though our society does not allow us to have as much time for our close relatives, I believe it is a worthwhile effort to keep it going, especially since I have a young daughter.

The biggest change in my relationships recently has been my divorce from Frank. As much as it surprised my friends, I think I surprised myself the most. My background is very conservative and I am Catholic; there is no divorce in our family. Certainly I've always thought marriage was forever. It took guts to make the decision, since that is the hardest part of all.

When I got married I was very young, twenty-one years old, and still innocent in many ways. I came to this wonderful country for Frank. I never had any big plans to be a career woman, and had never been surrounded by a career-oriented society. I never expected I was going to be as involved in my profession as I am now. I guess it was all meant to be. I became a career woman, although I never wanted to be one, and now I love it. Working has become a very important part of my life.

It is not easy these days to be a wife, mother, and career woman at the same time. I've learned that we all are responsible for our own happiness. My life is full of responsibilities; I can't afford to be pushed down because of an unhappy marriage. I tried to save our marriage for several years, but without success. I tried to fix it and used all methods I could think of, but I failed because I needed his cooperation and he never saw it as being necessary.

Compare us with a pair of beautiful tulip bulbs. When Frank and I got married we were the same type of flower bulbs, but we did not know which type of tulip our blooms were going to be. These bulbs were exposed to the same weather conditions, watering, nutrients, sun . . . and we bloomed differently. It is very sad indeed. Frank is a good man and I am okay, too, but we don't have the same outlook anymore about life.

Do I feel guilty about my decision? Yes and no. Yes, because I've made a promise in the church, "for better and for worse till death do us part." And no, because I know I've tried everything I could to keep our marriage intact. I've learned to forgive Frank as well as myself for it.

My biggest concern is Natalie. She was born truly out of love, we wanted her so much. Our family could have been so perfect, but life decided to tear us apart. Nevertheless, both of us love Natalie very much. She is our sunshine in the middle of an iceberg. Frank and I both try not to let Natalie suffer too much through our divorce. I've tried to verbally explain to her that "Mommy and Daddy do not want to live together anymore, but we both still love you very dearly." I've learned she can only understand so much and I plan to tell her each year a little more, whatever her little mind can handle. I don't want her to grow up resenting the fact that we never told her the truth. Our consistency and communication are going to be the most essential part of Natalie's upbringing. I want her to grow up as a happy human being on her own, which is what my parents have managed to give me. It's hard to share happiness with someone we love—or anyone else—if we don't have the happiness in ourselves.

Right now Natalie is very young. Hopefully she can cope with her situation better because of it. So far she does not seem to mind it. She still sees her daddy regularly and I still encourage her to love and respect him. I believe it is better for a child to be exposed to both parents living separately but happily than to live in a family where both parents are arguing all the time. Arguments take much more energy than they are worth.

My family has been wonderful. They understand and stand behind me all the way. They continue to give Natalie and me their love and support. As a family we pull together in a time of crisis; this has given us all a sense of strength that can withstand any life turbulence. I personally always compare myself to a rubber tree: you can bend me down but you cannot break me.

For the future, I don't really know. My immediate plan is to get myself more involved with my profession, build my independence. Right now my dad is living with me. Still having a man around certainly has made things easier. What happens when he leaves? I have to learn to check my car oil and water myself if the tires are low, I've got to know how to pump them. God forbid that my tires should blow up on the freeway, since I've no idea how to change them. As a wife I had always taken for granted that my husband would take care of certain things. It is a strange feeling, sometimes, to be alone. I liked being married, I thought I already had a companion for the rest of my life. What happens now?

I guess I've lots to learn still, but in the meantime our life is certainly much more peaceful. No more tiring arguments, and I am in charge of my own life. I will make it a happy one for both Natalie and myself. I do hope to still be friends with Frank for Natalie's sake and also hope that he will find happiness for himself.

Danielle gave me some wonderful advice: Follow your heart and don't let other people influence you, since you know your own situation best.

Susan ❧

It has been interesting for me watching the different relationships developing in my family. Dick and I each handled Natasha very differently and she obviously got something different, but essential, from each of us. For the first three years there was an obvious preference for Mom. She loved Dick and missed him when he wasn't at home, but when she needed something she went to Mom. Just how strong this preference was varied from time to time. I wasn't really surprised by this while she was nursing. The surprise was that it got worse, not better, after she was completely weaned.

During one period of time when Natasha was around age two she absolutely would not let Dick lift a finger for her without going into a full tantrum. He couldn't even help her to the bathroom, brush her teeth, or get her something to eat, let alone comfort her when she was upset or hurt. Yet, even then, when he left for work in the morning she would often say to me that she missed her daddy and didn't want him to leave. (These were some of the millions of times that I have wondered what was going on in that little mind of hers!)

At first Dick and I just let it go, knowing that with time Natasha's attitude would change and she would be anxious for Dick to be involved with her life again. But as Ariana's birth grew closer, Dick, knowing that he would have to do a lot with Natasha after Ariana arrived, began preparing her for that eventuality. He insisted on helping her. Gradually the tantrums became fewer, and by the time Ariana arrived, it was not much of a problem. She still showed a preference for me, but she let Dick help without too much fuss. Since then there has been a gradual shift toward Daddy. Now, even when we are both available, she actually seeks out Dick some of the time. There is a much stronger attachment developing for Daddy, which is delightful to watch. It was enhanced during our recent vacation because Dick took both girls to the pool every morning while I worked on this book in the room. He did it as a favor to me, but I think that it turned out to be a huge benefit to the three of them. I plan occasionally, even when it isn't essential, to be away for an afternoon or evening when I can leave Natasha and Ariana with Dick. When I am around they still focus most of their attention (both positive and negative) on me, so these times away give Dick an opportunity to really be with his children and for them to really be with him. He likes these times, although he admits that he doesn't think that he could do it for too long. It is exhausting to be the focus of all of their attention!

As usual, Ariana has been different from Natasha. She has shown less reluctance to rely on Dad for attention. Although she seeks me out more often than Dick, she has shown almost no reluctance to let Dick take over when I'm busy or too tired. On occasion, when Ariana is very hungry or very tired, only Mom will do, but these times are rare exceptions. In fact, Dick is much better able to do certain things for Ariana. Most notable is getting her to go to sleep. Unless she is hungry she never fights him; she almost always gives me a fight.

No matter how much the feminist in me wants to believe that dads and moms are interchangeable in their children' lives, my observation over the past four years has been that this just isn't so. Dick and I are both an essential part of our children's lives but we fill different needs. Would it have been different if Dick had been the primary caretaker and I had been away at work each day? I don't know. I'm not sure that it is that easy to explain the preference for Mom that we have observed in our house.

Natasha's relationships with her extended family have also been interesting to watch. It was apparent that she understood at a very early age that her grandparents, aunts, uncles, and cousins were special people. She reacts differently to each of them according to their different personalities, but it is apparent that she understands that they are all family. At this point in her life I think that a visit to see Grandma Betty and Grandpa Burt is highest on her list of priorities.

At a very young age, however, Natasha began to show some favoritism among relatives. I didn't expect this to show up as early as it did, and I wasn't prepared to handle the situation when she rejected someone who loved her and wanted her affection. I have not handled any of these situations well. I first noticed it when she demonstrated a preference for her cousin Kevin over his brother Brian. Recently she defiantly refused to sit next to Brian in the car. When I insisted that she sit next to Brian, she threw a tantrum, and the result probably made Brian feel worse than if I had just quietly let Natasha have her way. There is no easy answer. I could easily attribute this to her immaturity and patiently wait for her to mature, but other people's feelings are being hurt in the meantime and that bothers me.

Around age two Natasha began to show some reluctance to give Dick's parents the warm response that they wanted from their grandchild. This was, of course, part of her rebellious stage. Sensing just how important it was to them, she exerted her power by withholding her affection. Interestingly, even when this was at its worst she was always anxious to see Dick's parents. My parents live farther away and thus far have been spared this coolness.

Natasha and my mother seem to have something really special between them. The comradery that I observe between the two of them goes beyond the fact that they are grandchild and grandmother. It is something really special and something that defies analysis.

Ariana is still warm and affectionate to everyone she meets. So far she hasn't shown any favoritism.

Somehow I expected my relationship with my parents to change once I became a parent, and I know that many moms' relationships with parents and in-laws have been strained over issues of child-rearing techniques. But I haven't noticed much change at all, perhaps because I was older when I had children and had already developed an adult relationship with them. I do get to see my parents more often now that they have granddaughters to visit. I have always enjoyed being with my parents but I enjoy it even more now because it is a real vacation for me when my mom is around. Natasha would much rather be with Grandma Betty than with me, and Ariana goes everywhere and does everything that Natasha does, so I truly get some time off when my mother is around.

I didn't notice any change in the relationship between Dick and his parents either, but I did notice a difference in Dick's parents. His father was eighty years old, his mother seventy-four, when Natasha, their first grandchild, was born. Color returned to their cheeks and they seemed to have a new reason for living. They now have three grandchildren and are enjoying them immensely! Dick's mom has been disappointed when we asked her not to let Natasha and Ariana have any of the mandelbrot or cake that she baked, but with many reminders she has honored our wishes. I know that there are things that she would probably do differently, but she has never tried to interfere and I truly appreciate the confidence that both sets of parents have shown.

The most obvious relationship to expect to find changed is, of course, between Dick and myself. And there has been a change. Fortunately, it is for the better. Dick and I married after we both had established careers. Dick owned a house and was financially secure. We were not like young couples who start life together with these major financial goals to accomplish together. I sensed that this difference left something missing from our life together— not of major significance, but I did notice. Then we decided to have children and the dynamic changed. Now we had a very important common goal and it definitely created a closer relationship. That closeness has only been enhanced by the actual presence of Natasha and Ariana in our lives. Now that which is the most important to each of us is the same: Natasha and Ariana. We watch them with the same amazement and with the same mystical feeling that we can't quite believe that we have

341

created these wonders. And we share in the joy and frustration of rearing children.

I was interested to observe that some things about Dick that never bothered me before we had children began to be of some concern to me when I thought about our children developing the same habits. This has not created any major difficulty for us but I'm sure that it could in some relationships. One area that did create some stress and that we are slowly working out is religious holidays. Neither Dick nor I are religious but I was raised in a Protestant household and Christmas was a major event in my life as a child.

Dick is Jewish and thus has a certain distaste for the celebration of Christmas. None of this was of any importance before we had children; I didn't mind not making a big deal out of it before Natasha and Ariana were born. Once they were old enough to begin to appreciate the festivities, though, I wanted to give them some of the joy I experienced from celebrating Christmas. Dick has been extremely tolerant when it comes to Christmas and I appreciate this, but Christmas is a family holiday and it just doesn't have the same pizzazz without him joining in— something I naturally cannot expect him to do.

There have been other added stresses. When we differ concerning how the children should be handled, we each feel equally strongly that we must convince the other that our way is correct. I can see how this could destroy an otherwise happy relationship, but Dick and I are lucky in that we usually agree when it comes to our children. Our philosophies are very much the same. We usually handle the same problem a little differently, but since our basic beliefs are the same we are able to accept each other's variations on the theme without getting too upset. On a couple of occasions we have gotten into major battles over how to handle Natasha. Ariana's turn will come, but she isn't yet at the stage where our differences become apparent. So far we have gotten through these battles without inflicting lasting damage on our relationship and have negotiated settlements somewhere in between our two extremes, most likely for the benefit of Natasha and Ariana.

I will tell you about the all-important relationship between Natasha and Ariana in Chapter 24. Watching this relationship develop and mature is a wonder to behold!

Dick's and my relationships with our friends has not changed as much as one might expect. We made a pact before having children that our social life would not suffer as a result of having children. For the most part we have kept our pact. We still have dinners out with friends and have dinner parties at home. One of my best friends has become like an aunt to our children. A couple we are very good friends with are the godparents of our children. These relationships have changed some it is true, they have grown to include our children, but I don't think that they have suffered.

It is fun to watch the relationships develop between the girls and our friends. They love to hear that we are having guests for dinner. Natasha and Ariana stay up during the appetizers and interact with our friends. Then they are sent off to bed and Dick and I enjoy adult company. Natasha and Ariana like to ask some of the guests to read their bedtime story. For a while it was difficult to prepare the meal for guests with both girls "helping" in the kitchen, but as they get older it is getting easier.

Another set of relationships we have had fun watching develop are the relationships between Natasha and Ariana and their friends. Ariana is still a little young to have friends of her own, but when Natasha has a friend over to play, Ariana considers her one of her friends too. They love having friends over, and for Natasha, at least, the more, the better. So far we haven't reached the stage of "best" friends and jealousies between friends. Whoever is over that day is the friend they love the best. But it is clear that Natasha's friends are very important to her. When we are away from school because we are out of town, she talks about her friends and says that she misses them. I suspect that this will get more intense as time goes on.

24

SIBLINGS

- Introducing the next pregnancy
- Bringing baby home
- When the older child regresses
- How we promoted good relationships between our children
- Sharing toys and attention
- Sibling rivalry
- When the older child hurts the younger one

Diana 🍃

Sosia was two years nine months old when Benjamin was conceived. It seemed of little importance to explain what was going to happen to her life when her baby brother arrived. My main thrust was to prepare her so that her skills would be mature enough that she could function well on her own. I concentrated on making her a bit more independent. I wanted to be sure that her vocabulary was large enough that she could express what was happening to her. And I also wanted her to be able to enjoy some "grown-up" activities that were at her age level.

We began to read books about the baby's arrival. Many of them were excellent. However, I found that some of these books are a little bit suggestive as to what the child is "supposed" to feel rather than addressing what having a baby is about. For someone as young as Sosia was, the information about what a diaper pin is and where a baby gets food is sufficient. The books about "When the baby comes I'm moving out" and other such topics are a bit frightening and confusing for little children. I found the books about animal mothers and what mama feeds the baby are more suitable.

I kept being told that Sosia's reaction would be so terrible and drastic that I think I may have been overly cautious and too suggestive unnecessarily. After all, giving a sibling to your child is really the most wonderful gift you can give. How many Sunday mornings are spent playing together that would otherwise be quiet and lonely? They really adore one another—most of the time.

Before Benjamin arrived Sosia and I visited other babies and had outings with them. We enjoyed the way the other mothers fed their babies and how the babies rode in their carriages. I'm sure all this helped Sosia understand what babies were like, but probably nothing could have prepared her for sharing her position in the family with a new baby.

I was offered some very good advice about how to handle the day that the new baby came home, making it as untraumatic as possible for the older child. I planned to spend most of my attention and time on Sosia that day. I tried not to carry the baby extensively, but to let others carry him. We explained that although I had been in the hospital, the new baby had not hurt me or made me sick. We had a special ceremony when Benjamin came home so Sosia would have a chance to share in all the excitement. We exchanged gifts from each child to the other with notes about how wonderful it would be to have such a terrific sibling.

After Benjamin came home we let Sosia be involved in everything that she could handle. One baby-sitter brilliantly let Sosia powder Benjamin's foot with a cotton ball, all the time stressing how little he was, just as Sosia had been when she was a baby. I let Sosia get me things—diapers, bottles, cotton balls. Any time I was taking care of Benjamin I let Sosia be a big part of it. She always shared feeding times.

I also made sure that Sosia had her own activities. She attended her prenursery school twice a week for two hours. It gave her a sense that, although the baby was receiving a big dose of attention, she was a much bigger girl with more wonderful privileges. Whenever it was possible I did something with just Sosia. Her prenursery school teachers suggested that I sit with Sosia once a day and do something simple with her like put a puzzle together. I thought I didn't have an ounce of energy left for such a feat, but I decided to give it a try. The first night, as we completed a simple, five-minute puzzle, Sosia stood up, came over to me, put her little hands on each of my cheeks and said, "Mommy, this has sure been fun. Let's do it again real soon." Needless to say, from then on I included a little chunk of quiet personal "just Sosia and me" time every day.

The house changes were a big part of having a new baby. Sosia was moved to a different room with "big-girl" furniture. We worked feverishly to accomplish this change well in advance of Benjamin's birth. Sosia was well adjusted to her new room long before Benjamin's arrival and was referring to her old room as the "baby's" before he was born.

I also tried to make everything everybody's. Gifts that came to the house that Sosia especially liked always seemed to move from Benjamin's room to Sosia's room, and since Benjamin didn't seem to mind, I just let it happen. Believe me, Benjamin was unaffected and it was very important to Sosia.

After Benjamin's arrival I tried to make sure that Sosia and I had a little time to talk about the baby and share him. As soon as it was safe I let the children do a lot of things together. They read books together, watched television together, and took baths together.

As I mentioned in Chapter 16, Sosia did regress after Benjamin was born. The baby gets a lot of attention and to the older child this looks unfair—until he or she realizes the good things that come with being grown up.

All moments were not rosy. Several times Benjamin was hurt by some toy flying through the air in his direction. I would let Sosia know in no uncertain terms that I would not let her hurt Benjamin, just as I would not let Benjamin hurt her. There were times when I felt I would go mad if they did not settle down and start getting along better. There were times when I felt that Sosia was egging Benjamin on to do things she knew would get him into trouble. But there were also times when I know Benjamin, although much smaller, was causing Sosia plenty of grief. I suppose it is just part of the down side of having siblings. But I feel that it is a huge advantage in the long run. They would be lost without one another. Their relationship is invaluable.

There is sibling rivalry. Sosia and Benjamin vie for attention and praise ad nauseam. I am sure that I did as a child and I am pretty sure that their children will do the same. What can we do about it except show them that they are both loved and respected?

Since my children are some of the oldest in our play group, I am often asked, "Diana, just when does all this sibling rivalry end?" I respond with complete authority, "When it happens at my house I will be sure to let you know!"

Jan 🐛

I loved Jaclyn so much, I thought, "How can I have any more love for another child?" Katherine assured me that you just do. And of course she was right. It seems silly to me now that I could have had such a thought. But I really did, and I readily admit it.

Jaclyn was just two weeks short of two when Jenna was born. Jaclyn was the baby, *my* baby . . . yet all of a sudden she was the big sister. And as much as Jaclyn had all the love in my heart, the minute Jenna was born I wanted to protect her and shield her from Jaclyn, who now seemed to me like an amazon.

I really had some mixed emotions. How could I have loved my first child so much, and then all of a sudden regard her as an intruder? In time (ahhh . . . time, a wonderful thing), everything worked out—my emotions, Jaclyn the amazon and intruder, and gurgling little Jenna. I love them *both*. I love Jenna as much as I

347

love Jaclyn and vice versa. But to be honest, it all took about three months for me to come to grips with the new baby and her older sibling.

Preparing for Jenna was easy. I had amniocentesis and knew it was to be Jenna. So we talked about Jenna, read books about babies (the best book was one called *Babies*, by Gyo Fujikawa), and visited friends with babies. I bought a doll for Jaclyn, took it to the hospital, and gave it to her when she came to visit the new baby. I told her the doll was her baby, and that it was a gift from her new sister. She took the doll and tossed it aside with little interest. (Didn't at least one book say this was a good idea?)

My pediatrician had warned me that many times an older child regresses when a new sibling arrives. I really didn't notice any jealousy from Jaclyn for about the first three months. And slowly it begins: "I want to wear a diaper like baby" or "I want to drink from baby's bottle."

And then it gets worse: "Mommy, put baby down." Bopping the baby on the head with a toy is mild compared to the kicking (with shoes on) to push the baby down, making sure the head smacks against the tile floor.

I'll never forget what Dr. Verby, our wonderful pediatrician, told me when I detailed to him all these glorious incidents. He said, "Think of it this way. How would you feel if one day your husband came home with a mistress and announced that from this day forth, the three of you were going to live under one roof in perfect harmony?" How would I feel? Yukkk! "What a horrendous thought," I said. "Exactly," was his reply. "That's how Jaclyn feels with a new baby. The only problem is that she is too young to verbalize her emotions. She takes out her frustrations physically by hitting, kicking, and pushing. Have Jaclyn take out her frustrations on a doll. Hitting a stuffed animal, a pillow, or the couch is much better than hurting her sister."

The hitting and kicking got worse instead of better. Jaclyn was sent to her room or made to stand in the corner. But we are now getting close to "better"—and the funny thing is, baby sister is now hitting back!

Katherine 🦆

When Jack and I became pregnant with Alexandra, I immediately began talking to Deren about babies and showing him little babies and any advertisements featuring babies I could find. I would enthusiastically tell him how wonderful it would be for him to have his own baby brother or sister to play with. Jack and I would gush. Deren was completely disinterested. He didn't seem to have any concept of what we were so excited about.

After my pregnancy started to really show in the fourth month, I would have Deren pat the new baby. I showed him books that portrayed beautiful babies in their mommy's tummies. He started to get a little interested.

I found several good books on bringing home a new baby. "The Berenstain Bears" series includes a good one. Deren became more and more interested. Some days he said he'd like to have a baby brother or sister. Other days, he didn't want to.

Deren really enjoyed patting my tummy and giggling about how fat I was. Jack and I would continue talking about the new-baby-to-be and about how lucky this baby would be to have a great big brother named Deren. We would remind Deren about all the things he could teach this new child and how he would soon have a new friend for his whole life. At age three Deren still was not too impressed and wanted to change the subject each time we'd bring it up.

The night before the big day arrived I had tucked Deren lovingly into bed the way I had each night during the "home stretch," as we'd called it. We had told Deren that Minnie would come to the house to spend the night with him when the new baby came. We set up this system so that Jack and I could go to the hospital, have the baby, and then have Deren come over immediately to meet and bond with his baby brother or sister. I didn't want him present for the actual birth experience in case there was a repeat performance of his birth—long and very painful! I didn't want Deren to think his little sister was causing his mother any pain or discomfort. I also knew I wouldn't be able to pay attention to Deren during the entire birth process and I wanted to spare his feelings and ensure that he got a good night's sleep before the big event. When I went into labor with Alexandra, Jack picked up Minnie about 2 A.M. and she crawled into bed with Deren.

About ten minutes after Alexandra's birth—which turned out to be short and sweet with just a minimum amount of pain—we called Minnie and told her to bring Deren right over in a taxi. Within one half hour they were there and Deren was quite curious and interested. We also had an enormous present (a stuffed animal) wrapped up for Deren as a gift from baby Alexandra, and he was thrilled about that. He ate all my French toast and drank my juice from my breakfast tray. I just wanted Deren and Alexandra to share some wonderful precious first moments together.

Deren stayed for about an hour and Daddy took him and Minnie home. Jack returned later to spend the day with us and brought Deren back over for dinner.

I remained exceedingly conscious of Deren and his feelings about being important and special in our family. I would try not to nurse Alexandra when Deren was around. I made extra efforts to have one-on-one time with him so he wouldn't feel left out or jealous.

Deren showed a polite interest in Alexandra at first. After she was about six months old and would smile and coo at him, she became irresistible to him. He didn't want to take his hands off her. He loved to hold her, laugh at her, and watch her sleep. She was very content with him as well.

Thank goodness Alexandra was not too demanding as an infant. She was happy to let Daddy hold her. Baby-sitters were not much of a problem for her, and she slept a lot during the first three months. This freed me up to be extra attentive to Deren. Gradually he became the one to make overtures to see his sister. Since he felt he was getting "his share" of attention, he became more and more happy to include her in activities.

Today they are seven and three and a half and very good friends. She worships him and can hardly wait until he outgrows a T-shirt or discards a toy her way. She's thrilled that it belonged to her big brother!

He thinks she's a pest or uses his crayons or sometimes gets more dessert or toys from the five and dime store, but basically he knows that Jack and I deeply love them both and that even though they get mad at each other, they don't have to be jealous about our love for them. Of course we continue to prove this by giving each of them lots of one-on-one time.

What is fascinating to me is how different Deren and Alexandra are from one another and yet how compatible they are. I enjoy watching them relate when they don't know I'm watching. It gives me a real warmth inside.

Susan ❧

Natasha has always been a very social creature. The more people there are around her, the happier she is. Even as an infant she couldn't be given too much attention. I didn't know what overstimulation was until Ariana arrived. Natasha enjoyed being passed from person to person and it never mattered if the faces were unfamiliar. Because of her character, we had no doubt that she would enjoy having a new baby in the house. I had heard all about sibling rivalry and I knew that we might have some problems when the baby first arrived, but we really didn't think that we would have major problems. We were right.

When it came to introducing the idea of a sibling, my only concern was that Natasha would get impatient. Nine months is a very long time, especially to a twenty-month-old. I thought about not telling her for a while, but I wanted her to share in our excitement and it just seemed right to tell her, so we didn't wait. I don't think that telling her early created any problems. I would do it the same way again. I don't remember exactly how we told her, but I think we just asked her how she would like to have a baby brother or sister. She immediately liked the idea. I told her that it would be a long time before our baby would come, but that one of these days we would have one. That was fine with her. After that we didn't talk about it much for a while.

When I was feeling particularly rotten during the first three months I would tell Natasha that I was very tired. She would ask why, and I would answer by saying it was because of the baby growing in my tummy. (I know the theory about using anatomical names and lots of times I do, but in this case, tummy just seemed appropriate.)

Sometimes we would ask whether she wanted a sister or brother. At first her answer would vary, but soon her answer became consistent: she wanted a sister. Fortunately, that's what she got. After we had the amniocentesis and knew that we had a little girl on the way, we selected a name. From that point on we talked about Ariana. Natasha talked to Ariana through my navel. She would say something like "Ariana, Ariana, can you hear me? Kick me, Ariana." She loved feeling Ariana kick!

We talked a lot about Ariana during the last three months. I told Natasha how little she would be and that she wouldn't be able to play with her for a very long time. We talked about how fragile Ariana would be and that she wouldn't do anything except lie there, sleep, nurse, pee, and poop. I told Natasha that she could help me change Ariana's diaper, but that she must never do anything for Ariana if Daddy or I weren't there to help.

Diana lent us a few books that talk about new babies in a positive way. These were the only books we read on the subject. I gave Natasha every opportunity to talk about concerns she might have regarding having a sister, but I tried hard not to suggest problems that might never arise. I did tell her that when Ariana arrived I would have to spend a lot of time with the baby and that would mean that I wouldn't have as much time to spend with Natasha. I asked her how she would feel about that. She wasn't very concerned.

I was very happy to be having another baby, but I did feel a little sadness as the time grew near for her birth. This would be the last time that it would be just Natasha, Dick, and me. I wanted to savor the moments. There seemed to be something so special about our family of three, and Ariana was still an unknown to us. But Natasha didn't seem to share any of my sadness. She was *ready*! We visited other new babies. When Jan gave birth to Jaclyn, Natasha and I visited her in the hospital. Jan very kindly let Natasha sit on her bed and hold Jaclyn. Natasha was instinctively gentle. It was beautiful to see the excitement in Natasha's face as she held a brand-new baby and caressed her soft skin.

I also made arrangements for us to visit the birth center where I was planning to deliver. They had a wonderful "mommy" doll with a baby attached to an umbilical cord that could be pulled out through the doll's vagina. The umbilical cord was attached with Velcro, and they had clamps to use when we "delivered the baby." I thought it was great and was eager to show Natasha what was going to happen when Ariana was born. Natasha was more interested in the Velcro.

I explained to Natasha that when it was time for Ariana to come, she would stay at home with her baby-sitter and Daddy and I would go to the hospital. The doctor would help the baby come out of my tummy and then Daddy would pick Natasha up and bring her to the hospital to see Ariana and me and we would all go home together. I didn't even think about the possibility of my having to stay in the hospital.

Naturally, things didn't go as planned. Ariana was in severe distress and arrived by emergency cesarean. I was concerned that Natasha would have trouble with the idea of my having to stay in the hospital, but she handled it like a champ. We explained that Ariana and I would stay in the hospital for a few days because the doctors had had to open my tummy to get Ariana out quickly. Natasha looked at my bandage with minimal interest. She was far more interested in holding Ariana.

My mother was planning to stay with us for a while after Ariana's arrival, as she had done when Natasha was born. I'm sure that's why Natasha didn't mind when I stayed in the hospital. Who needed Mom when Grandma Betty was there? Natasha visited Ariana and me in the hospital every day. She loved holding her baby sister.

When I came home from the hospital I was ready for the sibling rivalry that I had heard so much about to manifest itself. Natasha was an angel. She was gentle beyond belief and loved helping. She seemed so amazingly able to handle the whole situation. When she needed attention she asked for it. One day I was holding Ariana and Natasha said, very nicely, "Mommy, put Ariana down and hold me." I did. One of my greatest disappointments about the cesarean was not being able to pick up Natasha. She was used to running up and jumping into my arms. Now the only way that I could hold her was to sit down and constantly remind her not to touch my stomach. It definitely detracted from our hugs, but Natasha seemed to handle that, too, although she did forget a lot.

The only problem we had with Natasha was that she wanted to help too much. She wanted to do more than she was capable of doing. We had some tears of disappointment over her being told that she couldn't do certain things with Ariana, but overall everything was peaceful.

Three months went by and I had forgotten about sibling rivalry except to mention from time to time that we were very lucky to have been spared. Then we got our dose. Natasha started to exhibit the classic signs of sibling rivalry. She started to bite Ariana, started to wet her pants, and in other ways started to demand attention in a negative way. I tried not to overreact. Every time she tried to hurt Ariana, I would talk to her. I told her that we wouldn't allow her to hurt Ariana, and then I asked her why she did it. I asked her if she wished Ariana would go away. She almost always said no, that she would miss Ariana if she went away, but she couldn't tell me why she wanted to hurt Ariana. I told her it was okay if she didn't like the attention Ariana was getting, and even if she didn't like Ariana sometimes, but that she must *never* try to hurt her. The worst part of this stage lasted only about two or three weeks; then Natasha stopped wetting her pants and the attempts to hurt Ariana became fewer.

I never left the girls alone together for more than a minute or two until Ariana was almost a year old. Even when Natasha didn't intend to hurt Ariana, she wasn't aware of her own strength and sometimes hurt the baby unintentionally. I was always concerned that she might drop Ariana while trying to pick her up. From other stories about sibling rivalry that I have heard, we had a very minor case. Ariana was never hurt seriously and Natasha always told us what she had done.

The interesting aspect of sibling rivalry that I wasn't expecting is how quickly the baby begins to be jealous of the attention the older sibling gets. Some time before Ariana was a year old she

354

became aware of the attention that we give Natasha and now always demands attention at those times too. If I pick up Natasha, Ariana wants to be picked up; if Natasha gets something to eat, Ariana wants the same thing; if Daddy kisses Natasha, Ariana looks up, ready for her kiss. By the time Ariana was a year old I would say that the rivalry was equal. They want the same toy, the same food, the same drink, the same attention from Mom and Dad. It doesn't matter who got the item or the attention first, the other one comes running for her share. And for Ariana it's more than a desire to get her share of our attention. She wants to emulate Natasha. Ariana tries to copy *everything* Natasha does and is sorely disappointed when she cannot.

The flip side of sibling rivalry is the closeness that exists between the two. It is enormously satisfying to watch them play together and show their affection toward one another. Ariana is very affectionate and she tries to comfort Natasha when she is upset about something—even if that something is that I have just reprimanded her for being mean to Ariana. Ariana will go to Natasha, put her arms around her, and give her a hug and a pat on the back. That is one of the most precious sights in the world. Other times there are hugs and kisses between them with no apparent precipitating event. Natasha is developing a very protective attitude toward Ariana and has, on more than one occasion, told me that I am mean to Ariana as she comforts her little sister. They obviously care a great deal for each other.

As with one child, having two creates lots of problems, but the joys it brings far outweighs the problems.

Chapter 25

TWINS

- Managing two newborns
- Breast-feeding two
- Twins and double trouble
- Traveling with twins
- Encouraging sharing
- Disciplining two
- Dressing twins

Averil Haydock 🐦

There are so few books on twins. I hope that by relaying my experiences raising William and Oliver I can give some insight. I do not wish to be considered an adviser, nor do I profess to have done it all "the right way." We all read books, talk to other parents, talk with our pediatricians and do it the best way we know how. Having twins is a real joy, and believe it or not, I think in some instances easier than a single child. For the most part, though, it is double trouble!

I may at times find it difficult to separate the upbringing of Oliver and William from that of Zoe, Oliver, and William. Zoe is now almost three and a half and the boys are almost two and a half. We fall somewhere between rearing twins and triplets. There are only thirteen months between Zoe and the boys so it's pretty darn close! I have often thought how "easy" it would have been to have just Zoe, or just William and Oliver, because it is the three together that create the most friction. Any combination of two is a breeze compared to the full threesome, when someone invariably gets left out or gets in the way. The other day a veteran mother of four said that four children is easier than three because they can then pair off. Does this mean that Tim and I should produce another? I'll have to give that idea a good hard thought!

William and Oliver are fraternal twins born three minutes apart. William was the first born and he sure let everyone know that he had arrived! From the moment they were born they were as different as night and day. Willy is heftier, more aggressive, more vocal. Oliver has always been the calmer, more peaceful of the two. Even when I was pregnant, Willy kicked and moved around more. Oliver was quiet and often moved only when nudged by his next-door neighbor. William is very demanding, always wanting everything immediately, full of life and character. Oliver is patient and gentle. One of Oliver's many nicknames was "Our Gentleman." Even now, Oliver often will be off in another room reading his latest favorite book, entertaining himself. What I have found to be so interesting about having twins is that babies really do have such incredibly distinct personalities from birth. William and Oliver have lived under the same roof and have been brought up with the same values, but they are totally different. It proved to me that we all are what we are, our personalities formed at conception (genes!) and then only embellished by our environment and our upbringing.

As newborns, twins can be a handful. It takes a while to get a grip on a method of breast feeding that you feel comfortable with. I did attempt feeding them simultaneously, but it just didn't work for me. Just as I would get them both in a comfortable position (*I* never got comfortable!), one of them would do a big poop or need to be burped. I quickly decided to feed them alternately—breast-feed one while the other had a bottle, and then switch at the next feeding time. William was a very rough nurser and I had to wear a breast shield (a rubber nipple that you place over your own to protect it from your ferocious baby). The other thing I found to be useful for nursing twins was the electric breast pump we rented from our local pharmacy. It works much faster than any of the other pumps, and you can then store that milk in the freezer for an emergency or when you're going out.

If at all possible you should have someone at home with you the first month or two. I honestly don't know how I would have managed on my own. Just as I would start nursing the boys, Zoe would suddenly be dying of hunger and thirst. Tim was very helpful with Zoe and we had a wonderful lady, Kessie, who stayed with us. I think it's especially important to have help if your twins are small and need extra attention (very common with twins, as they often are premature). We were very fortunate to have big healthy babies; Willy weighed in at nine pounds six ounces, Oliver at eight pounds one ounce. They were the biggest twins ever born at that hospital!

I think if you have just the twins it is manageable with your husband or mother helping out in the beginning, but with three children under two, it's a different story! If you do decide to hire outside help, it's important to conduct an interview with them and to spend a bit of time together. You want someone who can fit into your life. When Kessie left us we were very fortunate to have found Yvonne, a pretty young Jamaican girl who lives with us five days a week and extra days when necessary. We all are very fond of her and she is terrific with the children and helping around the house.

From the day we came home from the hospital, William and Oliver have shared a room. As William was an extremely vocal infant, I was concerned that he would wake Oliver. The pediatrician said definitely leave them together and they would get used to each other's noises in no time. True enough. Oliver somehow managed to sleep through all the racket! For the first several months we had them in individual baskets placed in the same crib. That way they were very close together. We had colorful mobiles hanging over the crib and cute, fluffy animals all around the sides.

I was very fortunate to have three children who were excellent sleepers when they were little (that changed when they turned two!). All three of them slept through the night by the time they were two months old. We wrapped them very tightly in their blankets, which I think was comforting and reminded them of the womb. Until they were fifteen months old they had a morning nap and an afternoon nap. When, on their own accord, they cut out the morning nap, they would sleep for three to four hours in the afternoon. In the evening, after their communal bath (which is always a fun time, with lots of toys and splashing and swimming), there was not too much of a struggle to get them into their cribs to sleep. Read a little story, say prayers, give them their "blankies," and kiss them good night. Oliver and William went to bed perfectly happily. After all, when the lights went out they had each other. We have always kept either an extra crib or an extra bed in the boys' room so that Zoe can sleep with them if she wants to or if we have visiting children. Since they've all turned two, it's as if the word "nap" were an archenemy, and if they had their way bedtime would not even be mentioned until at least ten o'clock.

Around two years of age they begin to be manipulative and use little methods to stay up just a little bit longer. They do also start being scared ("Mummy, there's a tiger in our room!"). As I've always been afraid of the dark myself, I'm particularly sensitive to this. I usually end up lying down in their room until they fall asleep (at which point I usually have fallen asleep myself!). Sometimes if they wake up in the middle of the night I'll bring them into our bed and we all fall back to sleep. I know a lot of mothers think that's the worst habit to encourage. However, my feeling is that if it's comforting for my child, and Tim and I don't mind, why not? Zoe slept with us almost every night for a year (she would creep into our bed in the middle of the night) and just recently has weaned herself away from that. She now sleeps in the boys' room every night, or in her room when she has a friend for the night.

It is really exciting to see twins grow and conquer new obstacles. When Willy and Oliver were four and a half months old they were scooting around all over the place in their walkers. It was like a bumper-car rally as they'd crash into cupboards and each other and find it so amusing.

The twins attained different skills at various times. Willy was slightly ahead of Oliver communicating, whereas Oliver was the first to crawl. It was always just a matter of a couple of weeks before the other one would catch up. Naturally the imitation factor is very strong with twins.

Twins do get into all sorts of things that you never hear about with single children. I have two stories that come to mind, which at the time were terrifying but in retrospect are funny. Last winter, when the boys were one and a half years old, we were all busy working inside and outside the house. There was a lapse of communication, as I thought Tim was watching the boys and he thought I was watching them. I went out to see what headway Tim was making on painting the house and I didn't see the boys anywhere.

"Timmy, where are Oliver and William?"

"I don't know, Ave. Aren't they with you?"

Panic set in, and we raced around looking for them, my heart going a million miles an hour. As it turned out, they were halfway down Mount Holly Road, Oliver in his blue car, Willy in his fire engine. Thank God we live on a very quiet dirt road, where most of the neighbors have children and are conscious of driving slowly and carefully. When I caught up with them and admonished them with a few strong words, they looked up at me and grinned. That's twins for you.

The other story comes from the mother of two-year-old twin boys. She had put her boys in their room for a nap and was in her kitchen cooking. I imagine all was quiet so she thought they must have fallen asleep. When she answered the telephone she was appalled to hear her neighbor tell her that her twins were climbing around on the roof! Her heart must have flip-flopped. There must be great moments of scheming between twins. What can they do next to most frighten their mothers!

The inside of our house had already been childproofed for Zoe, so it was ready for the boys when they were old enough to get into trouble. We had stair gates, top and bottom. I was always concerned that they might push each other or trip over each other and go tumbling down the stairs. We had safety locks put on kitchen drawers where there were sharp knives, matches, scissors, and other dangerous items. Those gadgets have been so effective that most adults can't even open them! All our medicine is in the medicine cabinet above the sink in our bathroom or in a closet in our bathroom that is kept locked. All the poisonous cleaning liquids are under the kitchen sink where there is a safety latch. There are always some dangers that you just haven't thought of. You do get to know what kinds of things each child is curious about and therefore take the necessary precautions. None of my children ever seemed particularly interested in playing with wires or outlets, so once we had explained the danger to them a few times we didn't worry too much more about it. But all my children love to climb, anything—bureaus, shelves, swing sets, ladders left leaning against the house (a good way for them to get up on the roof!).

Until your twins can feed themselves (a milestone in "twindom"), you'll be very busy at mealtime. I found it easiest to use one bowl or plate and one spoon when feeding William and Oliver. First William, then Oliver, then William, and so on. I must say, William had the most insatiable appetite of any baby I had ever seen. I've never seen a happier baby than when William had finished a big meal! I started them on solids at four months (Willy would have liked to have started sooner, but the pediatrician advised against it). First a little cereal, then some vegetables, them some fruit, and eventually some meat. William usually had three spoonfuls to Oliver's one, which worked out just fine as Oliver was far more interested in his milk than he was in the food. Until they were six months old we fed them in their infant seats or in their walkers. Then they graduated to their high chairs. When the three of them finished a meal the kitchen table and floor looked like a tornado had swept through. My advice to all mothers is—get a dog! Your postmeal cleanup will be cut in half (Zoe's dog, Mickey, won't go near the fruit, unfortunately). The other bit of advice I have is to feed your children as many healthy things as possible when they're little because later on they do get picky and you cannot force them to eat something they don't like. When Zoe and the boys were little they all ate lots of freshly ground fruits and vegetables (the boys had orange complexions from all the carrots they ate), and almost no sugar or salt. When we traveled we would use the commercial baby food until they were old enough to eat cut-up veggies, meat, and fruit. Zoe didn't know about her sweet tooth until she was about two years old, but once she had a taste she dreamed about candy

361

and cookies every day. The boys picked it up earlier because of Zoe. You don't want to cut sweets out completely, but I think it's important to keep the sugar intake to a minimum for their teeth.

As for brushing their teeth, my kids started when they were about one and a half, and we started it in the bath, easier than trying to reach over the sink to spit out. So far they all still think it's fun to brush.

The other bathroom activity, toilet training, has not become much of an issue yet with Oliver and William. Off and on they have both shown a bit of interest in going on the "potty," and there are days when they wear undies, but they're not quite ready yet. When Zoe was two and a half her older cousins came to visit for three weeks and she trained herself then. I really think it's important not to push it (I have seen long-term problems in some cases). Your child will let you know when he or she is ready.

Most often Tim and I are at home with the children, but we also enjoy our times away together. Once a year Tim and I take a vacation. Yvonne stays at home with the children and usually a family member comes to visit. There is a wonderful couple, Dorothy and Don Fiaceo, who help drive the kids to school. I would not be able to leave and enjoy myself if I didn't have this great backup group at home.

When we go away the first twenty-four hours are tricky, still fretting about the kids, but once we're really away we have a ball. It's so important to have that time together and to talk and laugh and relax away from the daily routine of home life. Don't forget, once your children are grown and away at college, it's going to be just you and your husband again. Tim and I usually take a ten-day vacation, and when we get home we take the kids on a vacation.

This past summer the children and I traveled quite a bit, visiting friends and family, and Tim would try to join us for the last few days. It's quite a production when we hit the road. Just this summer we sold our old station wagon to buy a bigger one, with the third seat in the back, because we couldn't fit into the other one if we were all traveling together. The boys sit in their car seats waving out the rear window. Yvonne and Micky share the middle seat, and Tim, Zoe, and I sit in the front. Last, but certainly not least, all our gear gets strapped onto the roof rack.

No matter how short a trip you go on, make sure you have favorite toys, blankets, snacks, and books. Recently, when we flew down to visit my mother in Virginia, I made the mistake of saying to myself, "Oh, it's only an hour's flight. We don't need all their things." Everyone was miserable, as the trip turned out to be about seven hours door-to-door.

Flying is still a bit complicated. There are not enough arms to carry Willy, Oliver, and Zoe *plus* all the carry-on luggage. And it's very expensive. Consequently most of our family trips are by car. As the children get older, it gets much easier. Even now it's better because we don't need to take any port-a-cribs (we put mattresses on the floor) and the kids can walk greater distances on their own. If we stop at a restaurant en route, they can feed themselves and hold their own glasses without too many spills.

Tim and I do not take the kids out for meals very often when we're home as it's more of a production than it's worth. Much easier and just as much fun to be at home and occasionally have friends come home from school. Our house is well set up for lots of children because there is a big playroom adjacent to the eat-in kitchen. So now while we're cooking we can see the kids fighting over their toys!

Which brings me to the dreaded subject of sharing. Any time you have more than one child you have to learn how best to deal with this issue. What I have attempted to do with Zoe, Oliver, and Willy is have some toys that belong to each one individually, and then the rest are to be shared. When there is one toy that they all want at the same time and huge screams burst forth, I first try to calm them down and then explain that whoever had it first should have their turn with it and then pass it on. More often than not it works. The boys love having Zoe in their room, but she doesn't always reciprocate. I try to explain to them that Zoe likes to be alone in her room sometimes, and that they shouldn't worry about it because she loves them anyway. Sometimes no matter what you say or do it doesn't work, and there have been times when I've simply let them work it out.

The subject of sharing brings me around to that tricky topic— discipline. The first year of a child's life is a time of nurturing and learning. They're still experimenting without knowing right from wrong. Between the ages of one and two you can definitely rationalize with them and even begin to deal with matters more

363

directly. By the time my children were one and a half I found they responded quite well to explanations of do's and don'ts. (For instance, I'd go to the fire screen, touch it, pull my hand away quickly, and say, "Fire. Hot. Ouch! Don't touch.") By the age of two *I* think you can be very firm. Tim is a very strict disciplinarian, and I mostly agree with his ideas. A blatant act of wrongdoing is reason enough for a good talking to, and if that doesn't seem to have any effect, then a spank on the hand, a "to your room," and up they go. I don't think Oliver has ever been sent to his room, but Willy has spent many an hour there, as has Zoe. The rule is that they stay in their rooms until they are ready to come down and apologize. The other day Willy was spitting in Zoe's face and then poked her in the eye (sweet children!). After spending several minutes in his room he calmed down, came down the stairs, and said, "Sorry, Zo Zo." End of discussion.

One has to be careful not to scold if there's any doubt concerning who was the instigator. If a fight breaks out between the children and I don't know who started it, I tell them they had all better behave themselves and be nice to each other, and that the next time whoever starts the fight will be in big trouble. Always follow through on your threats, otherwise they'll catch on and test you to the brink! It is so important for the parents and other adults involved in the rearing of your child to be consistent and in sync with one another. Always back up the other disciplinarian in front of the children. If you feel the other person handled it incorrectly, talk about it when the children are not around.

I think it's been pretty difficult for Zoe to adapt to having not one but *two* baby brothers. When the boys were infants Tim or I or both of us would take Zoe out to lunch or on errands or on an outing with friends. In fact, she has spent far more time alone with us than either of the boys. Recently we have made an effort to take the boys out one at a time. In the summer Tim will often take one of the children when he goes to play golf (they love riding around in the golf cart!). I took Willy to a birthday party in the city, and Oliver came with Tim and me for an overnight trip to visit his aunt and uncle and little cousin. They all adore having the time alone with us, and it's nice to not have to share our attention three ways! The two left at home aren't terribly pleased at first, but they end up having a wonderful time.

When the boys were little it always amazed me how insensitive some people were to Zoe. Someone would come to visit and say, "Oh, aren't the twins adorable!" I'd always interject with praise for Zoe. Now that they're older it doesn't happen as much, and Zoe has such a dominating personality that you'd be hard pressed not to notice her! It's been fascinating to see how the three of them go through different stages of pairing off. It used to always be Zoe and William (he always responded to her commands). Lately it's Zoe and Oliver (she even sleeps in his bed at night). It's incredible how child development is such a series of stages, some the best and others . . . not the best. But as Susan Keel once pointed out, a stage rarely lasts longer than a few weeks, then it's on to a whole new phase.

Many baby books seem to put a big emphasis on dressing twins: "Do dress them alike if you want to." "Don't dress them alike if you want them to establish their own identity." I haven't found this to be a big issue yet. Sometimes Willy and Oliver dress alike, sometimes not. The older they get, the less they are dressed alike. If they have matching outfits, they're usually different colors. They both have red boots, but their sneakers are different. Oliver and Willy look so different and have such different personalities that I suppose I've never been concerned about a loss of individuality, especially due to the way they're dressed. Sometimes Zoe and I will wear the same color clothes and I'll say, "Look, Zo, we're twins!" Any of Zoe's "unisex" clothes, like blue jeans or T-shirts, have been passed on to the boys.

When Oliver and Willy were younger people were always asking me if they interacted a lot or talked to each other in their own language. Yes, they did, but I don't think more so than siblings of different ages. However, what Yvonne and I have noticed recently is that if one boy is crying in another room, the other will get very concerned. Last night after the kids had their bath, I was applying some ointment to Willy's eye and he didn't like that so he was getting quite worked up, crying and struggling to get away. Well, Oliver tugged at my dress and said, "What Mummy doing to Beamy?" (Willy's nickname). I thought it was so sweet that he was being protective of his brother.

If you're pregnant with twins, or if you already have twins, you may be familiar with the twin organization that I have found to be helpful and fun. There's a national office for the Mothers of Twins Club, located in Rockville, Maryland, but most communities have a chapter in their area. The mothers convene once a month at someone's house with all the twins in tow and we all sit around comparing notes while the children play. I had one of the meetings at my house, and my mother, who was visiting at the time, couldn't get over the fact that ten children under the age of five could play happily for two hours with not one tear shed! If need be, this organization is also very helpful if you are looking to buy or sell any equipment or clothes for twins. But most of all it's fun and reassuring to see others going through what you are. Double trouble, double fun!

Well, it's time now to close my chapter. I'm sure I've left out a million things but I hope I've been able to add a little insight into the world of raising twins. No matter what anybody says, the rules do bend when you have more than one little child. You don't have two sets of eyes to watch both all the time, and you don't have two sets of arms to hug or carry them when they want it. In that respect twins have it tougher than a single child, but the beauty is that they do have each other and they are so close. It's such a special relationship. And just think, you have two beautiful children to love. Lucky you. Lucky us, we have Willy, Oliver, *and* Zoe!

Chapter 26

SEX AFTER CHILDBIRTH

- Making time for making love
- When you don't want any more children . . . for now
- Having "dates" with your spouse
- Being too tired
- Getting interrupted

Is there sex after having a baby? Most definitely, yes! (There are siblings, don't forget!) Is sex the same after having a baby? Well, no, not really. But the changes aren't too terrible. To me, the most unhappy difference is the lack of those leisurely mornings in bed on the weekends, making love and falling back to sleep. Now either there are four in our bed or one of us is summoned long before I am awake enough to have any desire for sex.

The good news is that the nighttime sex is just as wonderful as it was before children. There have been those occasions when we have been interrupted by crying from the other room that just cannot be ignored. I go to comfort the little monster and invariably return to the music of snores. Oh well, tomorrow is another day.

But don't expect to be back to great sex right away. There's some healing and recovery time needed. After my first child was born I couldn't wait to get back to having intercourse. My episiotomy was healed but still painful. Lots of lubricant helped, but more time would have helped more. I found that some lubricant was necessary for quite a while after both children were born. (I've learned that breast feeding causes less vaginal secretions.)

When my second child was born by cesarean we waited until the pain from the incision stopped before resuming intercourse. I was less impatient this time, probably because getting up with two babies drained all my energy—who had enough energy to be sexy? But it wasn't that long before we were having intercourse again. I recovered quickly from the cesarean. The only pain and discomfort I experienced was from the incision, but I've heard that other women have more discomfort for quite some time. I think that it makes a difference which type of incision you have. The so-called bikini cut is great for wearing swimsuits again, but the recovery is longer. Since my baby was in distress they didn't have time for the bikini cut. I recovered quickly but no more bikinis for me.

Even after everything is healed, don't be surprised if your sex life isn't back to normal right away. The fatigue of caring for babies makes less energy available for other activities—even sex. But don't despair. We are enjoying sex again—so will you.

There are moments, I have to admit, that I crawl into bed too tired to even think of being intimate, cuddling up with my spouse, or having sex. There are nights I am so tired I couldn't even tell you how to spell the word! It's the farthest thing from my mind. I just want to pull the covers up and let sleep take over my aching body. I feel just awful when I realize that weeks have gone by without my initiating any lovemaking. My only salvation is that my husband appears to be as pooped as I am to be uninterested in what has produced the greatest joys of our lives. (And how can the greatest joys of one's life leave you too darn tired to enjoy what brought them into the world?)

I can't give you any clear answers. I can tell you that our passionate lovemaking has often given way to immediate sound sleep. And the funny thing is, I am not complaining that my husband may not be as "active" as he was once. When I am tired I am *grateful* for his disinterest in the matter. I do hope we can—one day—get back some of the passion we seem to have on hold.

Once I did feel rather guilty about not having the prescribed sexual drive that one feels one should have. I talked honestly about our "lack of" with my obstetrician. Interestingly, he said studies have shown, when one is under stress and fatigue, sex is virtually nonexistent. As a working mom I know those words well. I am certainly not proud of them, nor am I pleased with what stress and fatigue are doing to our passion. But I do accept it for the time being, and am trying not to feel so terribly bad about the entire situation. Heck, I'm too tired!

When passion does arrive, there's a new wrinkle in our love-making these days, and that is avoiding getting pregnant. After all those desperate months of working on getting pregnant, *not* wanting to conceive is a new effort. Right now, two children is just right. In my heart I would love two more children, but can only my heart have them and raise them?

After being on the pill for eleven years, I do not plan to take it again. And being thirty-seven, soon to be thirty-eight, it is not medically recommended. The alternatives? You know them as well as I do. Perhaps you even dislike them as much as I do. We're pretty much practicing rhythm, and if the moment arises in a possibly fertile time, my trusty can of foam comes in handy.

Is there really sex after childbirth? Yes, but it's a challenge. Although there is always an abundance of love, there is, unfortunately, a limited supply of energy. A crying baby, children's demanding schedules, a time-consuming job, and running the household often leave me without enough energy to sustain an interest in sex. If this sounds like you, do not despair. Be patient with yourself. Most important: acknowledge the importance of your sexual identity.

There are numerous solutions to a less-than-perfect sex life, and often adjustments are needed along the way. What worked with the schedule of a nursing infant may not be effective with a toddler's schedule—and schedules and appointments are critical here. Spontaneity and "mood" sex find themselves temporarily falling by the wayside.

Some strategies are "dates." We make a date for dinner and a movie, hire a baby-sitter to see the little one through the bedtime routine, and then come back home to a cognac and a little romance. (Here it helps to have a baby-sitter who prefers to drive herself home. Second best is sending your husband off to drive her home while you "set the mood.") This is a period of calculated romance, but it continues to be fun and exciting.

I know some women who set the alarm and cuddle up for some early morning romance. Others take an afternoon nap, either religiously or sporadically, so that they'll have more energy when they need it.

Creativity, a sense of humor, and patience on the part of both partners helps immensely! The object of sex is to be of comfort to one another. You don't always have to experience an earth-shattering orgasm. Sometimes being close and being loved is enough.

The sexual side of a relationship does change some, even

drastically, after children. The best idea is to prepare for it all in a creative way and face the fact that sex with children in the house will probably be a different experience than before children were an issue. Alterations have made our romance everything that it once was and even more.

When the first baby was born I was so sore and uncomfortable from the episiotomy that I couldn't imagine enjoying the process of lovemaking again. I was afraid to trust that my body would heal. The incision was painful, and I didn't want to look at it in a mirror—but by not actually seeing it, I believe I imagined it was far worse than it was.

My doctor was positive and optimistic. He encouraged me to actually look at my incision and engage in sexual relations six weeks after birth. He said I'd be completely healed by then. I gave him a horrified look and said, "Fat chance!"

However, he was right. We had our first lovemaking at six weeks and I was shocked! My body worked fine and it wasn't painful!

The biggest problem we have in our family is finding a private time for lovemaking. It seems that each time we shut the door, the children are pulled to our rooms as if by a magnet. They bang and shout, "Let us in!"

There also doesn't seem to be a great time for sex because at night I'm too tired and in the morning I'm still too tired. Having and caring for children takes an enormous amount of energy.

In some ways, having children is one of the best forms of birth control. They are continually in and out of our bed during the night with various excuses ("I have to pee," "I'm thirsty," "I'm scared," and the list goes on).

We came up with a wonderful way to have our love life! Because our children are afraid of the dark and afraid of sleeping alone, we tuck both children in the same large bed, turn the light on low, and put two glasses of water on each side of the bed. They have each other, they're not lonely, and they usually stay in bed for five nights out of seven. Before they shared a bed they would come into our beds nearly every night at any hour. With such a lack of sleep, I would feel chronically tired and this certainly can have an effect on one's sex life.

So because we are sleeping more regular hours now, it is easier to keep ourselves energized with more privacy for our lovemaking.

We also plan regular times when we go off for special evenings to keep the romance strong in our relationship. We have also discovered the middle-of-the-day "quickies" and other ingenious ways of getting together. In the meantime, we hug, kiss, and cuddle a lot as a couple and as a family. Next to roughhousing these are some of the children's happiest times—ours too!

Chapter 27

THE DADS SPEAK UP

- Fathering—in the fathers' own words
- How many diapers Dad changed, and whether it made any difference
- Adapting to new schedules
- The economics of childrearing
- Fathers and "quality time"
- How the fathers feel about our new family relationships

Melvyn D. Bert, M.D. &

Watching my children grow and develop is exciting. Every day is a new chapter; every month a new book; every year an encyclopedia. Their growth is a process that I enjoy watching very much. I always make sure that I'm a part of their development, that I'm included even though my schedule is very demanding. I always keep in mind that my family life and my children are the center of my life. Although I do not feel that the hands-on everyday care and maintenance of the children is really a job that I am needed for, nor one that I enjoy, I do feel that playing with my children and being there to share their day-to-day experiences is a very important role and a very pleasant one.

Today fathers play a much more active role in the lives of their children. Sosia and Benjamin were a welcome addition to my life. I make sure I have some time alone with my children every day and have a daily exchange with them. I find that for every minute I share with my children there is an enormous return of love and satisfaction. As they develop I find that I enjoy them much more. The satisfaction and exchange of love grows deeper. Although they are still extremely dependent, the dependency is based more on interaction and is much more rewarding to me. Bonding with them as infants was wonderful, and I felt it was important to let them know that I was an important part of the family, but I did not feel that diapering and physical maintenance was a significant part of the fathering experience. The relationships that I now have with both my children are rich and rewarding, and the fact that I changed very few diapers means little in our relationships today.

Diana's decision to stay at home was a wonderful choice and I loved it. It meant that the entire family could benefit from high-quality care. As the years have passed, we both have realized that it was the best possible decision she could have made. We both agree that it is very important that one parent be with the children a good part of the day. I found that picking baby-sitters and working with them was one of the hardest parts of being a parent. It was very difficult for me to entrust my children's care to a stranger. Having Diana available to mother was just wonderful. I feel that extended day-care facilities can't possibly offer what the parents can offer, and in my experience other care-givers were not as motivated as Diana.

With the addition of our children we experienced changes in our relationships at home. We had less time together. When we did have time together, there was a lot of interference and less spontaneity. We couldn't just pick up and go, as we had before the children. But those changes were anticipated. Being prepared for the changes made them quite tolerable for me. The necessary changes in the household, the addition of high chairs and playpens, were just part of the experience.

The experience of being a father is truly wonderful. It is

wonderful having your children love you, and it is wonderful returning that love to them.

John M. Dusay ❧

We have totally changed from owls to larks. Owls, as you know, are night creatures. When the sun goes down they come out. Since Katherine is a psychologist and I am a psychiatrist, and we are in private practice, we usually were able to schedule our hours to our own preferences.

Before Deren and Alexandra were born we would start work around ten o'clock in the morning and work straight through to midday, schedule a break, and then work late, usually until ten at night. We loved it and our patients did too! They could consult with us after their nine-to-five work hours and not miss much time from their occupations.

As owls Katherine and I really came to life later in the day, and when our more larklike acquaintances would be pooping out, we thrived. About ten or eleven at night we would head for our favorite restaurant—one that stayed open until two or three— and they knew us well. Our Caesar salad was ready to be tossed, the fresh catch was waiting for us. We would chat with the other late-nighters—jazz musicians catching a snack, some off-duty politicians or policemen, an occasional hooker taking an hour off, and a few "larks" who were having a night on the town and trying to keep their eyes open. We loved it! Benny, our favorite waiter, would tell us the recent jokes he had heard during the day while tossing our salad. We read the late papers and found out what the early birds would not know for hours. Our life-style was absolute bliss!

After our grand repast we would whoop it up, go to a jazz club, drive around the quiet city, take in the sights while the real tourists were soundly sleeping in their Holiday Inn beds. We almost always finished off the wee hours by dropping in on our favorite sourdough bakery and buying the extra-dark loaf right off the baking tray in the oven. Katherine loves the fluffy, warm, moist inner parts of the bread and I love the dark crunchy crust.

I have been watching both my children's development closely. They seemed to wean, walk, get the first tooth, talk, and toilet train on schedule; however, in the very important developmental area of eating sourdough bread, they have waxed and waned. Early on Deren seemed to be following in his proud father's footsteps. He definitely preferred the crust. However, when his baby teeth started falling out, his preference was for the soft insides. Now that his permanent teeth are en route, he is leaning more toward the crust. Will he be like his daddy? Or will he be like his mother—and leave me more crust? Alexandra fortunately has identified with her mother and is a confirmed softie even at age three.

These observations are admittedly frivolous, yet they underscore one of childrearing's greatest joys. The "little things" count the most. Our lives are enhanced by the inquisitive minds of our children.

Recently we took a train ride at Disneyland and excitedly pointed out the dinosaur to Alexandra, who quickly corrected me by saying, "That's not a dinosaur. It's a brontosaurus!" Now she has a T-shirt collection of Tyrannosaurus rex and Triceratops, among others. I just turned fifty and discovered that I can learn something new every day from a three-year-old.

Many books tell you almost everything about having a baby, except the most important thing of all: babies wake up at the crack of dawn. You can try everything—blackout shades, music tapes of the gentle Pacific waves rolling in, absolute quiet (phone off, doorbell silenced, thick drapes in the room)—nothing works. Babies can "smell" that first ray of sun. They "hear" it coming up, and they come bouncing into our bedroom, full of life, vigor, and conversation, carrying teddy bears, cars, books, and dramatic tales of their not-too-innocent dreams.

With the arrival of children we surrendered to a lack-of-sleep schedule. The biological need for cuddling, nurturing, and nursing babies is an absolute joy and necessity. Katherine would breast-feed the baby and doze off; I became the one who was relegated to walking up and down the hall to fetch the hungry little one and return the child to his or her crib afterward. I was the only sign-up for the late-night diaper-patrol duty. I'm not complaining, because that was always easy for me, a natural owl. I could change diapers in the dark, in thirty seconds flat, even with one hand. I would contemplate how curious it was that a necessity like changing wet diapers could almost take on an art-form quality.

Perhaps the greatest friction that developed between Katherine and me was during the period in which we made the transition from owl to lark behavior. Katherine became a lark long before I did. She had to change for biological reasons. Both babies are ravenously hungry at the crack of dawn and their mother supplies their breakfast. Where our irritations would show up was mostly at night. I was still a confirmed owl and wanted to go out for the night, while Katherine was sleeping like a lamb, immovable and unwakable. I would implore, "You can't go to bed at 10 P.M.! Try the news, try reading, try anything, but stay up!" She couldn't and wouldn't. She was totally exhausted from nursing and child care. I was more energized from horsey riding the kids, rocking them in the rocking chair, and playing hide-and-seek with them. I was able to fit both children easily into my work schedule, and wrongly assumed that Katherine could do the same. Whenever she had a break she wanted to take a nap. I felt frustrated during these early months and went through some lonely nights. I experienced concerns such as "Doesn't my wife love me? Why can't we make love—it's only midnight? What happened to jazz clubs, late movies, and dinner?" The babies thrived on their inborn time schedules, Katherine survived, and I became more of a lark—even happily so!

Katherine and I, being older professionals, could have hired some more helpers to do the routine childrearing, but we decided to do most of it ourselves. We enjoy sharing and growing with our children, especially in the "mundane" everyday things. We truly feel that the little things provide the special times that create the challenges, solutions, and joys of having a baby.

Now I have become one of those curious creatures who bounces up at the crack of dawn, figuratively beats his chest, and actually eats breakfast before eight in the morning! This is usually accomplished with one babe in arms, a box of Rice Krispies, and the morning newspaper (first edition). Instead of my muffler and wool evening jacket that I'd wear out on the town, now my main attire is a well-worn, nearly threadbare bathrobe and slippers. As Deren and Alexandra continue to get a little older, their marvelous conversations become our topics of interest—questions of life and death, poo-poo and pee-pee, and why Grandpa's teeth come out—and each month the questions become even more scintillating and profound. At first we watched the development of their motor skills. Now language and knowledge are marvelously unfolding. "Where do babies come from? How do they get in Mommy's tummy? What does it feel like when you put the seed in?" Whew! I now expect something new every morning—before 8 A.M.!

We still work hard (maybe harder). We still live in the same house (much more of it), and we still love each other (even more). Our lives have changed dramatically—and for the most part, for the better!

Maybe in my retirement (a long ways away), I can experiment with being half lark and half owl. Up early, to bed late, and midday naps. For now I have happily discovered the sunrise—after having a baby!

John Zimmerman ❧

They can be the cutest angels—my "little guys," as I like to call them (also "the rug rats" is another favorite of mine), and they do say the darndest things. On the other hand, they can really put your patience to the test. I've often remarked that it's a good thing you start out with them as innocent cherubs, because at age two there are moments when you wish you could send them back!

I always look so forward to seeing the children when I get

home from work at nights. I also feel guilty about working long hours and not spending more time with them. The great big smiles, outstretched arms, and squeals of "Daddy's home!" from three-year-old Jaclyn and mumblings of "Da-da, Da-da" from nineteen-month-old Jenna make the workday hassles melt away.

I was present at both births, and I felt then that their births were the most remarkable experience I have ever had. But watching them grow up—and so fast too—is another experience I feel fortunate to have had. I have a fifteen-year-old daughter by a previous marriage, and have always felt cheated in not having been able to see her grow and be with her daily.

That probably has a strong influence on how I view Jaclyn's and Jenna's developing personalities—children change so quickly. I just want to slow the world down to a crawl so that I don't miss a thing. Those times when Jaclyn got the great idea of giving herself a haircut; the swimming, gymnastics, and music lessons (before they can talk); and the Halloween costumes are moments that can't be replaced. The only way I've been able to cope is by shooting hours of video tape, so much that I can never hope to be able to edit it into any semblance of order (so that it might be watchable by anyone other than the closest of relatives).

Jaclyn and Jenna are two of the best reasons I have in trying to break a twenty-year habit: smoking! It hasn't been easy, I assure you, but every time I light up and one of them walks into the room, I feel guilty. I want to be with them a long time. I want to see them grow up, date, even teach them to drive, see them go away to college.

For a long time—nine years, to be exact—Jan and I didn't have any kids. And now we can't imagine our lives without them. They're great to give horsey rides to (I'm the horse); they are perfect targets to tease (I *love* to tease); they are sleeping angels; they are the very, very special people of my life.

Richard L. Katz ❧

At the time Sue and I decided to have our first child, Natasha, economics did not appear to play a major role. How wrong we were! I had already been an attorney for over twelve years at the time, and I was making a fairly substantial living. Susan, also an attorney, was relatively new to the business, but doing quite well. Our combined income enabled us to enjoy most of the things life has to offer. Although Susan's income contributed approximately 25 percent of our total, we did not realize how important that contribution was until she stopped working. While I never regretted asking Susan to stay home for the first two years of Natasha's life, the loss of that income did have a dramatic effect on our lives. Not only did we lose the added cash, but our expenses rose with the addition of the new member of our family.

In addition to the usual expenses for food and clothing, other expenses started to creep into the picture. Monthly doctor visits, child care, additional insurance, and increased home expenses had an impact. While each item by itself seemed to be an insignificant amount, the cumulative effect was far more dramatic than either one of us had anticipated. Fortunately, my income was high enough to enable us to maintain a fairly full life-style, but if I had to do it all over again, I would prepare a budget! By the time our second child came along, I was better prepared.

The second child, however, adds another element of expense that I should have anticipated. With the first child it was relatively easy to continue our traveling as we had in the past—and traveling is very important to us. When the second child came along it was far more difficult to squeeze the whole family into one room. So now when we travel we have to pay for an additional room (and most places do not give you a discount because the room is occupied by children rather than adults). Also, once your child exceeds the age of two, the additional airfare adds a significant wallop.

The good news is that children do not eat as much as adults and it is generally fairly inexpensive to feed them. When we eat out, most of the time Sue and I merely order a dish for each of us and have our children share our meals. Once in a while Natasha will insist on her own full portion, but overall the cost of food on our vacations has not dramatically increased.

Another hidden cost in travel is the size of the automobile you rent. Not only do you have two extra bodies along, but the additional luggage requires you to rent a larger car than you might have otherwise done. In the United States the cost of upgrading is not terribly dramatic, but if one travels to Europe, full-sized cars are very expensive to rent. Altogether, I would estimate that the cost of traveling with our two children has virtually doubled the cost from when we were childless. This is especially true if you factor in the added cost of baby-sitting while on vacation.

I realize that the current trend, particularly among Yuppie women, is to have the child and go back to work as soon as possible. Our own experience leads us to believe that this is a grave error. Sue and I feel that our decision to have her stay home for the first two years was a correct one. It is clearly apparent that the children need their mother at home. No amount of arguing is going to convince me that a father or other care-giver can replace Mom. It is clearly apparent that the soft hand of a woman is necessary during the early years of childhood. There is simply no way you could replace the nurturing that Sue has been able to give our children. Indeed, I am at times jealous of her ability to provide this necessary ingredient. During the first two years of Natasha's life it was impossible for me to replace Susan. Natasha simply wouldn't allow it. Many times I offered to do some of the chores that Susan routinely did for Natasha—helping her dress, feeding her, holding her hand when we crossed the street, combing her hair—but with rare exception she insisted that Mom do it rather than Dad. We realized that sooner or later she would start looking to me for some of her everyday requirements, and sure enough, later Daddy became the favorite. Now, at age four, Natasha has be-come smart enough to use us both whenever it pleases her. In

381

fact, she seems to revel in her power to anoint the successful parent as being her slave for the day.

Even if you believe a child can get sufficient nurturing from two working parents during "quality time," I still would recommend that you reconsider the alternative. Babyhood is a time in your child's life you should not miss observing. When we decided to have a child I programmed in time to enable me to work at home so I could observe the early years. I have not been disappointed. Watching Natasha grow into a functioning self-assured woman/child has been wonderful! Watching her learn how to walk, talk, and experience the joy of some newfound discovery was so pleasing as to render me speechless on occasion. Tears would come into my eyes frequently from such observations.

Before Natasha was born Sue and I solemnly promised each other never to regale our friends with "Natasha" stories. The wails from Natasha after birth had barely stopped before that promise was broken, and our vow has been breached more times than Elizabeth Taylor has been married. If there is one constant in the world, it is the bragging rights that parents (and grandparents) have about their children. This malady is so endemic that Jews have even coined a word for it—"kvelling."

It has now been over four years since Susan has worked a full-time job. This is remarkable in light of the fact that Susan was sure she would not be able to stay home longer than six months without going crazy. It turned out that she enjoyed motherhood so much that staying home for two years was a piece of cake. There was, however, one major problem. Susan's view of herself changed dramatically. She hated the idea of having to say that she was now a housewife/mother. In fact, she still refuses to accept the role of housewife. It is apparent that she is affected by society's dismal view of housewives/mothers. To counteract this Sue has always tried to go to her office at least one day a week. This has helped satisfy her ego. If this paragraph sounds as though I take a dismal view of this activity, it should not. I am well aware of the need of all of us to feel good about ourselves. Unfortunately, society has not yet granted motherhood the same degree of respect that is awarded successful professionals. I feel the feminist movement is to blame in part. Although much feminist literature tells women that being a mother is perfectly acceptable, the promotion of equal status for women in the working world has reinforced society's dismal view of the nonworking mother.

In any event, I have personally done everything in my power to give my wife the message that I view her job as a mom as an important one. Nevertheless, I occasionally get accused of assuming she has lots of free time because she is at home. I, of course, feel I've been unjustly maligned. The point is, both parents should be acutely aware of their changed psychological state. There is no doubt that each spouse perceives the other in a much different light after the child is born, and particularly if one spouse is no longer working.

As much as a mother loves her children, occasionally she is going to need a break from her everyday chores. This will mean getting away not only from the children, but also her husband. Susan, fortunately, has needed this break only occasionally in the four years that we have had children. On a few occasions I have had the responsibility of taking care of the children without my wife's help for an entire day. The demands they make on your time are incredible. Getting used to this fact is one of the more difficult adjustments of parenthood.

My brother and I grew up in New York City. During the week my father was working and was rarely around the house during the day. On the weekends, therefore, my brother and I looked forward to spending some time playing with him. I can recall many winter Sundays when my father was comfortably ensconced in his easy chair reading *The New York Times,* an enterprise that to us seemed to take the entire week. Unfortunately for my father, my brother and I did not recognize his need to sit and relax on his only day off. We would constantly tug at his sleeve, asking him to join us in playing in the snow. He would send us out of the house, promising to join us shortly. He never did. I promised myself that when I became a father I would not repeat his error. It has been another difficult promise to keep. Learning to be unselfish with your time has absolutely been *the* most difficult lesson to learn. Hopefully, however, my children will not grow up feeling the same disappointment in their father I felt in mine.

How does one discipline a child who is loved beyond loving? Not easily! I have yet to discipline my daughters without feeling a pang of remorse. Nevertheless, it must be done. There is no question in my mind that children not only need discipline, but crave it. I have yet to see a truly happy undisciplined child. I have carefully observed children whom I believe to be undisciplined and, almost invariably, the child is irritable and often arrogant. Too much discipline, however, can create a morose child. Therefore, finding the proper balance is another difficult parental obligation. Sue and I are constantly agonizing over the proper degree of control. Natasha has been an extremely high-spirited child and we are constantly concerned about breaking her spirit. So far, so good.

Everyone told us that having a second child would quadruple the time required to deal with the children. They were wrong. I wish it were only a multiple that small. The good news, however, is that having two has doubled our pleasure. Ariana's personality is completely different from Natasha's. (Thank God! Having two of Natasha would have been impossible.) Ariana has been a much more easygoing child than her older sister. On the other hand, she has not been as advanced physically or mentally as Natasha. This has caused the inevitable comparisons between them. It is easy to advise others to "avoid this pitfall," but one would be less than human if one did not make such comparisons. I have, however, vowed never to say "Why can't you be more like your sister?" Any sibling who has ever heard those words has a right to cry "foul!" I can't be more like my brother, because I am not my brother. Love me for who I am, not for who you'd like me to be. Enjoy the differences in your children—they enrich your life.

In most cases when people get married they have come from very different households. Hopefully one of the things that got you together were basic principles of life you have in common. Before Sue and I were married, we had long discussions about basic moral issues. Incredibly then, as now, our mores are mirror images of each other. Even though I was raised in a Jewish household in New York and Miami, and Sue was raised in a Presbyterian household in Southern California, our parents instilled the same basic moral values. It has helped significantly in setting goals for our children. It is extremely important, even before the birth of your first child, to set out your principles of discipline and childrearing. Also, we find it helps to have one parent in charge of goal-setting for the children. In most instances when there has been a disagreement I have accepted Susan's position. There have been a few instances when I felt so strongly about a solution to a problem that I *insisted* that we deal with it my way. We have always, however, managed to keep such discussions out of earshot of our children. We also strive mightily never to contradict each other in front of the children.

Another one of the more difficult problems in rearing children is doing what's best for them rather than for yourself. For example, a child both likes and needs to make noise. It is readily apparent that this is a normal part of child development. It is also readily apparent that very few people enjoy the screaming that children do around the household. In order to reconcile my needs and those of my children, I have allowed them to scream, but with the volume turned down somewhat. There are many other examples of learning to be unselfish. I constantly ask myself whether or not my decisions regarding my children are made on the basis of my needs or theirs.

Recent headlines concerning child abuse have created a certain amount of paranoia in our society. As the father of two daughters, I am constantly in fear of being accused of sexually abusing my children. I admit to taking great satisfaction in fondling the buttocks of my children. Those buns are so squeezable, they are simply impossible to resist. Am I sexually abusing my children? Not in my mind. Am I concerned that somebody might accuse me of such? Yes. Do I stop squeezing their "tushies"? No. Do I demand hugs and kisses from my children? Yes. When I change my child's diaper do I not only wipe the poop from her tushy but also from her vagina? Yes. Am I concerned that someone may view this activity as wrong? Yes. Will it stop me from doing it again? No.

Both my wife and I periodically walk around parts of the house nude. Obviously my children have been interested in my male appendage. Indeed, they have been interested to the point of using it as a handhold. Unless one is unusually small and thinks this might help it grow, this is not an activity that I recommend highly. Be that as it may, it took quite a while to convince Natasha that it was not appropriate behavior. I also had to deal with the inevitable questions about the differences in the sexes much earlier than I had anticipated. Children's curiosity about the sexual parts of our bodies is a never-ending source of amusement.

One of our children started masturbating at a very early age and has used every hard object in the house as an artificial aid. Attempting to deal with this problem delicately has taxed the limits of our minds. If you find yourself in this situation, I have no suggestions other than to say that the problem will go away of its own accord in time. We do, however, ask our daughter to engage in this activity in the privacy of her room, which often does stop the activity as she hates being alone.

As human beings we have a tendency to emphasize the downside in life. There are seemingly many more half-empty glasses than half-full ones. Nevertheless, the upside of having children clearly outweighs the downside. The lack of privacy and sleep are clearly downside results of having children. The joys of watching your children grow up and become members of a loving family unit is the upside. When I come home from work after a hard day at the office and one or both of my children leaps into my arms, it makes my day!

Chapter *28*

FAREWELL AGAIN

Diana ❧

We were sledding with our children recently and my sister-in-law looked over at me as we watched them glide down the hills and said, "Can you remember what gave meaning to your life before you had children?" Although I had a complete and wonderful life before having children, Sosia and Benjamin have indeed given my life meaning that I never felt before. There are meanings that I never saw in life, purposes that I had never realized.

There are days when I feel as if I had basked in sunshine all day just by sharing time with my children. There are also days when I have to wear sunglasses because the very thought of sunlight is enough to send me for the eye drops. There are days when I marvel at the simplest wonders of life, and there are days when I scream like a lunatic while I look under beds for the lost ants from the ant farm. There are days when I wouldn't trade in my life for a zillion dollars because it is so rich, and other days when I would do anything just to be able to read the paper without a child on my lap. The tough times are when all those wonderful/awful things are wrapped up into one day, and, WHEW, I can just barely make it through!

The good far outweighs the bad side of being Mom. I am proud of the job I do, and happy that I am able to devote my

387

time and attention to doing it well. I'm proud of two of the best kids on the block. Me? Prejudiced? Just call me Mom.

We come now to the place where our paths must part again. I hope the time that you have spent with us has given you a giggle, an idea, some consolation. Though the road of parenting is rich with pleasures, there are pitfalls along the way. I wish you success in stepping over them. I hope that the tantrums and messes will fade in your mind, but that you will remember the cuddles and ballet recitals. I hope that you will remember us when it seems like it was a bad idea to have children in the first place. We are all parenting too. We are all striving to find answers to the questions we ask.

We are rearing children for future worlds—worlds of peace, worlds without hunger. Let's all remember to bring up our children to contribute to the worlds of which we dream. Let's remember to watch their toys and their media input so they know the values we strive for. Let's remember to give them so much love that they will know how to give it when it comes their turn. Let's remember to give them the tools and morals that will help them bring about the values of a world of peace.

Let's also remember that we are all human. There will be days when we might swear, days when we will be horrified at our efforts to be parents, days when we would gladly turn in our resignations, if we just knew where. But let's remember that we can say we are sorry. We can lose some of the arguments. We can be human. No matter how the parenting went that day, we can change it and improve it tomorrow. Our relationships with our children will grow and change every day. Let's all strive to meet the challenge of being the best parents we can be.

Jan 🍂

THE BEST:	Jaclyn and Jenna.
THE WORST:	"Mommy, I'm thirsty!" At three in the morning.
THE BEST:	The unconditional love you have for your own child, and their love and unconditional faith in you.
THE WORST:	"Mommy, I peed!" At four in the morning.
THE BEST:	Jaclyn's new boyfriend at school. Jenna singing "Twinkle, Twinkle Little Star." Both girls having a tea party together—happily—for two minutes.
THE WORST:	"Mommy, there are monsters in my room!" At five in the morning.
THE BEST:	Jaclyn learning to count. Jenna swallowing a penny. (This is good? No, but it turned out to be better than swallowing a nickel. Pennies are more easily passed.)
THE WORST:	"Mommy, can I sleep in your bed?" At six in the morning.
THE BEST:	Hugs and kisses every time I come home.
THE WORST:	"Mommy, can I change into play clothes?" At 6:07 in the morning.
THE BEST:	Jaclyn and Jenna.

As in our first book, we don't need to say good-bye or farewell. The lives of our babies are just beginning, and so are our own. I'd much rather continue to carry on our conversation. Is your little one sleeping through the night? Are you? Uh-huh, another ear infection. Right, a special treat after going to the potty successfully.

The best reward I got from our first book was hearing from so many of you. *Thank you* for taking the time to write. Having a baby . . . and then another baby . . . are two experiences I feel blessed to have had. I hope you have found some comfort, perhaps shared a laughed, and maybe even learned a time-saving hint from this book. It has been a joy to write . . . and an even greater joy to remember.

Katherine 🐦

I would love to have lots and lots of children. The best parts of life are truly getting hugs and kisses from my husband and kids. I can't get enough of touching the children and their perfect little bodies. Each age has been unique and exciting. I often say to Jack, "I wish we could freeze them at this stage. There's nothing more wonderful!" I really enjoy each of them for where they are.

The worst of it is that there is seldom a break from childrearing. Even when I am working or away from Deren and Alexandra, I think of them. They can be rude, cruel, demanding, and have temper tantrums. They put a real bite in the family income and it's hard to imagine that it will ever let up. From the moment they're born it's difficult to get a good night's sleep.

The upside is the thrill I get seeing my child go through different stages and knowing that I went through these same phases to get where I am today. It's fun to watch the "repeat" performance.

I'm pleased I'm an older parent and that I waited to have kids. I got in my career, traveling, and wild times during the thirty-five years that I waited. I also like seeing the physical parts of myself, my husband, and the grandparents in each child. I love having both a boy and girl. They are completely different in their developmental timing, dispositions, and interests, and I've tried to rear them in a similar way.

I had never experienced emotions of such happiness or anger before I had children. They offer the best and worst in life. However, the *best* certainly overbalances the worst by a thousand to one—and those are excellent odds.

I've enjoyed sharing with you again. This is a completely different book from *Having a Baby*, particularly because the babies are born, alive, and kicking. There's so much more to talk about and describe. Babies in the tummy seem like more of a fantasy. When they pop out—a reality.

Jack and I will probably stick with having only the two children because our lives are manageable and we have one of each sex. Our lives are complete. They are both fun to talk to, laugh with, and play games with. Deren beats me in chess and I win in checkers! They continue to get easier to do things with and take places. We have both children on skis. We'll probably start our longer traveling vacations again in about a year.

Jack and I wish you joy, happiness, and success with your families and lives.

Mary 🦆

When Natalie was still an infant, one of my clients used to tell me, "The older she gets, the more fun it will be." I must say, she was right. Every step of Natalie's life so far has been fun. When she was a baby I often wished she could just stay the way she was and never grow up. On the other hand, I was also very anxious how she would turn out grown-up.

The worst of it all is that childrearing requires so much attention, time, and energy. Many times I cannot do the things I used to do or liked to do. On my trips to Europe I bought more things, especially clothes, for Natalie than for myself. But all has been done voluntarily and with pleasure. I love it.

The best part of all is being a mother, being able to give my love to my daughter and give her as much nurturing as she will need.

Susan 🙠

There are terrible moments and there are terrible entire days. The worst moments are having to say no for the twentieth time to the same request and wondering how I will ever get the message across, then wishing I hadn't when the cries of anguish come because they have finally understood; not being able to think because of the constant chatter; dealing with tantrums; and not being able to decide between brand X and Y in the store because every time I start to look at the label Natasha is pleading for me to buy something she has seen on the shelf, and by the time I convince her that the answer really is no, Ariana starts fussing because she can't quite reach the item she is trying to pull off the shelf. I console Ariana only to be greeted by another request of Natasha's, and the process begins again.

The worst days are the fussy days—the days when I've had no sleep because I've been up six times during the night feeding Ariana and handling a variety of requests of Natasha's. I get up in the morning wondering how I am going to get through the day only to be greeted by two whiny, fussy, complaining little twerps who cannot be consoled. I stare at the list of things that must be accomplished that day but cannot even focus on it because my head is in a fog and I can't hear myself think. The fog in my head never lifts but I finally make it through the day and Dick comes home wondering why I haven't remembered to pick up his cleaning!

But there are many moments and events that are extraspecial, like watching Natasha and Ariana hug and pat each other on the back, or having Ariana put her head on my shoulder and pat me on the back and sigh, "Ah," or having Natasha come to me and say, "Mommy, I love you sooooo much—as much as the whole house!" But *the best* is the overall picture. The best is being a family of four who love each other and care about each other and want the very best for each other. The best is the overall experience of having children and watching them grow and mature and develop into people who are the future of our world and knowing that the future is going to be better because of them. The best is the love I feel for these little wonders—a love more intense and more wonderful than I ever imagined was possible. And the best just keeps getting better!

Here I am saying farewell again when we are still just beginning to experience the wonderful life that we have together. If what we have experienced so far is any indication of what is to come, we are in for a real treat! I'm sure that you are too. You have come into our lives by reading this book. We have shared some of our most intimate experiences with you because we care. I hope that you have enjoyed reading about our experiences and that in some small way it has helped you to enjoy your family more, because no matter what else we do in this world, what really matters are the experiences we have with the people we love. Enjoy!

INDEX